UNIVERSITY OF KNOWLEDGE

GLENN FRANK, B.A., M.A., Litt.D., L.H.D., LL.D., *Editor-in-Chief*

PRINTED AND BOUND IN THE UNITED STATES
OF AMERICA BY THE CUNEO PRESS, INC.

Every Branch of Knowledge Man Possesses May Be Applied To Some Good Purpose

THE MEDICINE MAN

THE UNIVERSITY OF KNOWLEDGE
WONDER BOOKS

GLENN FRANK, EDITOR-IN-CHIEF

THE STORY OF PRIMITIVE MAN

HIS EARLIEST APPEARANCE AND DEVELOPMENT

BY

MABEL COOK COLE, A.B.

Author: "Philippine Folk Tales,"
"Savage Gentlemen," etc.

AND

FAY-COOPER COLE, B.S., Ph.D., Sc.D.

Chairman Department of Anthropology
University of Chicago

•

UNIVERSITY OF KNOWLEDGE, INCORPORATED
CHICAGO - 1940

GLENN FRANK
Editor-in-Chief

INTRODUCTION

This volume is the second of three volumes in which scholars of unerring authority of scholarship and exceptional artistry of presentation paint with broad brush strokes the background of the whole human venture. If we are to understand, with any richness of insight, the meanings of the modern world and the meanings of modern man, we must know something of the long past, out of which they came.

The physical world and all that is in it, aside from man, is the stage upon which man has played and, to the end of time, must play the comedies and tragedies of his existence and his enterprise. But the physical world is more to man than the wooden boards and canvas wings of a stage are to the actor. Its very forms of plain and mountain and desert, the rigor or blandness of its varied climates from arctic to tropics, its rivers and lakes and oceans, its plants, its animals, the thinness or fertility of its myriad soils, and a thousand other physical facts of the physical world have profoundly affected the nature and trend of human development that has come to its present phase in modern man as we know him here and now. We must know how this physical world and its varied factors that have so profoundly affected modern man came to be. It was this that the first volume of this series set out to do and did so admirably.

When we have burrowed into the long past out of which came the physical world as the stage upon which the human venture is to be played, our next concern must be the actors who are to take the parts in this play. The actors now are ourselves, but we, like the physical world in which we act our parts, came out of a long past. Modern man did not come to be the thing he is in any split second. He grew, slowly and laboriously, as the physical world grew. The flashing imagination that has given us the supreme works of art and letters, the patient and prophetic intelligence that has given us the methods and fruits of modern science, the practical genius that has fashioned the governments and industries of the world, and the mystical spirit that has given mankind contact with those values that lie beyond the flesh and economics—all these things—mark the long road that has had to be traveled from the dim and dawning intelligence of primitive man. If we are to understand ourselves, we must know this story of how modern man came to be what he is. This story is not just curious lore that is interesting to ponder, if we happen to find an idle hour in which to consider it, but knowledge we must have in order rightly to understand ourselves. Moderns that we are, our ancestors still live in us. They are in our veins, in our habits, in our manner of thinking and acting; all of them, our immediate parents to the sub-men of the morning hours of the race! It is this story that this volume has set out to tell, and it tells it magnificently.

When we have come to know how the physical world came to be, this stage upon which the human venture is played, and when we have come to know how the actor in this play, man, came to be, we must then turn our attention to the play itself. We must know the story of the early steps of civilization. That story is told in the next volume.

This volume, which tells the story of man through the ages, has been written by Fay-Cooper Cole and his wife, Mabel Cook Cole. Mr. Cole is the distinguished head of the department of anthropology of the University of Chicago. He is an active force in a long list of scholarly societies. He is not an arm-chair anthropologist. He has conducted various expeditions in far fields. He is equally at home in the science of exploration and the art of exposition. He is the author of a goodly list of books that have flowered from his research and exploration. He has served in important posts in the National Research Council and was the chief of the social science division of the Century of Progress exposition in Chicago in 1933-34. Mrs. Cole is an active partner in her husband's scientific interests. She has traveled extensively in the Orient. She has given particular attention to the Philippines, Borneo, and the Dutch East Indies, where she has made intensive studies of the women of primitive tribes. She has an interesting and important list of published studies to her credit.

The three volumes I have referred to in this introduction form a colorful mural which, as I have said, gives the background against which the modern venture is being played.

GLENN FRANK

MABEL COOK COLE

Author: "Philippine Folk Tales,"
"Savage Gentlemen," etc.

FAY-COOPER COLE

Chairman Department of
Anthropology; University
of Chicago.

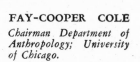

2

[X]

TABLE OF CONTENTS

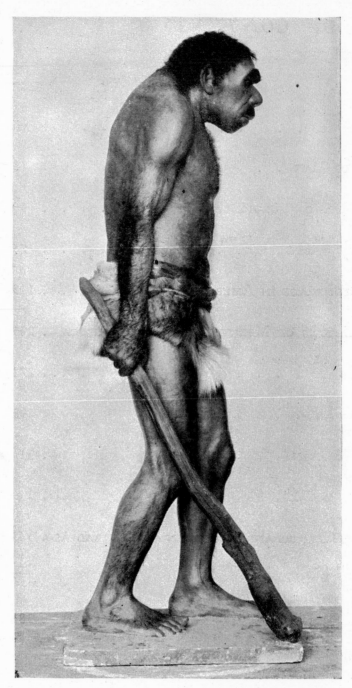

**NEANDER-
THAL MAN**

Neanderthal man,
while human,
differed greatly
from modern
man.

Courtesy Field
Museum of Natural
History, Chicago
Sculptor,
Frederick Blaschke

IN THIS VOLUME is told the story of man from the beginning. It is an epic of struggle and achievement recorded in the strata of the rocks, in the beds of ancient lakes, and in dark caverns once the homes of men.

Early writers have told us of a "golden age" when men did not toil, when nature supplied all their needs. But there never was such an age. It is as much a fable as the poet's "mossy beds of ease." When we know the facts we find that the moss is damp and full of bugs. Likewise, the early days of man were filled with hardships, with strife against the giant cave bears and other animals which would devour him, with struggles against the forces of nature.

Now the story is being revealed by the work of scientists who excavate the caves in which human beings once lived, who study great shell heaps left from ancient meals, and who painstakingly search the record to be found in long abandoned settlements.

A WORLD WITHOUT MAN

We have read of a world in which man had not yet appeared. Can you imagine such a world?

When man did arrive, he straightway set about destroying, changing, building. Man is the great killer. Other beings may kill for food, but not for sport, for territory, or for possessions. Man kills for food, for clothing, for fun. Only those animals he needs or fancies have a chance for survival. He has exterminated the buffalo and has all but driven wild game from the Mississippi Valley. Today hunters travel from New York or Chicago to Africa or to the Far North to hunt, to kill, for sport.

Had man not appeared, the world would have remained as nature shaped it. Great forests would cover regions now barren; grass-covered prairies would replace areas now desolate. No mines or cuts would deface the landscape, no smoking chimneys would darken the sky, no refuse pollute the streams.

But without man there would have been no fire to warm, no light to gladden, no homes to give shelter, no art, no religion —nothing we call civilization.

Man alone has speech. Other beings have calls; even chickens can warn of danger or indicate food, but, so far as we know, not even the apes have a language. Without language there can be no culture; each individual must learn by imitation, or by trial and error.

Man can communicate his experiences, can cooperate. Man speculates and tries to direct nature. He is an inventor. He alone has perfected tools and weapons, he has domesticated plants and animals, he has broken the soil. Far beyond all other animals he has learned how to control his environment.

MAN ARRIVED LATE

The geologists tell us that ninety-nine one-hundredths of the world's history was without man. As they study the strata of the rocks, they find convincing evidence that the upper layers are most recent and contain modern forms of plant and animal life. As they go down, they encounter older deposits and quite different types of life.

Such a study is possible where some great excavation is being made, either by man or nature. In our West the Colorado River has cut away the various strata to a depth of more than one mile, producing the Grand Canyon. As you stand on the rim of this great chasm, you see layer above layer of rocks, in different colors and containing fossil forms which existed in the countless ages of the past.

By observing many such evidences of stratification, the geologists have been able to divide the history of the earth into four periods. The first two show no traces of man or his near relatives, but, about the middle of the third, forms begin to appear which may be ancestral to man and the anthropoid apes.

In the third period great events took place, events which were destined to mold world history. In America the western mountain ranges were forming; the Colorado River was starting to dig the Grand Canyon. In Asia the great Himalaya mountains

Courtesy Field Museum of Natural History, Chicago

THE GIANT CAVE BEAR
Against such animals early men had to defend their homes in the caves.

Courtesy Atchison, Topeka and Santa Fe Railway

GRAND CANYON OF THE COLORADO
The story of countless ages is recorded in the strata of the rocks.

were rising, to form a barrier between North and South. Climates and vegetation were changing. It was a time of great shifts and development among the animals. The giant forms began to disappear while the small, active mammals started to develop toward those with which we are now familiar.

At this time the ancestors of the anthropoids appeared. They were small in size, with teeth and claws too weak to serve as defense against their enemies. But nature had provided them with larger and better brains than had been known before. They also were able to use their forelegs and paws as arms and hands. Large brains and free hands started their conquest of the world.

Of the earliest of these beings we know very little. In the Siwalik Hills of northwestern India there are great exposures of strata of Miocene times—that is, about the middle of the third period. In these rocks have been found teeth and parts of jaws belonging to animals which may be ancestral to man, the chimpanzee, or the gorilla. These beings are known as Sivapithecus.

In Germany and Austria teeth and jaws of a similar type have been discovered in deposits of the same age. There they are known as Dryopithecus, or the "oak ape," because one of the first specimens found had a fossil oak leaf adhering to the bone. Similar teeth of even earlier date have appeared in Egypt.

It is fair to ask: "Why are teeth so important in the study of fossils?" The first reason is that teeth are often preserved when all other portions of the skeleton have vanished. Secondly, the cusps on the molar teeth have a very definite arrangement, while the roots and pulp cavities of anthropoid apes and men have peculiar characteristics unlike those of other animals. Not only are the teeth of man-like beings peculiar, but they differ in number and in arrangement from those of most other living things.

Teeth are so important that scientists use them with great confidence in determining other types of animals. They are equally useful in tracing the story of man and his closest relatives. It is because the teeth of these fossil animals from India and Europe give strong evidence of being related to those of man and the anthropoid apes that science says we have here forms which may be ancestral. Even if we doubt that they are in the direct line of man, we can still say that man-like forms were beginning to appear toward the middle of the third period.

AN APE WHO DID NOT ARRIVE

The most striking discovery of one of these early anthropoids occurred in Bechuanaland of South Africa in the year 1925.

A great limestone cliff was being blasted away to secure materials for a local lime kiln. Frequently in the rock fragments the workmen would find bones of animals which apparently belonged to late Miocene times. This led to frequent and careful observation of the site.

Following one blast a peculiar stone, shaped like a human brain, appeared. The discoverers picked it up, but considered it just a freak of nature, for they knew that brains and flesh decay more rapidly than they can be replaced by mineral matter. They knew all the jokes about petrified men and decided to add one more to the list when they carried the specimen to Professor

International News Photo   Courtesy American Museum of Natural History

THE GREAT ANTHROPOID APES

ABOVE: Left, the Gorilla, largest of the modern Anthropoids. Right, the Chimpanzee, most intelligent of the group.

BELOW: The Orang-utan, giant anthropoid ape now found in Borneo and Sumatra.

Courtesy Chicago Park District

Raymond Dart at the University of Johannesburg. But the professor was not fooled; he recognized at once that it was truly a fossil brain much like that of man. He also realized that, if it belonged to the same deposit as that from which the bones were being recovered, it meant that man-like beings must have been associated with very ancient animals.

A group of scientists went at once to the quarry, where they looked in vain for the skull from which the brain had come. Finally they searched the face of the cliff and there, forty feet from the top and twenty from the bottom, they found a small opening into which the brain fitted perfectly. In great excitement they cut out a large block of the surrounding stone and carried it to the University. Certainly whatever the block contained must be as old as the cliff itself, for no animal could burrow into solid rock.

Day by day they chipped away the stone until finally there was revealed the face and skull of a young anthropoid ape. But it was no ordinary ape, for, though it was only about six years old, it had a brain larger, and in many respects more like that of human beings, than is possessed by the apes of today; also its teeth were more man-like than those of any other of these beings —ancient or modern.

Recently Professor Brom, a distinguished paleontologist of South Africa, discovered another skull of similar type, but this time it was an adult. However, the rock in which it was imbedded belonged to the fourth period after man had appeared.

These two skulls seem to indicate that in South Africa nature had produced a being far advanced toward man but that he never arrived.

These beings are known as Australopithecus—the Australoid-like ape—or as the Taungs Ape, because the first skull was found near the place of that name.

Apparently they are not ancestors of man, but they do give a hint of the development which was taking place toward the modern apes and man in that distant past.

THE FIRST MEN

When man did appear he was very different from human beings of today.

The story of the oldest human now known was recorded in a most unusual way, for nature made the record and preserved it for half a million years.

Java is a tropical island in the Dutch East Indies. It is famous for its scenery and for its many active volcanoes.

Several times in its history this island has been connected with the mainland by land ʰridges, over which traveled plant and animal life. This was the condition a half million years or so ago, just about the time the first glaciers began to push down over northern Europe and Asia.

At this time a volcanic cone rose in what is now central Java. A great eruption took place, but apparently this was preceded by a wave of gas which swept down one side of the mountain and killed every living thing—plants, trees, animals, and man, if he was there.

Such a catastrophe is not mere fancy, as the last great eruption of Taal Volcano in the Philippines proves. At that time a cloud of gas swept from the crater and covered the villages at one end of the lake. Everything alive was wiped out, and more than two thousand human beings perished inside a single hour.

Much the same thing happened during the ancient eruption in Java. Then quantities of blue mud poured out of the crater and swept down the mountain side carrying with it rocks, trees, and animals which had been trapped by the gas. Finally the waves of mud reached the lowlands. In the centuries which passed other eruptions helped build up the soil, while the wash from higher lands made deposits which now reach a depth of eighty feet above the blue clays.

Since the last glaciation the Island of Java has been slowly rising and as a result the rivers are cutting deep valleys.

Near the foot of the ancient volcano the Solo River has cut through the deposits until at low water it now exposes the blue clays laid down so long ago. In these clays quantities of bones of the animals and portions of plants and trees which per-

Photo by Cole

TAAL VOLCANO IN THE PHILIPPINES

ished have been found. It is because of the testimony of this plant and animal life that we know the approximate age of the clays and the deposits above them.

In the year 1891 Dr. Eugene DuBois, now Professor of Paleontology at the University of Amsterdam, made a discovery which has been the subject of more discussion than of any other thing ever found.

THE MISSING LINK

For years men had been talking about the many likenesses between man and the apes, but no beings had been found which seemed to bridge the gap, and so they came to talk of "a missing link."

When the water of the river was very low, Professor DuBois gathered bones which protruded from the clays, but when it was high he went to a place where the banks sloped up from the water and sank trenches until he again reached the blue clays. During his work he found hundreds of bones belonging to at least twenty-four species of animals long extinct in Java. One day, to his great surprise, he came upon a molar tooth which looked very much like that of man, yet had many characteristics similar to the teeth from India which we described in an earlier paragraph. Later he found another tooth and this led him to the belief that he had discovered evidences of a high primate close to man.

During succeeding months he extended his trenches over a radius of about fifty feet and was rewarded by the discovery of a skull cap and an upper leg bone. Later work produced another tooth, two more leg bones, and a few months ago the skull of a child was found in the same deposit.

SKULL CAP OF
PITHECANTHRO-
PUS ERECTUS

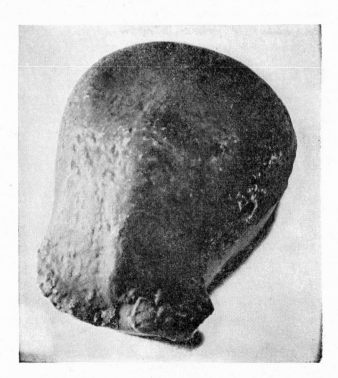

Courtesy Anthropology
Department, University
of Chicago
    Photo by
    Raeburn Rohrbach

We cannot go into a technical discussion of this discovery, but we should take note of a few of the most important observations which have led most learned men to the belief that we have here the oldest human being now known.

The teeth appear to be human although they have primitive characters. They also tell us that their owner did not chew like the apes, but in the manner of modern men. The chimpanzee, gorilla, baboon and similar beings have long canine teeth which project beyond the others, and when they chew these interlock so that their jaws must go up and down. All of the teeth of man are of about the same length, and when he eats he grinds his food by making his jaws go in a rotary fashion. This method of chewing wears the teeth in a very characteristic manner.

The skull cap looks much like that which a giant baboon might possess. It has a huge ridge above the eyes and behind this the forehead slopes rapidly backward. No human being of today has such brow ridges and no human forehead is as low. Another bony crest runs along the back of the skull in a manner characteristic of the great apes. Why then do we think it belongs to man?

Fortunately the clay had filled the skull cap and had kept the interior from injury. When now we take a cast of the interior of this skull we secure a true picture of the outer surface of the brain. We find that it is half as large again as the brain of the largest gorilla. In size it stands midway between those of man and of the apes.

The frontal portion of the brain is poorly developed and probably indicates a dull-minded individual, but there is considerable expansion of the portions above the ears, a region in which the brain of man alone has grown. The convolutions on the outer surface of the brain, while quite simple, are far more complex than in the animals below man. Finally, we come to the leg bone and we find that not only is it straight, but the lines of muscle attachment show that this being walked erect.

Because of the many intermediate features between man and the apes which these bones and teeth show, and because he stood upright, this being is called *Pithecanthropus erectus,* or "the erect ape man."

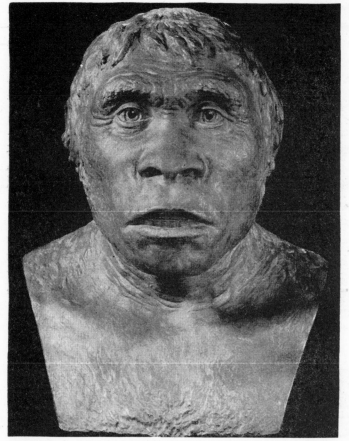

Some scientists have insisted that we have here the bones of a giant anthropoid far advanced toward man; more have come to the conclusion that Pithecanthropus erectus is a very primitive man just over the border line of the human.

It would not be safe to claim that the Java man is ancestral to modern man, though he may be, but apparently he is related to the man of China, next to be described.

We made brief mention of the skull of a child likewise found in the clays. Ordinarily brow ridges in man do not appear until maturity, but this little fellow has them well developed. It is evident that had he grown up he would have equalled the huge ridges of Pithecanthropus.

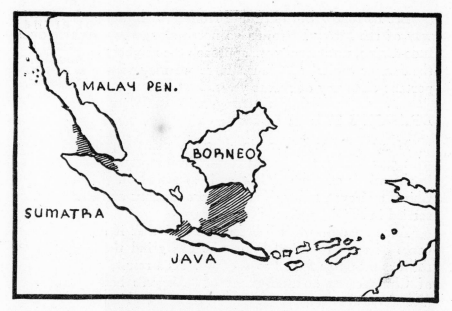

ANCIENT LAND ROUTES
Shaded portions of map represent old Land Bridge between Java and Sumatra and Mainland.

THE OLD LAND BRIDGE FROM
JAVA TO THE MAINLAND

Java and the surrounding islands stand in shallow seas. Each time that the glaciers locked up great quantities of water in ice, the surface of the oceans was lowered and many land bridges appeared. Such a bridge extended from Java to Sumatra and thence to the Asiatic mainland by way of the Malay Peninsula. Geological evidences of these ancient land routes are clear, but in addition to such proof we find in the Islands today many animals and plants which traveled overland. In Sumatra and Borneo we find the orang outang; the same type of tiger and elephant occur in Sumatra and the Malay States; while more than six thousand species of plants, similar to those on the mainland, are found in the Islands.

This discussion of land connections is important, for it means that an open road existed from India to Java and from there to China.

Let us follow this old route from Java to Sumatra, then by way of the Malay Peninsula go north along the coasts of Siam, Indo-China, until finally we approach the neighborhood of Pekin, the former capital of China. Here we may view the most important discovery of recent years.

DRAGON'S TEETH

Many Chinese believe in dragons, giant reptile-like beings with great heads and jagged teeth. So important was this being in the minds of the people that it appeared on the flag of Old China, and even today fanciful reproductions of the dragon are carried in religious processions.

Accompanying this belief is the idea that if one can secure bones of these mythical beings, he can grind them up and use them as medicine for all sorts of ills. As a result, the drug stores of China carry an assortment of "dragon's bones" and these

Courtesy Art Institute, Chicago

CHINESE DRAGON

usually turn out to be the bones and teeth of fossil animals. Foreign scientists visit the shops to see the bones and frequently they have found evidences of very ancient beings. Several times in recent years they came across teeth which appeared to belong to a high primate far advanced toward man. No one was able to learn the exact location from which the teeth had been taken, but it was assumed to be in northern China and hence it was predicted that this region would ultimately yield a great discovery.

All our readers are familiar with the expeditions sent to Asia by the American Museum of Natural History. The director of these quests—Dr. Roy Chapman Andrews—found dinosaurs and dinosaur eggs, but no fossil men. Another ardent searcher was Father Teilhard de Chardin. He found evidences of things made by man of great antiquity, but no skeletons of the owners. Finally the discovery was made.

PEKIN MAN

In 1927, J. G. Andersson, of the Chinese Geological Survey, was led to the site of an ancient cave by one of his coolies.

In the days of the first Ice Age, almost as far back as the time of Pithecanthropus, this was a cave of some size. Near the center was a deep fissure which led to the river far below. A tiny stream from the nearby hills flowed not far from the entrance and, at times of high water, it ran across the floor of the cave and emptied into the fissure.

During the dry season the cavern was fairly comfortable, but during the rainy period water oozed through the limestone walls and dripped from the ceiling. This water was charged with lime, but, as it spread over the floor of the cave and ran to the bottom of the crevasse, it deposited its load to form a stone known as travertine. Usually only a thin layer was laid down each year, but it served to seal in everything below it, and in the course of years the layers often became quite thick.

The details of this story are well known, for soon after the discovery of the site the Rockefeller Foundation provided funds so that it might be excavated by a group of qualified scientists.

Courtesy Field Museum of Natural History, Chicago

PREHISTORIC CAVE NEAR PEKIN, CHINA
Site of the discovery of Pekin Man (Sinanthropus pekinensis)

Into this cave came the animals of long ago seeking shelter, and here also came man.

The flesh-eating animals dragged in portions of their kill and man likewise carried the choicer portions from the hunt to his home in the rocks and cooked the meat over fires.

Here in ancient China we have the first evidence of a fire made by man. Far back in the cave, close to the walls, he built tiny camp fires, over which he held pieces of meat to cook them. He also had the first stone tools of which we can be certain. Around his fires have been found about two thousand very crude flaked stones. These may have served as knives, but they are so primitive that they might have been considered accidental products of nature, were it not for the fact that they are all foreign to the cave and its vicinity. It is clear that they were brought in for a purpose by an intelligent being. An ape may pick up a stone and use it as a hammer, but he neither fashions nor preserves any tool. Man alone makes tools and builds fires.

Close to the cave walls have been found quantities of hack-berries which were sealed in by the lime-charged waters. Here we have the first evidence of the storing of food by man.

Apparently the bones in the cave became sufficiently unpleas-ant at times so that the inhabitants disposed of them by throwing them into the fissure in the cave floor. Occasionally the stream would overflow and would wash sand and gravel into the opening, covering the bones. Then would come a long wet period when the lime-charged waters would deposit their loads and seal in everything below. In this manner the fissure was finally filled up and a deposit was laid over the floor. Ultimately the top of the cave fell in and for thousands of years the site was left undis-turbed.

When the scientists began to clear away the debris and to dig into the fissure, they found these evidences of occupancy by man and animals. They gathered more than two tons of bones of fossil animals which had lived in the early Ice Age. There can be no doubt as to the period in which this cave existed, and it can be said with certainty that everything in it dates back to that time when the first fields of ice advanced from the north across Asia.

ANCIENT HEAD HUNTERS

Now comes the most startling as well as the most important news. It appears that these early men may have been either head hunters, cannibals, or both. In the debris, along with animal bones, and in the fissure have been found portions of twenty-five or more human beings, but almost without exception these are skulls or portions of skulls. The most complete of these show that the lower portions had been broken away, probably to ex-tract the brains. What was the purpose of such an act? It may be that the brain was considered a special dainty, or these people of long ago may have had the idea that by eating this portion they gained the strength and valor of their victims. Certain primitive people of today eat the hearts, livers, or brains of their enemies in order to gain their good qualities, and such an explanation may be suggested for the cave people of China.

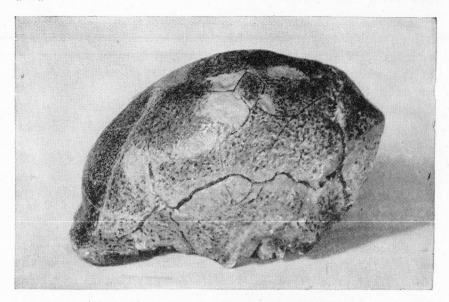

ABOVE: SIDE
VIEW OF THE
SINANTHROPUS
SKULL

●

BELOW:
TOP VIEW OF
SINANTHROPUS
SKULL
Note the huge ridges
above the eyes.

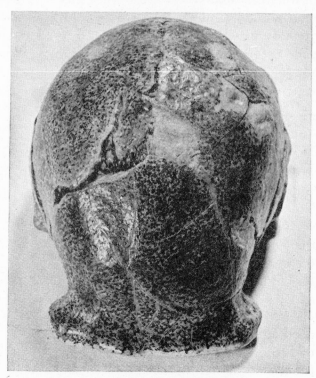

Courtesy Anthropological
Department, University
of Chicago
        Photos by
        Raeburn Rohrbach

What sort of man lived here while Pithecanthropus and his kind roamed the forests of Java?

From the teeth, many portions of skulls, and from three particularly complete heads, we know that these beings—who are called *Sinanthropus pekinensis,* or Pekin Man—were much like Pithecanthropus. The skulls were slightly larger and the forehead a little higher, but in some other respects they are even more primitive than the earlier find.

In general Java Man and Pekin Man are so much alike that we are justified in saying they are closely related.

MAN OF HALF A MILLION YEARS AGO

Judging by the evidence from the two discoveries, we can picture man of this early period as having heavy beetling brows, a projecting face, a chinless jaw in which were set teeth of a primitive character yet similar to those of later man. The forehead was low and the fore portion of the brain little developed, yet taken as a whole it was a great advance over all that had gone before. Man of a half million years ago had a better brain and a better mind than any other form of animal which has ever appeared in the world's history.

THE NEXT FOUR HUNDRED THOUSAND YEARS

Between the time of Pekin Man and the Cave Life of Europe, stretches a vast chain of years. Years in which the climate and animals of the northern regions were undergoing great change. Years in which man was slowly gaining control of nature.

Toward the end of the third period of the earth's history, the climate became cooler; ice fields began to accumulate in the far north and then to push southward. With the advance of the face of the ice sheet over Europe, the temperatures were further reduced. Heavy snows in the Alps and Pyrenees formed smaller glaciers which pushed down into the valleys until finally large portions of the land were covered. Plants and animals accustomed to a balmy climate were exterminated or driven southward, while the life of the Arctic regions took possession.

Courtesy Buffalo Museum of Science and Industry

A MOUNTAIN GLACIER
Great sheets of ice once covered large portions of Europe.

We call the period, from the time of the first advance of the ice up to about twenty thousand years ago, the "Ice Ages." But it was not a single invasion of the northern cold. After many thousands of years, the ice retreated as far north as Scandinavia and again the animals and plants of the South and East invaded the land. Then slowly the cold returned to be succeeded again by warmer conditions.

The record of these climatic changes is fully preserved in the strata of the rocks; it is told in successive layers of glacial deposits; it is recorded in glacial moraines. This record is a geological time-table by which we can date the advances made by man.

A similar story is known for America, but, since it has little bearing on human development, it is passed with mere mention.

In the strata laid down between the first two glaciations we begin to find evidences of man-made tools in Europe. We have already seen that Pekin Man made use of stone flakes, but it will be useful to watch the development of tools in one region.

Köehler, Yerkes, and other men who have made an intimate study of the great apes tell us that on occasion the apes will use clubs to knock down fruit, or will utilize handy stones to crush a nut or shell, but when the need is past the club or stone is discarded. Doubtless the first men likewise took advantage of whatever nature offered, but on that day when man deliberately fashioned a tool and, having done so, kept it for future use he started on the road which has led to civilization.

Fire and tools elevated man above the rest of the animal kingdom; they gave him advantages which no other beings possessed. Like other blessings, fire at times became a destroyer. When finally man began to put a high value on possessions, he prepared the way to the greatest curse man has known, the desire for possession which leads to strife and even organized warfare.

Crudely chipped flints have been found even in strata preceding the glaciers in Europe. Since they may have been made and used by man they have been called eoliths, or "dawn stones." However, many of these eoliths are doubtless the work of nature. Repeated heating and freezing, the striking of one stone against another as they were carried by a stream or avalanche, may and do produce chipping. Nature can chip stone, but it does not establish styles.

A SLAVE TO FASHION

As far back as we can trace man and his activities, we find that he has always been a slave to fashion. Once a method of stone-working was established, once a type of house was recognized, once a certain kind of garment was accepted, most of the people of that region followed the same custom as their fellows. Even today we dislike to be different from our companions, so we dress as they do, cut our hair according to the current style, eat off the same sort of dishes, even play the same games.

In the first interglacial period in France we begin to find a definite style in stone work. Some early inventor found that by striking a nodule of flint with another stone he could knock off flakes and produce an instrument which could be held in the hand. Compared with modern tools this was crude indeed, but it might be used to cut small sticks of wood for the fire, it could be utilized in cleaning the skin of an animal, it might even assist man in killing game or in defending himself in case of need.

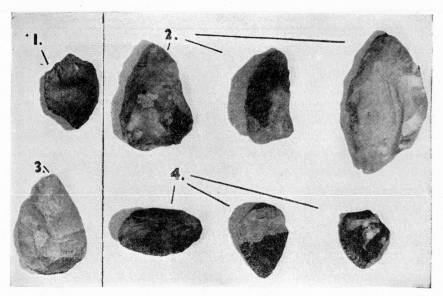

Courtesy University of Chicago   Photo by Raeburn Rohrbach

PLATE OF STONE TOOLS

1. EOLITH or DAWN STONE: Possibly one of the first tools made and used by man.
2. CHELLEAN HANDAXES: Crudely shaped tools which were held in the hand.
3. ACHEULEAN AXE: The edges are completely flaked indicating that the axe must
have had an handle.   4. MOUSTERIAN TOOLS: Neanderthal man had a variety of
tools made by using the flake instead of the core.

Judging by the large number of these stones which have been
found, it is apparent that a style had been started.

It is hard for us to realize how slowly culture developed in
those early days. In the next interglacial epoch, thousands of
years later, the same type of hand axe was still found in use. It
was much better made, the chipping was finer, but the idea was
still the same. Because the first of these tools were found near the
village of Chelles in France, they are called Chellean hand axes
and that stage is called the Chellean epoch.

Toward the middle of the third interglacial time a new idea
came into vogue. The axe was better flaked and sharpened all
the way around so that it could no longer be held in the hand.
This means that a handle had been added, truly a real invention,
for man's reach had been extended, he could kill at a greater
distance, he could strike a harder blow. At this time some of the
pointed flakes appear to have been used as spear points, while

others may have served as knives. This we call the Acheulian epoch because tools of this kind were first found near the village of St. Acheul.

We know little of the life of man of these times for he lived in the open, probably much like the pygmies of today. His frail dwellings were easily destroyed and all his possessions, except those of stone, have vanished. Yet we know he must have been in France in considerable numbers. Apparently he spent most of his time near the banks of rivers, for thousands of his tools have been found deep buried in the gravels of these streams.

Fortunately nature has preserved something of his story for us near Ehringsdorf in Germany.

In late Acheulian times a great game trail led through this region. At one point a wide, fairly level stretch of land bordered an ancient river. Back of this were limestone hills and cliffs.

Courtesy Field Museum of Natural History, Chicago

SCENE IN CHELLEAN TIMES
During the third interglacial epoch man was a hunter living in the open.

During the more favorable months of the year man made his camps on the level ground. When animals came to drink at the river, he killed what he needed and carried portions of the meat to his fires. Slowly a pile of refuse would accumulate around the camp. When the rainy season came on, waters from the hills would flow down over the camp and man would move away and live in the rock shelters. But the waters from the hills were heavily charged with lime which was deposited when the level ground was reached. Thus each year the materials left by man were sealed in limestone. Year by year, century after century, this continued until the deposit of stone reached a depth of more than eighty feet.

A few years ago a local company started to blast away the cliffs in order to secure materials for a kiln. As they did so, they encountered the camps made by men thousands of years ago. Some were near the top of the deposit, but others were found at all depths nearly to the bottom. Around these fires were the bones of the animals they had killed; there too were some of the utensils they had lost or broken, and, most surprising, the lime had covered portions of three human beings, so that finally we come to know something of the men who built the fires. Since these people are almost identical with the cave men, soon to be described, we shall mention them together.

Before we start to visit the caves, we should note that two more quite famous discoveries have been made in Europe, which tell us something of the people who preceded the cave dwellers.

A MAN WITHOUT A CHIN

Near Heidelberg in Germany a huge jaw was found deep buried in a sand pit, associated with bones of animals which flourished during the second great glaciation—three hundred thousand or more years ago.

The jaw itself is a huge affair, much larger than those of modern men, and it slopes away rapidly at the point where we have developed a chin. The lines of muscle attachment indicate that its owner had a heavy projecting face much like that of the apes, but here again teeth come to the rescue. All the teeth are

THE
HEIDELBERG
JAW
A massive ape-like
jaw with human
teeth.

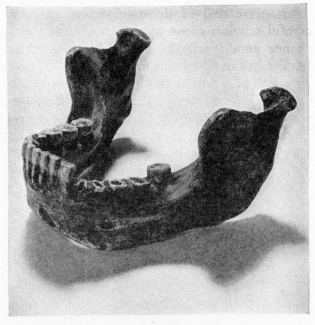

Courtesy University
of Chicago
  Photo by
  Raeburn Rohrbach

distinctly human and all are of the same height. Even so we
might be hesitant to call the owner a human being were it not
for the fact that the later cave men of Europe have the same
kind of jaws and teeth, only smaller. For these reasons this being
is called the Heidelberg Man.

A LADY WITH AN APE'S JAW

Another discovery which has caused almost as much discussion as that of Pithecanthropus is the Piltdown Man, found near
the town of that name in Sussex, England.

A river deposit laid down during the third glaciation, at least
150,000 years ago, has yielded a skull and jaw showing a most
unusual combination of advanced and primitive traits. The skull
is far advanced toward later man while the jaw and teeth are
much like those of a fossil chimpanzee. They were found together, the jaw seems to fit the skull, and both are in the same
stage of mineralization. If they did belong to the same lady—
for it is a woman's skull—she was unlike any of the known fossils of earlier or later time.

A great deal of debate followed this discovery and many careful scholars came to the conclusion that this was merely a chance association. This would probably have been the final verdict had not a second find been made in the same strata. Here a portion of a similar skull was again found along with a portion of a like jaw and teeth. The second discovery greatly strengthens the claim that beings with these diverse characters once lived in England. The final answer must await future finds in this region.

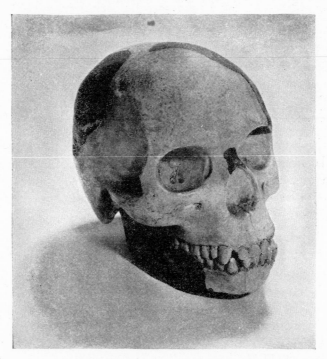

Courtesy University of Chicago   Photo by Raeburn Rohrbach

RESTORATION OF PILTDOWN MAN
This is the most disputed of all the discoveries of early man.

ABOUT fifty thousand years ago the ice sheet came back over Europe, and man who had been living along the rivers found it necessary to take refuge in caves and rock shelters. But other animals also wished to live in the caverns, and we can picture many fierce struggles for possession.

A FIGHT WITH A GIANT CAVE BEAR

In one cave there was found a skeleton of a giant cave bear with a stone axe deeply buried in the side of its head. The man who swung that axe must have been within arm's reach of the animal, for it would have been impossible to throw it with sufficient force to penetrate the skull. In this case we may suspect that the hunter lost his life, for the blow did not kill the bear.

NEANDERTHAL
MAN
Restoration based
on many skeletons
found in Europe.

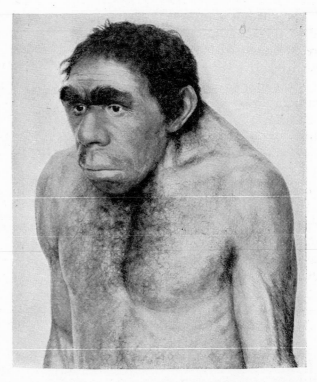

Courtesy Field Museum
of Natural History,
Chicago
    Sculptor,
    Frederick Blaschke

Although the axe was driven far into its head, it recovered and
the bone grew up around the blade. This skeleton is now preserved in the Museum at Trieste.

Several other skeletons of cave bears have been found under
conditions which indicate that they had been slaughtered, so it
appears that the struggle we have just described was not unusual.

LIFE IN THE CAVES

In such conflicts man had one great advantage. He possessed
fire which, for some reason, wild animals fear.

Near to the entrance of the caves have been found the remains of many fires. Small groups, perhaps families, would take
possession, would kindle flames to keep them warm and dry, and
over these they would cook the choicest parts of the game
they had killed. Having eaten, they would throw the bones to
one side.

They had no dogs or other tamed animals to act as scavengers, and so the accumulation of refuse would grow until even these careless housekeepers could stand it no longer. Then they would push back the ashes from the fires and cover it.

We can picture these people of long ago squatting in the dim light, chipping stone implements and probably making traps or cleaning skins. There is no evidence that they fashioned garments, but we know they must have covered their bodies with animal skins, for the cold became too intense to be endured without protection. All these activities helped to add to the accumulation on the cave floor.

From time to time the cave was deserted by its occupants. Perhaps the game was scarce, or death occurred and the people fled in terror, or mere whim directed a change. Whatever the cause we know that like other hunters they were often on the move.

No sooner had they departed than rodents and other animals moved in, and by their activities built up a layer of debris known

Courtesy Field Museum of Natural History, Chicago   Sculptor, Frederick Blaschke

NEANDERTHAL FAMILY
These people walked in a semi-erect position.

as a rodent layer. In some instances drip and rock falls from the cave roofs also helped to bury the evidences left by man. But after a time he would go back and the process would be repeated.

In this manner he left a record of his life and times much like that we are establishing in our city refuse heaps today.

WHAT A DUMP HEAP TELLS

At the Century of Progress in Chicago was a series of exhibits showing how the story of the past is revealed. One illustrated a section of a city dump. What was going into the pile in 1933? Electric light bulbs, parts of automobiles, radios, and other articles of daily use. What went in at the time of the World's Fair in 1893? None of the things just mentioned. In their places were oil lamps, wagon wheels, horse shoes, phonographs of early pattern, corsets, and many other objects of a nearly forgotten past. Finally appeared the refuse left by the Indians.

"THE CITY DUMP"

In our dump-heaps we are preserving a record of our lives which the archaeologists of the future may read.

Courtesy Logan Museum, Beloit College

THE MOUSTERIAN AGE
Neanderthal hunters stalking the mammoth.

In our dumps the archaeologist of a thousand years hence will be reading the intimate story of our civilization, just as we now learn of the life of the long ago. Our books may vanish, but this record will remain.

By examining the bones of the game the cave man killed and ate, we know the types of animals which flourished in his time, and from these we are able to determine the climate. Let us visit a few of the sites from which the record of cave life was gathered.

At Krapina in Hungary is a rock shelter which shows nine distinct layers or strata above the cave floor. At the bottom is river gravel, but the stream is now eighty-two feet below the entrance. This means that an infinitely long time must have elapsed while the brook was cutting the valley to this depth. Above the gravels we find evidences of successive levels of occupation. In these occur bones of the cave bear, wild cattle, beaver, and the rhino. Man-made tools appear, and here also are portions of ten human individuals. Many of the bones are split and broken, and some show signs of fire. Perhaps we have here evidences of a cannibal feast.

At La Chapelle-aux-Saints in France is a cave in which was buried the body of an old man. With and near him were flint implements, shells, and bones of the reindeer, bison, fox, horse, rhinoceros, and several kinds of birds.

In a grotto at Spy in Belgium were several layers of deposits. In the lowest were human bones and utensils associated with bones of mammoth, woolly rhino, cave bear, and cave hyena.

Many other caves have been excavated, but these samples will show how the animal life indicates climate. Those at Spy just mentioned are typical of a region of intense cold, while those at LaChapelle belong to a milder period.

DEAD MEN TALK

In the deposits laid down during the advance of the last ice sheet there have been discovered forty-two skeletons in Europe, fourteen in Palestine, and quite recently eleven have been excavated in Java. All conform rather closely to one physical type, and this differs so greatly from later man that we treat them as a unit. Because the first skeleton of this group to be discovered

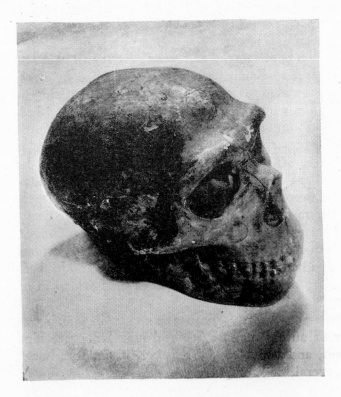

SKULL OF
NEANDERTHAL
MAN

These very primitive people lived in the caves of Europe 50,-000 years ago.

Courtesy University
of Chicago
Photo by
Raeburn Rohrbach

came from the Neander Valley, this people has been called the Neanderthal (Neander Valley) race.

All but a few of the skeletons which have been discovered have been buried with food and objects of daily use. This is a most significant fact, for it means that those people probably believed in a life after death and that they were providing the departed with objects they might use in the future world. This is the first evidence we have of a belief in immortality, the first hint of religion.

Association of tools with the dead also tells us definitely of the implements in use at the time of the burial. Still more important for science is the preservation of this large number of skeletons. Heretofore, we have been dependent on chance preservation. Now the story becomes more complete. These skeletons range from children to adult men and women and give us an excellent picture of Neanderthal Man who lived in Europe fifty thousand years ago.

WHAT WE KNOW OF MAN OF FIFTY THOUSAND YEARS AGO

His head was long and low and narrow. Above the eyes was still a huge ridge of bone, not so immense as in the ancient men of Java and China, but far greater than found in any living race. Hidden below these ridges were large round eye openings. The face was long and thrust forward like a snout. The low, flat nose opened onto a long upper lip in a sort of trough, such as we observe in a chimpanzee or orang outang.

The lower jaw is interesting, for it is like that we saw in Heidelberg Man, except that it is smaller. Like Andy Gump and Uncle Bim these people had failed to develop a chin.

The sloping forehead indicates a rather low mentality, but the posterior portion of the skull shows great development. When we take casts of the interior of the skulls it is clear that these people had brains much inferior to later man.

All the Neanderthalers were of stocky build, with short arms and large hands. Their heads hung forward on thick necks, giving the appearance of stoop shoulders. Always the thigh bone was bent and the muscle attachments show that men of this race walked in a semi-erect position.

A more detailed description would show even more clearly that the Neanderthal people were exceedingly primitive, but enough has been said to indicate that they were quite unlike any living race.

NEW TOOLS

About the time that Neanderthal Man went to the caves a new method of stone working was coming into use. Man had discovered that by striking a nodule of flint in a certain manner he could knock off flakes the size that he desired, and that these needed no retouching on one side. The outer, convex portion, he shaped by striking off smaller flakes, and then he sharpened the edges by secondary blows which left little scars resembling the gnawing of a rat.

In this way he produced axes, knives, planes, spear heads, and many other objects. The work was crude but allowed for greater variety and was much more easily produced than the hand axes of earlier times. This industry was first recognized at La Moustier, in France, and hence the whole cultural epoch of Neanderthal Man in Europe is called Mousterian.

SLOW PROGRESS

As we look back over the long record from the first known tools of Pekin Man up to the end of the Mousterian times, we are impressed that human development and cultural progress were very slow. Nearly a half million years had elapsed, yet man was still a primitive savage without domestic animals or plants. There is no evidence that he had developed tools or weapons more effective than the hafted axe and flint tipped spear, or that he had clothing other than an animal skin to wrap around his body. But he was making progress; he was learning new ways of fashioning tools, and he had come to the realization that there was a difference between flesh and spirit; he had come to believe in life after death.

Courtesy Field Museum of Natural History, Chicago   Photo by Cole

THE FIRE SAW
A pygmy of the Malay Peninsula making fire by rubbing one piece
of bamboo across another.

Probably the most important of all his discoveries, so far as his ability to survive was concerned, was the making of fire. Since this is always a major interest, we will take note of the various methods used by primitive man in producing a flame.

MAKING A FIRE WITHOUT MATCHES

Man must have been familiar with fire from the beginning of his existence, for spontaneous combustion, lightning, or volcanic eruptions would introduce flames from time to time, but he had no control over them.

No one knows how the making of fire was first discovered. Perhaps in play, two men may have drawn a vine or strip of rattan back and forth across a rotten tree. If this were repeated rapidly at one spot the friction would probably set the wood on fire. This method was formerly practiced in Scandinavia and is still in use among the pygmies of Palawan, north of Borneo, and in the interior of New Guinea. There each man wears a rattan armlet which serves as an ornament, but when he needs a fire he unrolls enough to make a loop. Next he cuts a piece of bark from his clout and lays it on the ground. On this is placed a split stick of soft dry wood. He passes the loop between the cloth and stick, places his foot upon the latter and draws the rattan rapidly up and down, until the friction produces enough heat to ignite the cloth.

More wide spread is the bamboo saw used throughout Malaysia. A section of bamboo is split lengthwise, and across the back of one piece a groove is cut through. Bark, cloth, or other tinder is placed below this opening and then the thin edge of the other section is rubbed rapidly in the groove. Soon enough heat is generated to set the tinder afire. A pygmy using this method won the primitive fire-making contest against all comers at the St. Louis Fair—time, less than one minute.

The American Indian had learned that he could produce fire by twirling a hardwood stick rapidly between his palms. The lower end of the shaft was allowed to turn in a groove cut in a soft plank, until the saw-dust it produced was on fire.

A modification of this is the bow drill used in the house of the Eskimo. Here a loop of the bowstring passes around a hardwood shaft, causing it to spin when the bow is sawed back and forth.

Of the same general nature is the fire plow of New Guinea. A long piece of soft wood rests on the ground and against the body of the operator. A lengthwise groove has been cut and in this a hardwood shaft is plowed up and down. The friction produces a powder and heat to ignite it.

It is possible that when fashioning flint tools the maker observed that sparks were often produced. He may have noticed that, if he were using iron pyrites or similar stone as a shaping instrument, the sparks were brighter and more frequent. Quite possibly some of these sparks may have set fire to dry grass or other inflammable material and thus may have given the idea of

Courtesy Buffalo Museum of Science, Buffalo, N. Y.

FIREMAKING BY PRIMITIVE PEOPLE

Upper shelf, left to right: Fire by percussion, fire by bow drill, fire by concussion of air.
Middle shelf: Fire by hand drill, fire by sawing, fire by weighted drill, fire by plowing.
Lower shelf: Bow drill and hearth, weighted drill and hearth.

a fire-making device which ultimately developed into the flint and steel.

Most discoveries are the results of accidents, and it is man's ability to capitalize on these which has led to his present civilization. However, one method of fire-making, utilized by certain peoples in the Philippines and other portions of the Southeastern Orient, must have been a real invention. The so-called "fire syringe" is far too complicated to have been due to chance.

This device consists of a small churn-shaped piece of wood or horn into which a cylindrical hole has been bored. A carefully made plunger fits snugly into this. At the bottom of this piston is a small hole into which tree cotton can be crammed, while grooves cut near the end allow a few threads to be wound in. This tinder of cotton and thread is rubbed with grease, then the plunger is placed at the top of the opening and is driven in with a sharp blow of the hand. If it is immediately withdrawn, the tinder will be in flames. The compression of the air has caused it to be set on fire.

Primitive methods of making fire survived until a little more than a hundred years ago when our match was invented.

NEANDERTHAL MAN VANISHES

We have seen that the life of Neanderthal Man was one of constant struggle against the forces of nature. The intense cold must have made existence difficult; the caves in which he dwelt were dark and often damp and unsanitary. On the bones of some skeletons are registered evidence of rheumatism and other diseases produced by bad conditions or improper food.

As the last great glaciation began to wane, and the climate began to moderate, two invasions occurred which probably led to the extinction of these people as a race. The first consisted of vast numbers of rodents called lemmings. Even today these animals appear in droves, in northern Europe, and press steadily over the land until finally they reach the sea into which they plunge and are drowned.

Apparently these animals overran the land of the Neanderthal people, for we find great numbers of their skeletons in deposits of that period, and in many caves.

The second invasion was by a new race of men, the Cro-Magnon. With their appearance Neanderthal man vanishes.

We are accustomed to think of Europe as the center of the universe, but in the Stone Ages it was on the remote outskirts of human development.

While Neanderthal Man still lingered in France and Germany, new types had developed in regions to the east and south. Among these were the people we call Cro-Magnon. We do not know their exact homeland but we can trace them from the east, up the Valley of the Danube, and along the northern shores of the Mediterranean, as they made their way into Europe.

Very different landscapes from those of today greeted the newcomers. The ice still covered much of the land, but the North Sea was a meadow and the mammoth roamed from England to Alaska. The Mediterranean formed two inland seas with

COLUMBIAN MAMMOTH (ELEPHAS COLUMBI)

The mammoth lived during the time of the early cavemen. In Europe, stone weapons have been found lying in the ground with mammoth bones, and drawings of the beast were made by the cavemen upon the walls of their dwellings.

2

land bridges by way of Gibraltar and Italy; the Sahara and Arabian deserts were grassy plains.

Over much of Europe the woolly rhino, mammoth, cave bear, arctic fox, and glutton still roamed, but as the climate moderated the reindeer and horse became common.

We know a great deal about the Cro-Magnon people, for they buried their dead, and this has preserved for us seventy-two skeletons from western Europe, while still others have been discovered in Moravia.

In general they were tall, with long arms and legs, and unlike Neanderthal Man they walked erect. Their heads were long and narrow and high, the foreheads were dome-shaped, and there was no forward projection of the face. Very wide cheek bones, long narrow noses, narrow eyes, and "strong" chins gave to them an appearance much like that of modern man. In fact there is little doubt but that they belonged to our own species—*Homo sapiens*. Their large, well-proportioned brains indicate that they were capable of great cultural development, yet at the time they entered Europe they were still primitive hunters. They knew nothing of domestic animals; no dog accompanied them on the hunt; they had not yet learned the use of the bow and arrow; and no pots had been invented in which to cook their food. Judged by the standards even of the more primitive peoples of today, their life was very meagre. Here an important fact is brought sharply to our notice, a fact which will help to explain some of the events we are to witness in later paragraphs. It appears that no matter how fine a body we may possess, no matter how large or well-proportioned our brains may be, we will remain lowly primitives unless we have the background of history, of experience. Cro-Magnon apparently was as well endowed as we are, but his ancestors had not gone through the many stages which have led us from savagery to civilization. No writing preserved the experiences of the past.

We have stressed what Cro-Magnon lacked; we must not overlook what he possessed. That record is well preserved in many caves and loess deposits, and it is to them we shall now turn.

CRO-MAGNON
RESTORATION

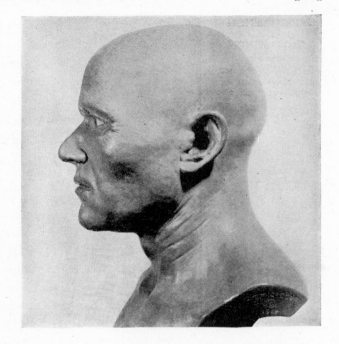

Restoration by
Dr. J. H. McGregor
Courtesy University
of Chicago
   Photo by
   Raeburn Rohrbach

CRO-MAGNON
SKULL

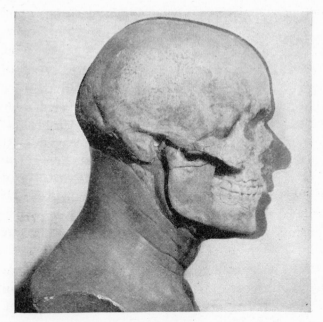

Restoration by
Dr. J. H. McGregor
   Courtesy of University
   of Chicago
      Photo by
      Raeburn Rohrbach

RESTORATION
OF
CRO-MAGNON
MAN
In Cro-Magnon we
first meet man of
our own species.

Courtesy American Mu-
seum of Natural History,
New York

AN UNSOLVED MURDER OF TWENTY THOUSAND YEARS AGO

Near Les Eyzies France was an ancient grotto. A few thousand years ago a landslide closed the entrance, so that its contents were quite undisturbed when it was discovered. At the bottom of the cave were found ashes of an ancient fire below blocks of stone which had fallen from the roof. Apparently the inhabitants were absent when this catastrophe occurred, for no bodies lie below the debris. After a time they returned and again occupied the cave, but for some reason they soon deserted it again and a sterile layer accumulated. Then came a long period of occupancy during which debris accumulated around the hearths.

In this layer were found five human beings, apparently buried. One was the skeleton of a woman who had evidently been severely wounded with a sharp edged instrument. Apparently she had lived for several weeks after the attack, for the bone had partially healed. Beside her was the skeleton of an unborn child. No further record of this tragedy is preserved, but we may surmise that the body was buried by friends, for necklaces and bracelets of perforated shells and ivory were placed with the dead. In this cave were also found engravings on bone, one of a woman, another of a bison.

Near Mentone in Italy a group of nine grottoes was discovered during the making of a railway cut. Here a number of Cro-Magnon burials were found. One had been arranged so that the head was resting on the left arm and hand. Near the neck and knees lay hundreds of perforated sea shells and a number of stag's teeth which had probably formed a necklace and leglets. Close beside the body was a bone dagger and a number of flint utensils. Over the skeleton red ochre had been sprinkled. In this same deposit were bones of the cave bear and the woolly rhino.

A nearby cave yielded four more skeletons of the same type, associated with bones of deer, ibex, leopard, moose, and other animals. Below the level of the Cro-Magnon burials were evidences of occupation during the Mousterian epoch when Neanderthal Man was in the land.

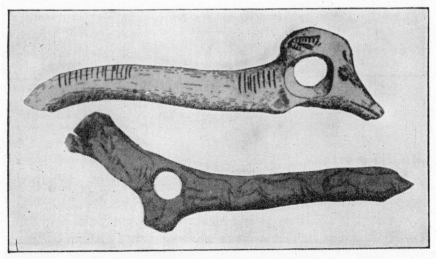

CARVED BONE UTENSILS
These may have served as shapers for the foreshaft of darts. (After Breuil)

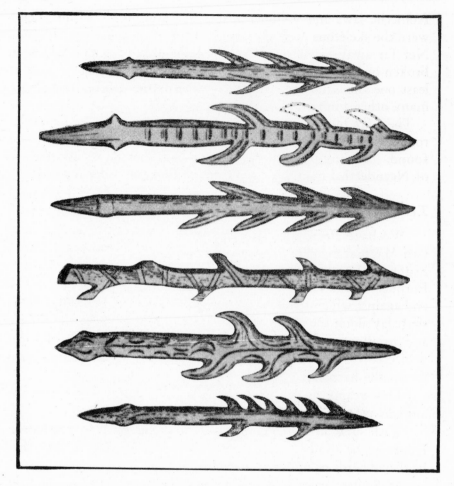

BARBED BONE POINTS
Such detachable points were doubtless used as harpoon heads. **(After Breuil)**

MIGHTY HUNTERS OF LONG AGO

At Predmost in Moravia hearths were found in and below deep layers of loess—fine glacial dust. Here lay blades and scrapers of stone, spear points of bone, daggers constructed from the leg bones of lions and bears, clubs and six figurines of mammoth bones, ladles of ivory, and necklaces made from the teeth of bear and other animals. Here also was a tomb constructed

from the jaws and shoulder blades of mammoths, within which
were the skeletons of twelve men and women and eight children.
Not far away was a pile of wolf skulls each of which had been
broken open to extract the brains. It is estimated that parts of at
least one thousand mammoths have been found here, along with
many other animals.

These are but a few of a large number of sites in which skeletons of Cro-Magnon man and evidences of his culture have been
found. In many places the levels in which they lie are above those
of Neanderthal man, but never do we find the order reversed.

THE CULTURE OF CRO-MAGNON

We have already noted some of the objects possessed by the
Cro-Magnon people. Probably the most important weapon they
had was the spear thrower and harpoon, an invention new to
Europe. This was a short lever of bone with a projection at the
end against which the butt of the harpoon or dart could rest. The
shaft lay along the throwing rod and was held between the thumb
and forefinger, so that it could be guided when the missile was
projected forward. Detachable bone points with barbs were used
to tip the harpoons.

This weapon is still in use by the Eskimo and is effective for
animals as large as the seal and the walrus.

With such an instrument man could kill game at a distance.
Doubtless he also had traps and pitfalls, and we may suspect that
he drove herds of animals over cliffs.

At Solutre in east central France is a layer of loess, ten feet
in depth, in which have been found objects and burials of Cro-
Magnon times. Here also were many fire-places about which lay
the charred, broken, and split bones of more than one hundred
thousand horses. It appears that the hunters of long ago drove
herds of wild horses over the edge of the nearby cliffs and
slaughtered them.

Of equal importance for food, and probably for clothing, was
the reindeer. In fact, that animal is so commonly found that this
period is frequently called the Reindeer Period. Mention has already been made of many of the other animals hunted.

Courtesy Buffalo Museum of Science, Buffalo, N. Y.

CRO-MAGNON CAVE MAN
These people occupied the caves of western Europe, mainly in France and Spain, approximately 20,000 years ago

Courtesy University of Chicago

CRO-MAGNON STONE WORK
Stone work of Cro-Magnon times was inferior to that of earlier epochs, probably due to the great development of bone utensils.

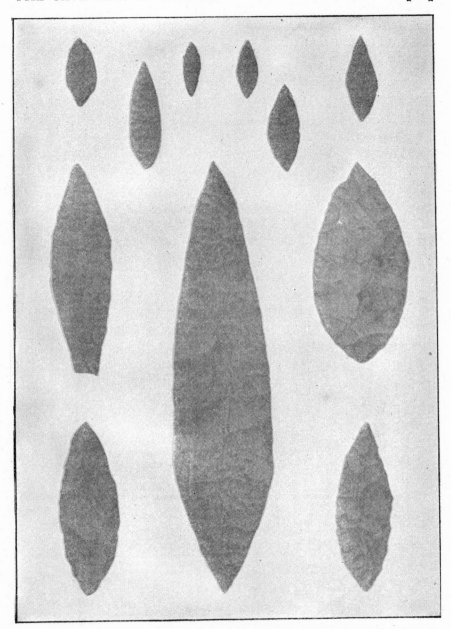

IMPLEMENTS OF THE SOLUTREAN EPOCH

During Solutrean times a great number of these "laurel-leaf" blades were made.
They are unusually thin and beautifully chipped.

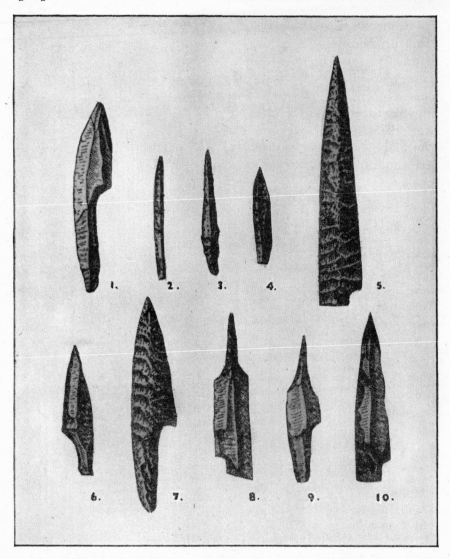

SOLUTREAN TOOLS
Pressure flaking first appears in Solutrean times. By its use symmetrical
leaf shape tools were produced. (After MacCurdy)

Stone work was of less importance than in previous times, probably because of the greater use of bone. Apparently the stone hatchet was no longer made, but many small blades, which served as scrapers and knives, were produced by a slightly different process. A piece of flint was smoothed off so as to make a level striking platform; then, by well-directed blows, thin narrow blades were detached. These were usually employed as they came from the block, without secondary chipping. Because of the ease of manufacture, they were cast aside as soon as they became dull or broken.

During one short period, the Solutrean, a new type of stone work, made by pressure flaking, appeared, but its range was limited and its period brief. We shall encounter this method again in later times.

Bone knives and skewers were common, and hundreds of bone needles and "buttons" suggest tailored garments. Bone whistles and flutes indicate the birth of music, while shallow stone lamps like those used by the Eskimo show that man was no longer entirely dependent upon the campfire for light after dark.

Compared with what had gone before, this age was a great advance; compared with what followed, it is extremely crude. In only one field did Cro-Magnon show his great potential ability, and that was in art.

CAVE MAN ART

Primitive people of today generally have some idea of art, of design. Even the lowly pygmy beautifies his body with scars arranged in patterns, while his wife wears a bamboo comb or arm band on which are incised designs.

Some of the headhunting tribes of the Philippines make elaborate carvings of beings represented in their folklore, while neighboring tribes show all their artistic ability in their weaving.

Hunting people often depict the game they are seeking, and then use these figures in magical rites to make the animals plentiful and more easily taken.

Writers have long debated whether art started when men sought to make reproductions of the plant and animal life about

Courtesy Field Museum of Natural History, Chicago

MAGDALENIAN BAS-RELIEF OF HORSES
Cro-Magnon man depicted the game which he hunted, in pictures, carvings and models.

them, or whether aimless marks and scratches suggested forms with which they were familiar. In other words, was art at first realistic slowly becoming conventionalized, or did it start with lines and dots and later develop into real pictures?

EARLY
ATTEMPTS
AT ART
Hands,   silhouetted
against a color, from
the cave of Castillo.
    (After Breuil)

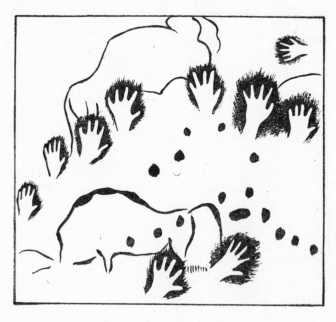

Perhaps the art of the cave men may throw some light on the discussion, while the practices of the present primitives may help to explain the pictures on the rocks.

There is no evidence whatever that the Neanderthal people had any art. This does not deny the possibility that they may have made designs on perishable materials but, if so, none have survived.

The first known attempts to represent any objects are found in the caves of Europe after the arrival of Cro-Magnon. There on the walls we find imprints of human hands. In some cases they had been dipped in pigment and pressed against the walls, but more frequently the palm was spread on the rock and then was outlined in charcoal. Here an interesting custom is shown, for in many cases it is evident that joints of one or more fingers are missing. It occurs too often to represent a single accident. What does this mean?

In parts of Africa it is the custom to knock out the front teeth or to amputate a finger joint when a boy reaches manhood. Apparently some such custom existed here. But why such a practice? Usually there is an explanation, but the real answer for the continuance of such a rite is custom.

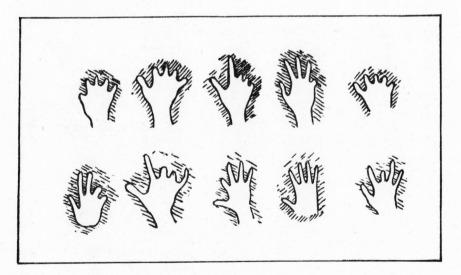

CRO-MAGNON STYLE?

These prints show joints of one or more fingers missing. Did this custom represent some Cro-Magnon rite? No one knows.

Why do our men shave or women bob their hair? We may answer that it is more comfortable, but remember that our grandfathers and grandmothers also wished to be comfortable, yet the men wore beards and the ladies prided themselves on their long tresses. A few years ago American audiences laughed when a lecturer showed Malay girls with their fingernails and toenails colored yellow, but in this year of grace our young women have blood red nails and carmine lips.

The first animals to be shown are outline drawings. These are crude, and, like pictures done by children, often have one leg showing through the other. Nevertheless the figures are in good proportion and many indicate action. From this stage on development is steady. Animals standing alone or in groups are drawn and engraved on the smooth walls of caves or are placed on objects of daily use.

In the earlier stages only outlines in one color appear, but later shading was attempted and then a combination of colors. Oxides of iron were employed to produce red and yellow, while carbon, white clay, and mineral pigments mixed with animal fat were added as desired.

A few figurines of human beings have been found. Most of these belong to the early stage of Cro-Magnon occupancy and seem to indicate that at the time of their entry into Europe these people must have been familiar with a people much like the present Bushmen of Africa. These figures are of short fat women with huge hips. Strangely, the faces and feet are never finished.

Aside from these human representations, nearly all the art is devoted to animals whose bones are found around the fires. Some of these are shown with darts or spear points piercing their bodies, and this suggests that one purpose of these pictures was to cause the animals to be plentiful and easily killed.

Most of these drawings and engravings are in recesses of dark caverns where the work had to be executed and viewed by the light of flickering torches or primitive stone lamps. It is possible, of course, that some of these pictures were done to while away the long hours spent in the caves, but we may suspect that at least part of them were used in magical practices.

THE BISON OF ALTAMIRA

A famous colored representation of a bison found on the cave ceiling at Altamira, Spain.
(After Cartailhac and Breuil)

Several cases of modeling in clay have been discovered, from time to time, but they have been so far destroyed by the action of men and animals that little can be told about them. However, one cave has yielded figures which proclaim Cro-Magnon a real sculptor.

CLAY BISONS

The only entrance to the French cavern of Tuc d'Audoubert is the opening through which the underground river Volp emerges. In winter this is filled with water, but in summer it is possible to wade in and, by using hooks to grasp the side walls, push one's way against the current, until finally a large gallery is reached. This opens into a cave on the walls of which are engravings of horses. At one place is a small opening or chimney which can be climbed with difficulty to reach a small chamber on the walls of which are figures of bison. Still above this is a third level,

Courtesy Field Museum of Natural History, Chicago

CLAY BISONS
Two unusually perfect figures of bison discovered in a cave in France.

the entrance to which had been closed by stalactites. The discoverers of this cave broke down these ancient barriers built up by nature and found themselves in a large cavern. There on the floor were bones of bears, flint implements, and finally, in a deep recess, were found the sculptured figures of two clay bisons. These were moulded in high relief against a rock. Each was about two feet in length and was complete, even to the indication of hair, made by fine incised lines. Two smaller animals had been started but never completed. Beside the figures were bits of clay bearing the finger prints of the sculptors, and on the clay of the cave floor were imprints of their naked feet. You have the feeling as you look at the sculptored bison that the artists have just stepped out for a moment, yet the cave has not been visited for thousands of years. These figures compare favorably with the work of modern sculptors and indicate something of the ability of the makers.

The question is often asked, "How do you know when this work was done?" The answer is fairly easy. In the first place the animals depicted are those whose bones are found around the fires, associated with objects of Cro-Magnon culture. Many of those animals are now extinct but are typical of the days when the ice sheet was retreating. Again much of the art work is engraved on the bone objects used in every day life, objects buried with Cro-Magnon skeletons or found around their camps. In some cases the paintings and engravings on the walls of the caves have been covered by refuse and deposits built up in later times. Reindeer, cave bears, mammoth, the ibex, and similar animals left Europe at the end of the Ice Age. It is exceedingly unlikely that later races would attempt to depict animals with which they could not have been familiar.

"THE STAG HUNT"
From the "Cueva del Mas d'en Josep." (After Peake-Fleure)

Toward the end of Cro-Magnon supremacy, a new type of art work, which seems to be related to that of the Bushmen of today, appeared in Spain. Apparently it spread or was carried from Africa, for it only penetrated a short distance into Europe.

So-called shadow pictures show bodies of men and women, often as mere lines to which are added heads, arms, and legs. Many of the men carry bows and arrows, a weapon not known until the end of the Cro-Magnon times, and are shown in lively action. One figure seems to be that of a woman climbing a tree; a raised hand and circular lines about her head suggest that she may be warding off little black objects which seem to be flying about her. One writer labels this drawing "a woman robbing a bee tree."

FIVE THOUSAND YEARS OF CRO-MAGNON

For at least five thousand years Cro-Magnon was dominant in Europe. It is evident that he underwent some changes and some physical deterioration while in the land, for the later burials indicate a smaller people than those found at Mentone. It is possible also that he may have intermarried to a certain extent with other

MURAL PAINTING
In the Rock Shelter of Cogul, Lerida, Spain. Probably final Magdalenian.
(After Breuil and Cabré)

SHADOW PICTURES FROM THE SPANISH CAVES
A type of art, resembling that of the present day Bushmen, is found in the caves of southern Spain. Such drawings probably belong to the final stage of Cro-Magnon man's occupancy of Europe. (After Breuil)

peoples. At any rate, we know that he was not the sole possessor of Europe throughout his stay. In one of the caves at Mentone, Italy, already mentioned, are deep deposits built up primarily by man. Here have been found several Cro-Magnon burials, immediately below one of which, at a depth of 29 feet, was another grave containing two individuals. These people were not typical Cro-Magnon, for they were slight of build and had many characteristics which we today would call Negroid. They were not true Negroes, but it seems certain that they were related to that race. Everything indicates that this burial is of about the same date as that of the nearby Cro-Magnon graves, so it appears that the races must have met at this point.

About the middle of Cro-Magnon times there was a short mild period, which is known as Solutrean. It was a time of terrific wind storms when glacial silt and dust-loess—were carried great distances, but it was also a time when man could be in the open. In the deposits of this period have been found several skeletons which

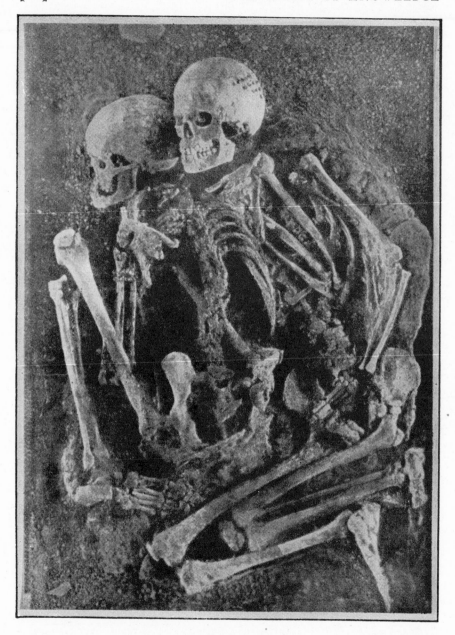

GRIMALDI MAN
Two skeletons showing negroid characteristics were found below a Cro-Magnon burial
near Mentone, Italy. (After Vernau)

have heavy brow ridges and narrow faces. They may be an invading people from the East or a divergent branch of Cro-Magnon. The Mammoth Hunters of Moravia, found in the deposits
at Predmost, likewise differ somewhat from the classical type already described.

SNAIL EATERS OF NORTH AFRICA

While Cro-Magnon flourished in Europe, a rather similar culture existed in northern Africa. There the milder climate allowed
man to live in the open. He was a hunter, as the many bones of
animals about his camp testify, but his chief source of food was
snails. He gathered millions of these and, having withdrawn the
meat, tossed the shells aside. In time these accumulated to form
great heaps, many feet in depth and covering several acres. Implements like those of Europe appear throughout the mounds but
a number of burials indicate that the inhabitants belonged to the
Mediterranean race. Here also was found the body of a woman
showing Negroid characters.

SUMMARY OF THE ICE AGES

If now we review what we have learned of man during the Ice
Ages, we see that human development has not been in a single line.

Pithecanthropus and Sinanthropus may be ancestral to, or
closely related to, Neanderthal Man; but Cro-Magnon is at best
only a distant relative.

Survival during the periods of intense cold was not easy for
a being without a natural covering of fur or one not physically
equipped for struggle with savage beasts. But the human brain
overcame these shortcomings and allowed man to survive against
all competitors.

THE TRANSITIONAL EPOCH

With the final retreat of the glaciers great changes occurred.
Animals accustomed to live under severe climatic conditions migrated to the North and Northeast, and it is possible that many of

·NEST OF HUMAN SKULLS
Found in the Transitional layer at Ofnet. Here long heads and round heads
appear in the same burial. (After R. R. Schmidt)

the hunters who depended upon them for food followed the herds out of Europe. However, some evidently remained and intermarried with the races which later occupied the land. Modern forest trees and plants appeared and with them came new forms of animal life.

At this time we find evidence of the modern races of men.

NESTS OF HEADS

In a cave at Ofnet in Germany have been found successive strata built up during the occupancy of Cro-Magnon man. Above these is a deposit in which bones of modern forest animals replace those of the reindeer, mammoth, and other fauna of the Ice Age. Here also appear tools of the transitional type soon to be described. In this deposit are two groups of heads arranged much like eggs in a nest. Some of these were evidently cut from the bodies soon after death, for the neck bones, bearing the marks of stone tools, are still in place. In one of these nests were twenty-seven skulls, in the other there were six. Nineteen of these were of children, ten were of young women, and four were of adult males. They must have been part of a sacrifice, for they are carefully buried and offerings of utensils appear with them. Of special interest to us is the fact that none of them is of the typical Cro-Magnon type, but all clearly resemble modern man. Some have long heads, some round, while others are intermediate. Several other discoveries of bodies apparently of this epoch likewise testify to the arrival of the modern races.

Courtesy Logan Museum, Beloit College

LAKE DWELLERS OF SWITZERLAND
These people built their homes over the waters of the lakes and
thus were safe from their enemies.

BEFORE saying more about the looks of these newcomers it will be interesting to see what they brought with them and how they lived. The milder climate not only allowed them to live in the open, but changed conditions often forced them to make their camps along the banks of streams and lakes. The great herds had vanished and in their place came deer, wild boars, bears, lynx, foxes, beavers, rabbits, and water rats. Man killed and ate all of these, but they were not sufficiently numerous to supply many hungry mouths, and so the hunters had to seek other foods. In other words, they became primarily food gatherers and fishermen.

We have already seen that great shell heaps exist in North Africa. In the Transitional these became common in Europe, especially in the region of the Baltic Sea, where some exceed a thousand feet in length and are fifteen to twenty feet in height. In the debris around these old camps we find the bones of many fish—herring, cod, and eels—and of such birds as the eagle, goose, duck, partridge, and swan.

The stone tools of earlier epochs were largely replaced by tiny flints in geometric forms. Some of these may have been set in bone or wooden handles and have been used as knives or saws, others may have been employed for boring holes in bone fish-hooks and harpoon points. One use for the smaller flints is indicated by the discovery of harpoons with side grooves into which the tiny flakes were set.

In Cro-Magnon times excellent harpoon points were constructed from reindeer horn, but that animal had now vanished from Europe and in its place the horn of the stag was used. This was more porous and necessitated inferior, flat-sided points. Bone fishhooks and pins were made, but there was a complete absence of needles, ladles, and other fine objects of bone and ivory so common in preceding times. Art also shows decline; in fact, about all that can be called art is found in geometric designs and dots painted on pebbles. What this represents or how the stones were used is quite unknown.

Taken as a whole, this epoch was inferior to that of the Cro-Magnon Cave Dwellers, but at least two notable advances had been made. The newcomers possessed the bow and the arrow, and in some regions the dog had become their friend and companion. Judging by the evidence found in the shell heaps, the dog appeared at first as a camp follower, a scavenger, but later he was accepted by the family and we find his bones buried with those of his master. The Transitional is notable also in that it is at this time that the modern races first appeared in Europe.

WHAT IS A RACE

Probably no word in the English language is more important than race, yet none is more misunderstood. One man speaks of an Aryan race. But Aryan simply means a person who speaks an Aryan or Indo-European language, and people of many races from Russia to India come under such a grouping. Another tells of a French race, but France is a nationality and people of three races make up her population. Today we hear a great deal about the Jewish race, but this also is without justification. The Jews once formed a nation, and today they are a religious group or

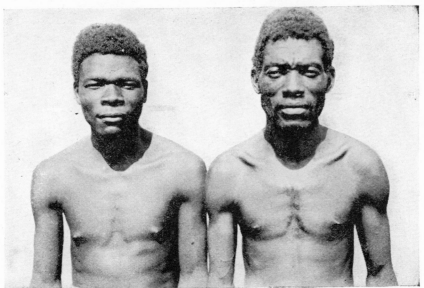

Courtesy Field Museum of Natural History, Chicago   Photo by Frederick H. Rawson Expedition

NEGRO TYPES

Dark skin, very curly hair, broad noses, and thick everted lips are characteristic
of the Negroes. Ovimbundu tribe, Elende, Angola.

caste, but they are not a race. Probably the ancient Jews were
Mediterraneans, but following the break-up of their kingdom
they roamed far and wide. In North Africa they converted whole
tribes of the Mediterranean Berbers to their faith; in the Caucasus
they were joined by many Armenoids, while in the region of the
Black Sea the Khazars, a people of Alpine Race, officially adopted
the Jewish faith in 740 A.D. Two centuries later the empire of
the Khazars was destroyed by the Slavs, and its people were scattered over Central Europe where they were recognized as Jews.
Today most Jewish people belong to the Alpine race, but many
are Mediterraneans and Armenoids, while some are Nordics.

The term race means a group of people who have in common
certain physical characteristics which distinguish them from all
other people. It means that they once lived in the same region or
territory and that they have a common ancestry.

It is hard for us to think without prejudice on the subject of
race. But if an explorer from another planet could see all the
existing types of man on this world and then attempted to describe

2

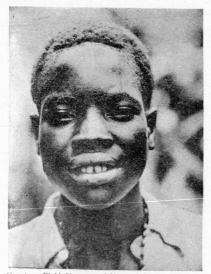

Courtesy Field Museum of Natural History, Chicago
Photo by Dr. M. Kuesters in collection of Museum
für Völkerkunde, Munich

Courtesy Field Museum of Natural History, Chicago

NEGROID TYPE   MONGOLOID TYPE
The Negroid possesses a long, narrow, and low head; the Mongoloid has a
short, broad, and high head.

them to his fellows, he probably would divide them up first according to color. He would say that most black men have curly or frizzly hair. He would remark about their long, narrow, low heads, their broad flat noses, their thick lips, projecting faces, and weak chins. Doubtless he would take note of one exception to his general description and would tell of the pygmies—little blacks with round or bullet-shaped heads. Such people as he would mention under his black grouping we call Negroids.

Coming to the "Yellow Men," our explorer would tell of their short, broad, and high heads; he would take special notice of their wide cheek bones and slanting eyes; their long, straight, black hair would offer strong contrast to the Negroids and would certainly get notice. His "Yellow Men" would be our Mongoloids.

In describing the white people he would doubtless take note first of their long, narrow noses, their thin lips, and the lack of projection of their faces. He would explain that while they are much lighter in color than other peoples they range from a pinkish white to dark brown; their eyes also are variable and may be blue, gray, or brown. Hair is light, brown or black, and may be straight

2

ARMENOID TYPES
A Kurd of Pizdher tribe from Sulaimaniya, Iraq.

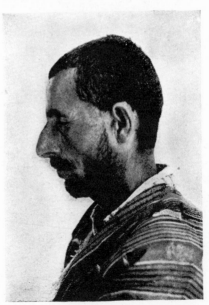

A Kurd of Surchi tribe from Rowandiz, Iraq.
The Armenoids form a sub-race of the Alpine division. Their heads are round and high and their prominent noses are usually convex.

All Photos Courtesy Field Museum of Natural History, Chicago

**MEDI-
TERRANEAN
TYPE**

Sulubba male from
North Arabian
Desert.

A typical member of
the Mediterranean
race has a long, nar-
row head and face,
and a dark complex-
ion.

Courtesy Field Museum
of Natural History, Chi-
cago

or curly. The head is either long or round, but always it is high,
and the forehead is full or dome-shaped. Despite the great range
inside this grouping, it has enough in common so that we call it
the Caucasoid.

If now our observer wished to draw lines more sharply he
would divide the Caucasoid people into the Nordic race of Northern Europe, the Alpine race of Central Europe, the Mediterranean race of Southern Europe and North Africa, and the Hindu
race of Northern India. For each of these divisions or races he
could indicate real differences, yet all have so much in common
that they belong in the same stock—the Caucasoid.

It would be possible to divide the other stocks in a similar
manner so that under the Mongoloid he would place the northern
Mongoloids or Chinese, the southern Mongoloids or Malays, and
the aboriginal inhabitants of America—the Indians.

In like fashion he could divide the Negroids into the typical
or Guinea Coast Negroes, Bushmen, Hottentot, Pygmies, Oceanic
Negroes, and others.

Courtesy Field Museum of Natural History, Chicago
Photo from Josef Weninger, Anthropological Institute, Vienna

Courtesy Field Museum of Natural History, Chicago
Photo from Josef Weninger, Anthropological Institute, Vienna

ALPINE TYPE
Austrian

NORDIC TYPE
German girl from Silesia

The Alpine type is characterized by a high, round head and broad face. The Nordic head is long and narrow, and the complexion is fair.

Enough has been said to make it clear that, in speaking of a race, we are putting together those who are alike in physical traits, and are separating them from those from whom they differ. This is the only proper use of the word, and it never should be confused with language or nationality or religion.

Until the white man began to overrun the whole world, less than five centuries ago, the major groupings—or stocks—tended to inhabit definite localities. The large Negroids were chiefly in Africa and Melanesia of the South Seas, while the pygmies were in the Congo regions and in the southeastern Orient. Mongoloids were in Asia except for one race—the Indian, who occupied North and South America.

Caucasoids had their stronghold in Europe, but they were also in North Africa and Northern India.

II—6

HOW THE RACES DEVELOPED

All the evidence at our command indicates that the existing races of man belong to one species—*Homo sapiens*. This means that they are closely related and at one time must have had a common ancestor. Why, then, are they now so unlike?

We have just considered some of the striking differences between the races, but before we proceed further we should also take note of the fact that all living men are very much alike. Bone for bone, muscle for muscle, blood vessel for blood vessel, we are so much like the Pygmies of Africa that a surgeon in operating on them or us would proceed without hesitation. This is what we would expect in two beings of similar ancestry. When we study the blood of the Negro, Chinaman, or Frenchman, we find the same blood groupings; and if they mate, they have offspring who may, in turn, marry and have children. The relationship, then, must be very close.

But why is the skin of one people black, while that of another is white? Why does the man of dark skin usually have a wide flat nose and the man with white complexion have a thin, narrow nose?

As far back as the time of Darwin it was recognized that variation occurred in all forms of life. If one observed a litter of puppies he saw at once that they were not all alike. Of course he could say that, since two families were represented, the differences in the offspring might be only family traits. However, some of the variations apparently were new, and had not been observed in either family.

The matter was made more difficult when one observed the flowers, leaves, and fruit on a single tree or branch. Here again considerable variation was evident.

Without doubt some of these differences were reversions to the condition of older times, but Darwin came to the conclusion that variations were constantly taking place and that these caused slow but steady change.

Lamarck and his associates believed that these changes came about as a result of need. Thus, with a shift in climate or physical

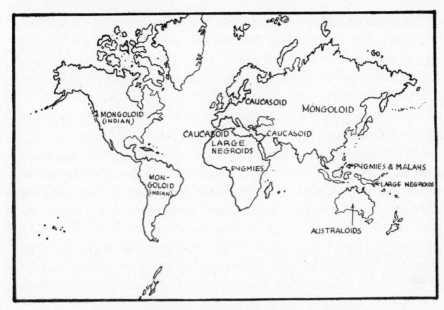

MAP SHOWING THE DISTRIBUTION OF RACES
LESS THAN FIVE CENTURIES AGO

environment, the plant or animal life would need to make certain adjustments in order to live. This, they said, was the cause of variation. They also believed that all changes which occurred in an individual might be inherited by his descendants.

A few years ago DeVris discovered that in addition to individual variations there frequently appeared sudden and radical changes which were inherited by some but not all of the offspring. These inherited variations were called mutations.

Further study showed that mutations might be good, bad, or neutral. It was also observed that they were more likely to appear with a change in environment. How does this affect man?

We all know that if we expose ourselves to summer sunlight we take on a darker color, called tan. If we go to live in tropical regions we also become tanned. This color apparently is furnished by certain glands which pour a substance called melanin into the blood stream. This is carried and is deposited between the two layers of the skin. Then the action of light on this gives the tan.

In most of Europe and North America the period of tanning is restricted to the summer months and no great strain is thrown on the system, but in the tropics, where tan is needed constantly, this causes a steady drain on those organs responsible for the delivery of coloring matter. As a result, many people with white skin are compelled to leave the tropics in a short time or suffer great physical injury or death.

We have seen that the Hindu of Northern India are quite typical Caucasians, much like the people of the Mediterranean region, in everything but color. It seems evident that at one time they lived to the north of India and were much lighter in complexion. As they moved southward they all took on tan. This ultimately caused such great injury to some of the people that they died or failed to have offspring.

We may suspect that among the survivors many mutations occurred. Some were injurious and the possessors failed to survive; some were neither good nor bad and might be continued in part of the population. It is probable that some of the people gave birth to children who had more efficient glands which gave the necessary color without injury. Such people would have a great advantage and would come more frequently to marry, as the less favored were wiped out in the struggle for existence.

Such a change takes generations to affect all the population, but apparently this accounts for the dark skin of the Hindu.

We have already seen that at the end of Paleolithic times mankind was living in small nomadic groups or bands, and we have also noted great climatic changes. Doubtless inherited variations, or mutations, were taking place then as we know they are now. But man was in such small groups that inbreeding, or close intermarrying, must have occurred, and thus any inherited changes were much more easily established than in the larger communities of later times.

Probably enough has been said to indicate how change can take place. That it has taken place is evident the moment we begin to compare people and divide them into races.

THE NEW STONE AGE IN EURASIA

Up to this point we have seen man himself being changed and moulded. The Old Stone Age gave us man and certain elements of culture, but the foundations for our civilizations were laid in the Neolithic, or New Stone Age.

Since the appearance of the modern races there has been little change in man's body, yet his cultures have grown and mingled.

The Transitional epoch showed us a changing climate; it presented man in small bands of hunters, fishers, and seed-gatherers. Under such conditions large groups can seldom gather for any length of time; the game and wild food are quickly exhausted, and the people are forced to scatter. Roaming bands cannot be troubled with many possessions; there is no incentive for building houses, for they will be quickly deserted; property in land is unknown, and there is little or no tribal unity. The head of the family or local group may have some authority, but chieftainship is usually weak in such a society. The whole tendency of this life

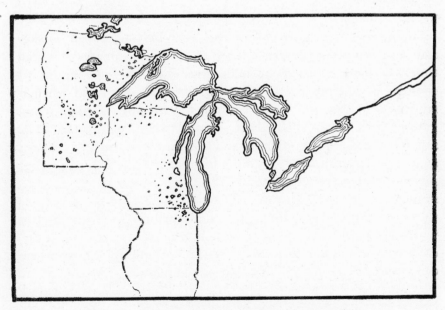

MAP SHOWING GLACIAL LAKES IN WISCONSIN,
MINNESOTA AND ILLINOIS

is to isolate people in small groups between which there are few friendly contacts.

In Northern Europe and Asia glacial lakes and thick forests made communication particularly difficult, but farther to the south the country was more open and this led to frequent meetings with other peoples. It is a matter of common observation that an isolated people is always backward and slow to change. Custom has such a strong hold that anyone who differs from his fellows is quickly made to feel uncomfortable and in some instances is removed from his tribe. There are many communities in the southern mountain regions of the United States which are still in the days of our Civil War so far as progress is concerned. But construct a hard road into such a district, so that it is put in touch with the world, and change comes quickly. So it was with groups of people in the early days of the New Stone Age. Left to themselves they made little progress, but where contacts were frequent each borrowed from the other and the way to civilization was opened.

A GREAT DISCOVERY

Somewhere in the region of the Near East—between Turkestan and Egypt—occurred one of the greatest discoveries of all time. Perhaps by accident man observed that some grains of emmer—a wild plant which he had gathered—sprouted when it lay in damp ground. Later he saw it grow and produce many grains which we now call wheat. It seems a simple discovery to be so important. Do not squirrels and other animals put away acorns and seeds which sprout? They do, but the squirrel does not recognize the young tree as related to the acorn, and man was so constantly on the move that he seldom had opportunity to observe the sprouting of the plant and the maturing of the grain. But when once he had observed the whole process he had made a discovery on which our civilization rests. Without agriculture there can be no cities, or concentration of population.

Having domesticated wheat, man tried other plants and with several he succeeded, so that he had an assured food supply. No longer was he entirely dependent upon what he could kill or find.

Courtesy Brooklyn Botanic Garden, Brooklyn, N. Y.

EMMER, THE ANCESTOR OF WHEAT
The discovery of agriculture revolutionized the history of the world.

BEDOUIN ENCAMPMENT
Nomadic peoples of the deserts and grass lands live in tents, which are easily moved.

More and better food meant a larger population. But the new discovery limited man's movements. If he was to raise crops, he must plant, weed, and otherwise care for the soil while the plants were growing; hence he must stay most of the time in one region. This allowed, in fact almost demanded, a concentration of population, and villages began to appear.

In our older books we were told that man was first a hunter, then a herder, and finally an agriculturalist, but the work of the modern archaeologist has shown that this order has to be partially reversed. Apparently the first tiller of the soil had no domestic animals other than the dog, and knew nothing about fertilization of the land he was farming. Wheat quickly exhausted the soil, and we find evidence that the early planters were often forced to move their settlements, just as primitive agriculturalists of today must do.

EL KANTARA—ARABS
Throughout history there has been strife between the city and desert dwellers.

In their movements some of the people entered the rich valleys of the Nile, the Euphrates, and other rivers where the yearly overflow enriched the soil. There they could remain, and there they established settlements which existed for centuries.

THE TAMING OF ANIMALS

About the same time came a second great discovery—the domestication of animals. Man already had the dog, and this may have suggested to him that other animals might be tamed. Apparently he tried everything, even the deer and hyena, but out of these experiments came domesticated cattle, pigs, donkeys, sheep, horses, and many others. None of these was used at first as a beast of burden; for many centuries even the horses were used merely for food.

In the rich valleys people were able to combine the raising of stock with agriculture, and this in time led to fertilization of the land. On the grassy plains the former hunters became herders. Their life was more certain than on the hunting basis, but they were much on the move and seldom had settlements of any size.

Where the agriculturists and nomadic herders met, there was a certain exchange of goods, but there were also many causes of conflict, and there began a strife which still exists. In Arabia the oasis dwellers live in walled cities to protect them against the wild Bedouin herders of the desert. Many were the conflicts in our West between the cattlemen and the farmers who would close off the range.

POLISHED STONE

So far as is known, no polishing of stone occurred during the Ice Ages. Early in the new epoch some workers began to grind and smooth the edges of their chisels and axes by rubbing them against other stones. They probably had learned by accident that such an edge was more effective than mere chipping. Then they came to realize that, if the tool was smoothed still further, it would cut deeper at each stroke. Up to this point the polishing of stone was purely utilitarian, but soon it became the style to

POLISHED AXE
Stone utensils with
the surfaces ground
and polished appear
in the New Stone
Age.

Courtesy Department of
Anthropology, University
of Chicago
Photo by Raeburn
Rohrbach

continue the grinding and smoothing over the whole utensil.
Finally they reached a point where they even polished hammers
and other objects.

Polished stone was not the most important advance of this
epoch, but, since it contrasted so sharply with the flaked tools of
the preceding times, it gave the name Neolithic, or New Stone
Age, to this portion of man's history. Not all the stone objects
were polished. Arrow and spear heads were produced by pressure
flaking. A bone point shaped much like our lead pencil was placed
against the piece of flint and enough pressure applied to throw off
tiny flakes. By this method very symmetrical points could be
produced. This was the manner of flaking tools used until the
metal ages in Europe and until long after the discovery in
America.

NEW POTS AND DISHES

Pottery likewise appeared at this time. It is difficult to understand why Cro-Magnon man, who modeled in clay, never invented clay vessels, but he did not. We probably shall never know
with certainty how the first dish was made, but there are certain
hints. Many of the early pieces of pottery bear on their surfaces

Courtesy Field Museum of Natural History, Chicago

COIL METHOD OF MAKING POTTERY

A Hopi Indian woman of northeastern Arizona builds up a pot by placing one coil of clay above another. These are pinched together and the surfaces are smoothed over.

the imprints of basketry. This suggests that clay may have been smeared inside baskets, which were then placed in the fire. When the basket had burned, a pot remained.

Once the idea of pottery was obtained, people probably experimented in ways of producing clay vessels. Out of many attempts two main methods had become established before the appearance of the potter's wheel.

One way, much used, was to take a mass of clay and shape it roughly with the fingers. Then a smooth stone was placed inside, and the outer surface was beaten thin with a paddle. Another method was to place rolls or coils of clay one above the other, pinch them together, and then smooth them off with a rubbing stone. Modeling and other ways are known, but the two mentioned are most widespread.

With pottery, foods could be cooked in new ways. Jars could also be used in storing grains and for holding liquids. At first utility was the chief concern of the potters, but later they began to decorate the exterior with incised or painted designs; finally they gave to their pots and dishes a variety of forms or styles. These styles are often of great help to the archaeologist in dating the deposits in which they are found.

WEAVING

Weaving was first known in Neolithic times. Simple plaiting of baskets may have given the idea for mats or simple garments made out of strips of fur, but the true loom is a complicated device, too intricate to be due to chance. This must have been a real, intentional invention, and apparently it was discovered at least twice in the world's history—once in the Near East and again in Middle America.

Real cloth revolutionized dress, and skins and beaten bark were discarded for materials made on the loom.

Other minor inventions appeared in various regions and spread from tribe to tribe and from region to region through trade. Evidences of these contacts will appear as we proceed.

HOW THE STORY OF THE NEW
STONE AGE IS READ

We have already seen how the record of man's life in the caves has been preserved. With the land free from ice, the caves and rock shelters were seldom utilized, but fortunately the story has been recorded in other ways.

The great shell heaps of the North give us part of the developments which began during Transitional times. In places these were also partially built up in later times.

At Maglemose in Jutland are huge refuse heaps, called Kitchen Middens. Here among the shells we find the beginnings of Neolithic culture. Fragments of very crude pottery tell us that this invention came early in this region, but they tell us even more. The archaeologist must be a sort of Sherlock Holmes, who takes advantage of every clue. In some of the bits of broken pots vegetable matter appeared, and when it was put under the microscope it proved to be domestic wheat. Evidently the woman who made the vessel was careless in the preparation of her clay and allowed a bit of wheat and chaff to become mixed with it. A somewhat more gruesome method of sleuthing gives us our first evidence of wheat in Egypt. While studying the dried body of an ancient Egyptian, archaeologists found chaff of wheat in the intestinal tract. These searchers have already told us of the ills from which early man suffered; now they even tell us how they digested their food.

The coming of domestic plants and animals is told in many shell heaps and in peat bogs. Careful excavation has shown the sequence and development of pottery styles while thousands of utensils tell of the increasing complexity of every day life.

SWISS LAKE DWELLINGS

The most complete story of the New Stone Age is preserved in ancient Swiss Lake villages. Early in this epoch the inhabitants of the region sought protection by making their homes over the waters of the lakes. Where a gently sloping shore offered a suitable location, they went out into the shallow waters and drove posts

Courtesy Swiss Federal Railroads

REMAINS OF PREHISTORIC LAKE DWELLINGS
Many villages similar to this one at Cour, near Lausanne, have been discovered
at times of low water in the lakes.

into the mud as far as they could with the tools they had, then
they piled stones around the bottoms to make them more secure.
When a number had been erected in this fashion they placed a
platform on the top, on which they erected a square or rectangular house. Something of the magnitude of this task can be under-
stood when we realize that a single village required thousands of
these piles, each one of which had to be laboriously cut with a
stone axe.

Instead of building up a refuse heap, as in the Kitchen Middens, the waste materials were thrown into the waters below the
houses where they became covered with mud. Occasionally a
good utensil would be lost, or an inhabitant be drowned and also
become part of the record. As in all towns built of wood, fires
sometimes destroyed a house or part of the village, and then quantities of materials would be lost. From time to time enemies
appeared and battles occurred in the shallow waters with the result that fully armed warriors were sometimes buried in the mud.

Courtesy Field Museum of Natural History, Chicago

RESTORATION OF A SWISS LAKE DWELLING
Many evidences of this life have been found buried in the mud
beneath the ancient settlements.

These people evidently paid great attention to fishing, but they also raised crops, and later in their history they had flocks and herds. To protect their animals from savage beasts as well as against raids of enemies, they built corrals out over the water and had piers or bridges which led from the land. The planks of such runways were not fastened down; so, when the animals were safely housed for the night, the boards could be taken up and intruders would be forced to approach through the water.

Some of these villages were evidently occupied for many years. Following a fire, the site might be abandoned for a time and then reoccupied. Today the record in the mud and marls is almost complete.

These ancient dwellings were quite unknown to the modern inhabitants until 1853, when a long period of drought caused the Swiss Lakes to fall to such low levels that the posts and other parts of houses were exposed. This led to the discovery of hundreds of lake villages extending from early Neolithic times up to the coming of the Romans. Some were tiny hamlets, but others are so large that it is estimated they may have housed a thousand people.

The mud and water acted as a perfect preservative, and today nearly every large museum of the world has a collection from the Lake Dwellers.

Near Zurich in Switzerland is a site which shows three successive levels. The first two villages were burned, the last was abandoned. Other locations give an even longer record.

In the oldest layers we find evidence that hunting and fishing were quite important, but few bones of domestic animals appear. Above these, the percentage of tame animals increases while game becomes rare. Eventually, domestic cattle, pigs, and goats are very common.

Much the same story is preserved in plants and fruits. Seeds of wild cherries, plums, nuts, and the like predominate near the bottom; but wheat, barley, millet, and other domestic plants become of increasing importance. The apple had been domesticated: in one house the woman had cut many apples into halves, evidently in preparation for drying, when her home was destroyed. Even loaves of bread were found.

Thousands of polished stone utensils have been recovered, and fortunately many are still hafted so that we know exactly how they were made and used. Fabrics of flax and wool, even the hair nets of the women are preserved, while bracelets and ornaments of beads, teeth, and animal bones tell of dress and ornament. We also learn of dress and bodily ornament from figurines which these people possessed. Designs on face and body suggest tattooing. Apparently the earliest style of women's dress consisted of two aprons, one in front and one behind, which later were united to form a skirt. Special garments were sleeveless shirts which extended to the knees.

An inventory of all the possessions of these people would be too long for inclusion here, but it would list many styles of pottery, baskets of various types, matting, fish nets, bows and arrows, and many other objects of daily use.

VILLAGES IN THE VALLEYS

At certain favored sites remains of Neolithic villages are found buried in the valleys. Here are traces of round or rectangular houses with sunken floors. Oftentimes the side walls are of small timbers and wattle work, but in some places they are of sun-dried mud. Ditches or palisades surrounding such settlements indicate

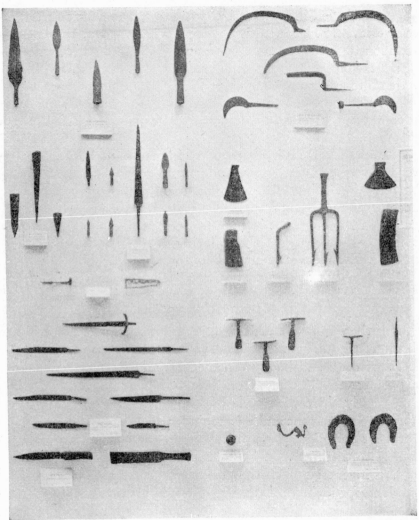

Courtesy Field Museum of Natural History, Chicago

SWISS LAKE DWELLER COLLECTION

Thousands of utensils, ranging from early Neolithic through the Bronze
Age, have been found below the lake dwellings.

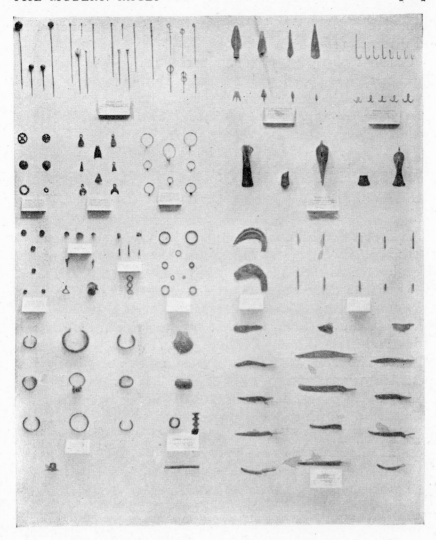

ORNAMENTS OF THE SWISS LAKE DWELLERS

Love of display is indicated by the pins, brooches, and bracelets recovered from beneath the Swiss Lake Dwellings. Fishing and hunting are indicated by hooks, spear points and the like.

the need of protection against enemies, for it is clear that warfare had made its appearance.

Usually such villages yield only broken materials in the refuse heaps, or objects buried with the dead. During the cold winter months when the ground was frozen the people could not dig graves outside, and so they sometimes buried their dead inside the dwellings close to the door or fireplace.

NEOLITHIC BEGINNINGS OF GREAT CITIES

Evidences of Neolithic culture have been found in the valleys of the Nile and Euphrates, but there the yearly overflow of the rivers has buried them many feet below the present surface. In these valleys a dense population through thousands of years has also done much to obliterate all traces of the early inhabitants. When, however, we excavate to the lowest levels of ancient cities, such as Susa in the Persian Highlands, Anau in Chinese Turkestan, or Knossos in Crete, we find there a culture similar in many respects to that which we have just described. Apparently the later civilizations of Europe and the Near East rest firmly on this Neolithic foundation which we have traced in the shell heaps of Scandinavia, in the valley villages of Central Europe, in the beds of the Swiss Lakes, and at the lowest levels of cities of great antiquity.

We need not review their accomplishments to realize how far these people had progressed on the road toward civilization. We should, however, take note that their type of life called for cooperation as well as division of labor. They had possessions which they wished to preserve, and hence they were willing to join with their fellows in defense. This meant that they must have submitted to some sort of authority, for men cannot live long together in a state of anarchy.

The hunter and herder can move if the game is scarce or water and grass are insufficient, but the farmer must remain at one place. He is dependent upon the proper amount of rain and sun at definite times, and we find that he develops religious practices which he hopes will bring him the favor of the gods. Among nomadic people we usually find the medicine man, but the priest and organized religion appear among a settled population.

ANCIENT MINERS

In the New Stone Age man had come to know the value of various stones for the manufacture of his tools. He would travel long distances or engage in trade to secure the materials he desired. He likewise had learned that flint deep-buried in the earth was better for chipping and polishing than that on the surface. This led to real mining operations. In places trenches were run along an outcrop until the proper stone was encountered; in other regions shafts were sunk deep into the ground. Often the shafts would be placed quite close together and then would be connected by underground tunnels and chambers. The extent of some of these operations can be appreciated when it is learned that thousands of implements, made from a flint occurring only in one limited region of France, have been found widespread over western Europe.

Apparently the chief mining tool was a pick made of stag horn. Many of these have been found, one with the body of a miner who had died in a pit. Doubtless tragedy often accompanied these mining operations, for the cuts were frequently in dangerous soil and were not provided with timbering against landslides and caving. In one shaft lay the skeleton of a woman who had fallen in head first and been killed.

THE CULT OF THE DEAD

Late in the New Stone Age a cult of the dead, associated with the erection of stone burial chambers, giant memorial shafts, and great stone structures, became widespread. Stone tombs ranging from rude slabs, which enclosed a chamber, to beautifully made structures are found from the eastern end of the Mediterranean to Great Britain and Denmark.

Single stones weighing tons were made to stand upright, to commemorate some important personage of the past.

Courtesy Field Museum of Natural History, Chicago

NEOLITHIC SUN WORSHIPPERS
Great structures of stone were erected during the New Stone Age.

In Brittany, in England, and in Scandinavia are huge engineer-
ing projects which exceed all works of man up to the building of
the pyramids. At Carnac in Brittany are rows and circles consisting of nearly three thousand stones ranging from two to twenty
feet above ground. These form parallel rows or avenues which
finally meet in similar cross rows to form rooms or courts.
Beyond these is a vast stone circle which is supposed to have been
a temple. At Stonehenge and Avebury in England are huge circles
of stones on the tops of which are laid horizontal stones weighing
tons. Smaller circles, and upright stones within the structure
proper suggest inner sanctuaries and altars, but their actual use is
not known. It is thought that they are related to the cult of the
dead, but this is not certain. Many fanciful explanations have
been given for these structures. They have been called the temples
of the Druids or even the lodge rooms of ancient Masons.

PRIMITIVE MAN AS ENGINEER

The first question which presents itself as one gazes at these huge rocks placed on end, or as capping stones, is how could primitive man without machinery handle such enormous stones. Fortunately there are primitive people in the world today who still carry on similar feats without machinery, and, by studying their methods and comparing them with those in Europe, we can answer the question.

First the huge stones, often weighing many tons, were drawn to the desired place by sheer man power. The wheel had not yet been discovered, but it is possible that they may have placed logs below the stones to act as rollers. When finally the stone was in place a hole was dug at its lower end. This was continued along the shaft until finally the center of gravity was passed and the stone slipped into the excavation in a semi-erect position. Long lines were then attached; the stone was pulled upright, and earth and stones were filled in at its base to hold it in position.

This explanation seems fairly easy, but the placing of the huge capping stones would seem more difficult. The primitive engineer

Courtesy Art Institute of Chicago

ENGINEERING FEATS OF PRIMITIVE MAN
Huge capping-stones were placed on top of stone pillars at Stonehenge, England.

solved this difficulty by building a hill to the top of the upright stones, then the cap stones were drawn into place and the hills were removed. Very simple when you know how.

On the little Island of Nias, off the west coast of Sumatra, the people even today erect huge memorial pillars and place great stone slabs on other stones, and the method in use is that just described.

MANUFACTURE OF STONE TOOLS

Since stone work has played such an important part in human history, we will briefly review the major steps in the development of tools and methods of making.

The eoliths or dawn stones were little more than sharp-edged stones or flakes, either produced by nature or rudely shaped by striking them against another stone. While these were doubtless used by early man, they can scarcely be dignified by the name of tools until the makers intentionally attempted to shape them for a definite purpose.

Such a shaping apparently occurred in the Chellean hand axe. A moderately large nodule, the unfinished end of which would fit into the hand, was made into a crude axe (pear- or almond-shaped) by striking and flaking it all around with another stone until a sharp zigzag edge had been produced. Doubtless some of the flakes struck off in the manufacture of the axe were used occasionally, but they were purely accidental.

The Acheulian hand axe is the same in principle. The nodule is still used, but the edge is now straight and is sharpened all the way around so that it can no longer be held in the hand. This means that a handle must have been added. Judging by the methods employed by stone-using peoples of today, this was probably accomplished by splitting one end of the proposed handle, slipping in the blade, and then binding the two pieces together, or by using a pliable material like rattan, one end of which would be bent around the axe head and be lashed down. Such device would allow both ends of the axe to be employed.

True flake implements, made from portions struck off the core, were used to a limited extent while the Acheulian axe was dominant. These probably served as knives or scrapers and can scarcely be called typical.

Mousterian implements represent a true flake industry, possibly a straight development out of the Acheulian. The axe continues, but it is smaller, and the edges and sides are carefully sharpened, sometimes by secondary chipping. In general, however, the core or nodule is replaced by flakes struck off the block. However, the toolmaker works over the outer surface before he detaches it by a single blow. The concave side is usually left unfinished, but the edge is sharpened on the convex side by removing small flakes. The result is an edge which resembles an object chewed by a rodent. Such forms are usually crude in appearance, yet require considerable skill to detach and sharpen. Most of these flints are tools rather than weapons and range from thin strips which served as knives and cutters to awls and points which may have been set in the ends of shafts to make lances. It is difficult to see how the stone products of this age could have been of great service in securing the large game on which we know Neanderthal feasted.

Cro-Magnon tools have the appearance of chance flakes, but their great abundance, as well as the discovery of blocks or platforms of flint from which they were knocked off, show that they were intentionally produced. They are usually small thin blades and appear to have been used chiefly as scrapers, chisels, or gouges. At times the edges are retouched as in the Mousterian tools, but this is not typical. They were used by Cro-Magnon man, and it is interesting to note that they increased in numbers as the art of engraving developed, hence they are often called "gravers."

The Solutrean epoch, which appears for a short time between the Aurignacian and Magdalenian, introduces a type of stone work which becomes of great importance in Neolithic times. This is known as pressure flaking. The striking or percussion method is replaced by the use of a small bone point which is pressed near the edge so as to remove small thin flakes. By this method beautiful blades resembling willow or laurel leaves were produced during Solutrean times. Throughout the Neolithic of Europe this was the manner in which lance and arrow heads were commonly produced, and this was the technique for making Indian arrowheads so commonly found in America.

In the history of stone work in Europe a so-called microlithic or tiny stone industry is next to appear. In this, small triangular, edged, or pointed flakes take the place of larger instruments. They are typical of the Transitional epoch and probably were set into handles of wood or bone to serve as knives, saws, and the like.

They do not introduce a new method of production, for they seem to be of the same general character as Magdalenian but are smaller.

We have already noted that such tools as chisels and axes were first sharpened only along the edge, but later were finished all over. Finally, style caused even stone hammers to be polished, while many ornamental and ceremonial objects were beautifully finished.

Here we are interested primarily in the method of producing polished utensils. Judging by tools in many stages of development which have been found, and also by observing present day Stone Age man, we can at least suggest how the ancient specimens were made. The miners roughly shaped out blocks of flint to shape and size suitable for transportation to the workshops in the villages. Here the axe maker broke the block into proper sizes and, having selected one, flaked it by the percussion or striking method into the desired shape. The next step was to remove the flake scars by pecking or repeatedly striking it with a harder stone. Each blow would cause tiny flakes to fly off until finally a fairly smooth surface was obtained. Next came the polishing by rubbing the surface with sandstone and water, or by placing wet sand on the axe and rubbing it down with another stone. Final smoothing and polish may have been accomplished by long continued rubbing on a rock of equal hardness.

Polished stone axes and adzes were produced with many variations in form in different regions, but they were of the same general pattern. It is interesting that they anticipated nearly all the forms which later were produced in bronze and iron. In fact, they looked so much like modern tools that the peasants of Europe thought they were "petrified" iron tools.

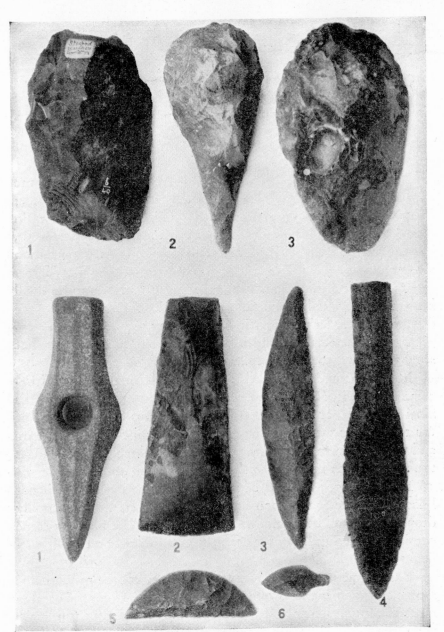

THE STONE AGES OF EUROPE

In the upper row are shown the crude chipped hand axes of the Old Stone Age. Below are the polished ax and adz, flaked saw-like blades and projectile points of the New Stone Age.

2

We may be inclined to pity Neolithic man for his lack of metal, but these stone tools were really very efficient. Sehested of Denmark, working ten hours and using one stone axe, cut down and trimmed twenty-six pine trees suitable for building a house.

THE COMING OF METALS

We have seen that the Neolithic, or New Stone Age, culture appears at the lowest levels of some of the great cities of antiquity; we have traced its development in the Swiss Lake villages, and in the shell heaps of Scandinavia. Important local differences exist, but basically it is the same, and on it all later European civilization rests.

It was Neolithic man who gave us agriculture and animal husbandry; it was he who first established towns and cities. He developed an orderly society in which many people could live together; he started trade and he probably introduced the greatest scourge known to man—organized warfare.

Before the end of Neolithic times the use of copper had become known in some localities. In the island of Cyprus, in the Sinai peninsula, and elsewhere, free copper was found in veins of the rock. This was beaten out into sheets or into strips like wire and was then shaped into rings, beads, and other ornaments. At times it was also beaten into the form of stone implements.

How man got the idea of melting and shaping copper is not known, but we may suppose that at some time he accidentally dropped some of the metal into a fire, or that he placed a stone consisting of a simple copper ore close to the flames and saw it suddenly turn to liquid.

Then came an extensive search for mines of free metal, or of simple ores, and as these were developed the use of copper became more common. Knife and spear blades, axes and even fish hooks were produced, but always by beating out the metal while it was cold. However, the knowledge that copper would melt very easily probably led to the next step. Some intelligent weapon maker conceived the idea that he might cut the form of a spear head in a piece of sandstone; he also realized that he might make

a pottery crucible in which he could melt the metal over a fire.
When this was done, he poured the molten copper into the mould,
allowed it to cool, and when it had hardened he had cast a metal
tool. It was not perfect in shape, but that could be cared for by
hammering.

The next step was to make a double mould, which when fitted
together would make a perfect form of the object to be cast. The
two sides were fastened together with pins, but when the metal
had cooled they were taken apart and the tool withdrawn.

In their search for copper the miners had somewhere encountered tin. Probably the chief source at first was from Persia
but later it was obtained from Spain and Britain. It was less
desirable for it was brittle, but it melted easily and could be used
in making ornaments.

Continuing our speculations, we may suppose that one day, by
chance, a bit of tin was added to the copper to be cast. The result
was epoch-making, for when the metal cooled it was no longer
copper, but bronze. The casters were quick to realize the superiority of the new metal, but it is evident that they did a great
deal of experimenting before they learned just the correct amount
of tin to add. Some early objects were nearly half tin, others had
very little, but in time they came to have about ten per cent—
the proper proportion.

One more major step had to be taken before the Metal Ages
could become a reality; that was the invention of a forge and
bellows. Somewhere either in the Near East or in Africa, the idea
was finally developed. All but two openings in the skin of a
small animal were closed. Into one of these a tube was fastened
while the other could be closed by pressing the hand over it. The
top of the skin was raised so as to fill it with air, then the hand
was pressed down over the top opening so that the air was forced
out of the nozzle. In time this was further developed with valves
and other conveniences until our bellows was produced. With
this device it was possible to keep a steady flame going, either to
reduce metals or to melt them for casting.

Man was already familiar with charcoal and in time he found
that the simple ores of copper could be reduced by mixing them

with charcoal and subjecting them to the steady heat produced by the bellows.

Once this discovery, or series of discoveries, had been made, a great search for metals began. Mines were opened in Cyprus, Persia, Austria and even at points more distant from the Near East. Ores were transported long distances and finished products given in return.

There can be no doubt but that the trade in metals was a major factor in bringing the people of the Mediterranean regions into contact with one another and with their neighbors. As they met they exchanged other ideas, and quickly the advances of one spread to the others. At this time a flood of new discoveries swept over the Near East—several systems of writing appeared, architecture developed, the chariot wheel and the potter's wheel became general, ships sailed or at least were paddled on the seas, trade routes were opened and a sort of currency developed. Later real civilization developed out of these beginnings.

Not only did manufactured objects travel but the methods of production likewise spread, though much more slowly. At first the regions of the Nile, Euphrates, Persian Highlands, and Crete were far in advance of the European mainland. When Greece and Italy had received the full benefits of the new era, the regions near the Swiss Lakes were lagging far behind, while Germany, Scandinavia, and the British Isles were just emerging from the late Stone Age.

The story of this spread or diffusion of culture is read in many ways.

THE SAFETY PIN GOES TRAVELING

An example of what often happened when an object traveled is afforded by the safety pin. In the Near East it looked like a safety pin and served all the purposes that such a pin should serve. But as the idea traveled north the artisans made it larger and more ornamental. By the time it reached Switzerland it was used chiefly as a dress ornament by the women, and when it appeared in Scandinavia it weighed one or two pounds and was purely for decoration.

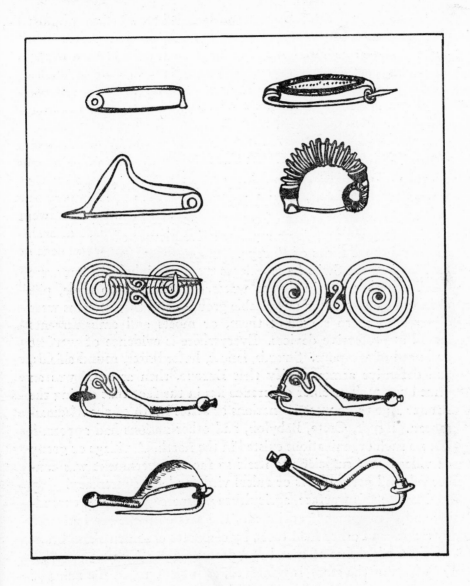

SAFETY PINS OF THE HALLSTADT EPOCH

From Salins, Jura. The two fibulae in the upper row have a serpentiform arch; those in
the lower are without spring. (After Piroutet and van Sacken.)

Trade routes both by water and land led to far distant lands; along the coasts of the Mediterranean and up the main rivers open boats of some size appeared. We know them chiefly from representations placed on pottery, although reproductions of them appear in some graves of the early Bronze Age. The horse and ass came to be used in the valley of the Euphrates, and, with the development of the wheel, trails began to develop into roads.

EARLY BRONZE AGE CULTURE

In the Near East the Bronze Age carries us to the portals of history. To the north civilization always lagged so it is difficult to describe "The Age" as of a certain year or century. Keeping this in mind, we can give a representative picture of the advances of early bronze times of Europe.

Many of the Swiss Lake villages were still inhabited but were usually farther out in deeper water. In addition to these, pile cities were constructed on suitable grounds and then streams were diverted so as to surround them, or moats and embankments served as protective devices. Everywhere is evidence of warfare and need of weapons. Swords, lances, hafted axes, round shields, and defensive armor testify that Europe, then as now, was an armed camp. The chief difference lies in the fact that during the Bronze Age there were no nations or states north of the Mediterranean. Egypt, Crete, Babylon, and other nations had appeared, but no such organizations existed in the north. A village or group of villages was sufficient to itself so far as government was concerned, and petty chiefs or rulers vied for local supremacy.

Despite this warfare, agriculture prospered, trade was extended, and development continued. The arts of peace are indicated by sickles and other field tools, by elaborate ornaments and beautifully made dishes of metal and pottery.

Much of the story is preserved, as heretofore, in the ruins of villages or below the lake dwellings. In the peat bogs of Scandinavia several burials of this age have been found in oak coffins. In these, fabrics and even flesh have been preserved. Such burials, together with art representations, tell us that the women wore skirts which hung in loose folds from their waists to their feet.

BRONZE AGE DRESS
Left: Male costume. Right: Female costume. (After Muller and Montelius)

Cloth jackets with sleeves to the elbows covered the upper portion of their bodies. Around their necks were bronze beads; on their arms were many spiral bracelets and rings of bronze, while ornaments of the same metal were attached to the jackets. Close fitting hairnets covered the whole head and neck.

No trousers as yet troubled the men. In their place was a four-cornered piece of cloth which wrapped around the body from arm pits to knees. A belt with elaborate buckle drew this garment in at the waist. The final article of dress was a round cap and a mantle which could be placed over the shoulders and be fastened in front by a glorified and magnified safety pin known as the fibula.

Evidently at least some of the gentlemen shaved, for bronze razors of quite modern type and tweezers are found accompanying the dead.

Sometimes collections of objects, known as caches, accompany burials, but these more frequently occur in the form of buried treasure. Apparently the owners hid them carefully away in times of danger, but never were able to return and claim them. Nearly eight hundred such caches have been found in France, and many more elsewhere. These consist of all sorts of things, but are principally ornaments, weapons, knives, and similar objects of bronze.

Apparently sun worship was widespread at this time, for the sun's disk alone, or placed in a miniature chariot, is often represented in offerings.

Taken as a whole, the Bronze Age is one of great advances, a time when the great civilizations of antiquity came into being. Roughly it extends from about 3000 B.C. to 1000 B.C. when it is replaced by the Iron Age.

THE IRON AGE

There is no sharp break between the ages of bronze and iron. Iron was known quite early, but it was difficult to shape or use. Nevertheless, it was so rare and so highly prized that even in the golden days of Egypt it was a fit present for the Pharaoh. Homer tells us that victors in early Greek contests were rewarded with pieces of iron. Even objects of gold were inlaid with iron, so highly was it prized.

In time men became aware that oxides and sulphides of iron could be smelted by using charcoal fires and the bellows. This made the metal more abundant but did not make it of practical use. When, however, a method of converting iron into steel was discovered, a new era began.

Courtesy Field Museum of Natural History, Chicago

MALAYAN FORGE

This type of forge is found from the Philippines to Madagascar, where
it was carried by early Malayan colonists.

STEEL

Perhaps the best picture of a primitive method of iron working is preserved for us by the Malayan blacksmiths of today. The
Malay people, from Madagascar to the Philippines, have developed
a forge somewhat different from that described in a preceding
section. This forge consists of two cylinders, made of hollowed
out logs, into which closely fitting plungers are worked up and
down. A bamboo tube leads from each cylinder into a clay nozzle
which in turn rests in a charcoal fire. As the plungers are worked
alternately up and down, a steady flow of air is driven into the
fire.

When all is ready, a piece of iron is heated and hammered
into the desired shape on the anvil. It is then put back into the
flame and is kept there until it attains a white heat. The smith
now removes it with tongs and holds it over a container filled
with water until it begins to turn a greenish yellow; then sudden-

ly he plunges it into the cold water, and the iron is turned to steel. The carbon of the charcoal, acting with the iron and water, produces the new metal.

How this discovery was made is lost in the ages of the past, but to it we owe our skyscrapers, our railways, steamships, airplanes, and many other of the most spectacular developments of our civilization.

We shall not trace the Iron Age in the Near East as there it is well within the range of history, but let us follow its introduction into Central Europe and view conditions there at the time when Greece led the world, or when Cicero and Cæsar were in Rome.

The Iron Age in Central and Northern Europe is generally divided into two epochs. First is the Hallstadt, which extends from about 1000 to 500 B.C.; then comes the La Tene, which goes through to the time of Christ.

The Hallstadt culture was widespread but had its major development in central and northern Italy and in Switzerland. The epoch gets its name from a great cemetery found near Hallstadt in the Alps. Here were about three thousand burials, approximately half of which represent cremations.

Despite the large population indicated by such a burial ground, and despite the fact that this is only one of several, there is no mention of this people in the history or legends of the Near East. Their lives are known solely from objects which they have left behind. Among these the most important for our purpose are wine pails or jars of bronze. On these the artisans of long ago have given us pictures of daily life. Here are shown dignified gentlemen wearing long straight garments which cover them from neck to ankles. Some of these dignitaries ride in chariots or on horses.

THE FIRST KNOWN BUGGY RIDE

One picture shows us a beautiful two-wheeled cart in which a gentleman is taking his lady for a buggy ride. But not all the women are so favored, for we are shown long lines of them carrying huge burdens on their heads. Hunters are depicted returning from the woods carrying game between them. Boxing was known, for we see lightly clad men apparently in contest, with the referee close by.

Much that is told us in the pictures is shown us in the graves. Warriors are buried with their chariots or surrounded with their weapons of bronze and iron. Pottery had reached a high stage of perfection and glass dishes and vases had appeared. At this time we also find the first examples of our modern pocket knives. A blade of iron was arranged so that it could be shut inside a bone handle.

Despite the size and extent of this population it is evident that the people did not construct permanent cities. Several of their camps have been discovered. These consist of large fields surrounded by ramparts, within which are rectangular houses of light construction.

THE LA TENE EPOCH

The second stage of the Iron Age of Europe extends from 500 B.C. to the beginning of our era. It is named from a lake village—La Tene ("The Shallows")—in Switzerland, although the culture extends across central Europe to France.

La Tene was a military stronghold, a pile village which was evidently destroyed and burned during a hostile raid.

In the mud below the shallow waters about the town have been found skeletons of soldiers, many with their skulls cut and crushed. Their swords and other weapons lie close by. Chariot wheels indicate that the raiders even drove out into the waters during the battle.

The culture represented at La Tene is also known from many burial grounds. It can be summarized as being a continuation and development of the Hallstadt but showing many contacts with Greece and Rome. Roman coins are numerous as are objects of Greek manufacture. The potter's wheel has appeared, also rotary stones for grinding grain. Horses are ridden, and the bridles and trappings are often very elegant. Personal ornaments receive great attention, especially the fibula or ornamental safety pin, earrings, and finger rings of gold. The mirror had long been known along the Mediterranean but it makes its first appearance in central Europe at this time. This is also the time of the introduction of the metal plow-share, iron scythes and sickles, and it also marks another product and need of civilization—locks and keys.

Europe of the Iron Ages had advanced far on the road to civilization, but it was still very backward when compared with the lands along the Mediterranean. Hallstadt and La Tene are after the time of Egyptian dominance; Ninevah and Crete had vanished, and Greece and Rome were at the height of their glory.

THE NEW STONE AGE IN AMERICA

UP TO THIS TIME we have been following the story of man chiefly in Europe and Asia. What of man in America?

If we look at a map of the world, we see North and South America roughly forming two great triangles, hanging in space.

North America approaches Europe and Asia at its extreme northeastern and northwestern corners, but South America is far removed from all other land bodies except the great Antarctic continent which is deeply buried under ice and snow. Since there is no evidence whatever that this snow-bound land has ever been the home of man, we can dismiss it as a possible route over which human beings may have passed.

THE FABLED LAND OF ATLANTIS

Many fanciful theories have been advanced to account for the high cultures found in Mexico and Central America. We have been told that there was once a great land of Atlantis, settled by a highly civilized people. Ages ago, it is said, this island met with a great catastrophe and finally sank. Before the destruction was complete, some of the people fled to Egypt and were responsible for the civilization there. Others crossed to America and from them came the Aztec, Maya, Toltec, and other nations found by the Spaniards. A similar legend is told for the Island of Mu.

It is a pretty story, but it belongs in the same class as Grimm's Fairy Tales.

We have seen how the cultures of Europe and Asia began and how they developed, up to the Age of Metals. Egypt and other great countries of the Near East built their fortunes on foundations laid down in the New Stone Age.

In recent years the claim has been advanced that people from Egypt or China crossed the Pacific to establish the American civilizations, but here again the facts tell a very different tale.

AMERICA NOT THE BIRTHPLACE OF MAN

A great deal of investigation and excavation has been conducted in North and South America. Geologists and archaeologists have been constantly on the watch for evidences of early man on this continent, but up to the present there is no authentic trace of any people resembling Neanderthal Man or any of the other primitive types. All skeletons, even those for whom some antiquity has been claimed, are of our own species, *Homo sapiens.*

In spite of what has just been said, recent discoveries indicate that man may have reached this continent before the retreat of the last great ice sheet.

EVIDENCES OF ICE AGE MAN IN AMERICA: THE COCHISE CULTURE

Recently, explorers from the Gila Pueblo Museum have traced a culture, hitherto unknown, along the Arizona-Mexico border. They have found ample evidence that this desert land was once well watered and was the home of animals long extinct in America.

Courtesy Southwest Museum, Los Angeles

ENTRANCE TO GYPSUM CAVE
In this cave near Las Vegas, Nevada, are evidences that man and the
ground sloth were contemporaneous.

In this region they have discovered ancient stream beds and
dry lakes along the edges of which were camps made by man.
Above the old beach lines are layers or strata in which appear
bones of the horse, mammoth, and other animals. At this time
hunting would have been possible, but it is interesting to note
that in the lower strata are evidences of a food gathering people
who paid little if any attention to the chase.

Around the old camps are found hammer and grinding stones
and cutting tools, but so far no weapons have appeared. Apparently the people responsible for this culture depended chiefly on
seeds and bulbs for their food supply.

No skeletons of this people have been discovered, so we can
only say that we have evidence that some sort of man was here
while the horse and mammoth were in the land and while this
region, now arid, had plenty of water.

Courtesy Southwest Museum, Los Angeles

THE GROUND SLOTH
Objects made by man have been found in association with the
remains of this extinct animal.

MAN AND THE SLOTH—GYPSUM CAVE

In the desert of southern Nevada, Dr. M. R. Harrington of
the Southwest Museum discovered a cave of great importance.
Near the entrance were deep deposits, while a less amount of debris was found in the more remote recesses.

Careful excavation revealed the fact that there were, in the
cave, six distinct layers which, in places, reached a depth of eight
feet. In the upper deposit were camp fires, corn cobs, fragments
of bows and arrows, and bits of pottery left by modern Indians
who came to the cave to gather gypsum crystals.

Below this was a stratum made up primarily of materials left
by wild sheep, but containing a few pieces of throwing sticks.
Then came evidence of an earthquake. Quantities of stone, broken
from the roof of the cave, covered the layer left by the sheep.

The real discovery occurred in layer five. Here the deposit

was made up primarily of dung of the ground sloth, an animal extinct in North America for thousands of years. In this were found a huge horny claw and the skin, tawny hair, skull and parts of the skeleton of a baby sloth. At various levels below and in the dung were charred sticks of camp fires, a "torch" made of bits of cane bound at the ends, parts of a painted throwing stick, a stone dart head, and a flint scraper. Here also were bones of a camel, broken as if to extract the marrow, and ribs of a sloth showing marks of a stone cutting tool. A part of this material had been covered and sealed in by a gypsum deposit, but most of it lay under such dry conditions that even the hair of the sloth was preserved.

In all, twelve positive evidences of man lay in undisturbed deposits, under such conditions that there can be no doubt but that man and the sloth were contemporaneous in this cave.

Courtesy American Museum of Natural History, New York

PROJECTILE POINTS FOUND IN NEW MEXICO

These symmetrical blades, known as Folsom points, have been found associated with fossil bison and other animals long extinct in America.

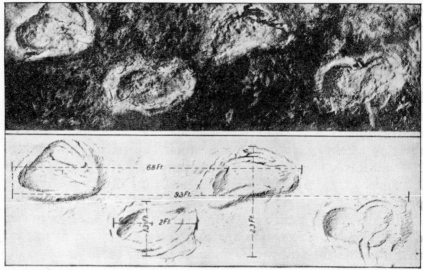

Paul's Photos, Chicago

FOOTPRINTS OF THE GROUND SLOTH
Upper: Replica of footprints found in the Carson City prison yard. Lower: The
diagram shows size of imprints, length of stride and width of straddle.

Covering the rock floor was a stratum made up of river gravels washed in when water was much more plentiful in this region. This is also indicated by the fact that the stones are partially cemented together with gypsum which had dripped from the cave walls. It was probably at this time that the stalactites of gypsum, which give the cave its name, were formed. In this lower layer were found bones of the horse, and a llama-like camel, but no traces of man or the sloth.

Geologists have come to the conclusion that the damp period in which the gypsum crystals were formed probably belongs to the end of the last glaciation; that the evidences of man with the sloth are probably immediately post-glacial. This gives to man a respectable antiquity in America, perhaps 15,000 to 18,000 years, but nothing compared with that of man in Europe.

EXTINCT BISON KILLED BY MAN

Near Folsom, New Mexico, a small stream had cut a narrow passage through about twelve feet of deposit. A ranch hand, riding by, saw large bones protruding from the bottom of the layer and reported that he had seen some dead cows. These "dead cattle" turned out to be the skeletons of a species of bison supposed to be extinct in America from the end of the Ice Age. Scientists from the Denver Museum and the American Museum of Natural History excavated the site and found thirty of these animals. They lay close to what was apparently an ancient water hole, and it appeared that they had been killed by some agency. That agency certainly was man, for at least fifteen projectile points of a very distinct type were found in association with the skeletons. Evidently man had slaughtered the beasts as they came down to drink, had skinned them and taken away portions of the meat. Apparently in removing the hide they had cut off the tails, for most of them are missing.

The projectile point found with these bison has come to be known as "the Folsom point." It is a long, thin, leaf-shaped blade, beautifully made by pressure flaking, with a longitudinal flake removed along each side from the base nearly to the tip. As a rule the base is so very convex that the sides appear as "ear-like" projections.

The best of the specimens represent such a high degree of workmanship that it is difficult to think of them as representing one of the earliest phases of human culture so far discovered in America, yet such is the case.

At Folsom no other evidence of human beings appeared, but near Fort Collins, Colorado, Dr. Frank Roberts of the Bureau of American Ethnology, found an ancient kitchen midden, or refuse place, buried under seventeen feet of deposit. Here erosion first indicated the location, but the camp was exposed by running a wide trench from the surface to the old land level on which it had been placed. Here nine more of the fossil bison were found. In one of these, part of a Folsom point was deeply imbedded in the vertebrae, indicating the cause of the animal's death. Around the camp were more than one thousand stone implements ranging from Folsom points to scrapers, cutting blades, hammer stones, and the like. This gives us some idea of the other objects made and used by these early people.

Near Clovis and Carlsbad, New Mexico, Dr. Howard of the

Philadelphia Academy of Natural Sciences excavated an old lake-bed deposit and the strata covering the floor of an ancient cave. Here, together with bones of the bison, elephant, horse, camel, and musk ox, he found the Folsom cultural complex, consisting of points, scrapers, knives, and gravers.

Other projectile points of this type have been found in various parts of the country but usually on or near the surface. The discoveries just mentioned, together with Gypsum cave, give clear proof of man's association with many animals typical of the late Ice Age. It seems definitely to answer the question as to whether man and the elephant existed together on this continent.

This, however, is not proof of "Ice Age Man" in America, for all the places mentioned are outside the glaciated district, and it is possible that in this western region some of the large animals may have lingered for a time after the retreat of the ice.

MAN IN THE TRENTON GRAVELS

Near Trenton, New Jersey, is a high river terrace overlooking the Delaware River. In the upper layer objects made by the historic Indians have been found. Below this was a deposit of yellow loam evidently laid down by water action. This in turn rested on glacial gravels. It appears that the yellow loam is either a late glacial deposit or dates from early post glacial times. This is important to us, for in it have been found a large number of tools, projectile points, and other objects made by man. These are all constructed of a dark gray slate known as argilite. Here again is a hint of early man on this continent. Other hints have come from Oklahoma, Nebraska, Florida, California, and elsewhere.

MINNESOTA WOMAN

The last case of early man to be cited will be the recent discovery in Ottertail County, Minnesota. Several years ago a geological study of an ancient lake bed had definitely placed the date of its existence at the end of the last great glaciation.

A roadway which led from higher ground into the old lake bed was rebuilt a few years ago, but at one point it was inclined to

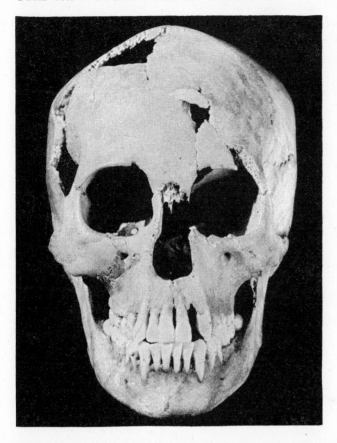

THE MINNESOTA
WOMAN
Front view of wom-
an's skull unearthed
in Minnesota by
highway workers.
Other portions of the
skeleton were later
recovered.

Courtesy Dr. A. E. Jenks,
University of Minnesota

buckle up during periods of freezing and thawing. To overcome
this, the pavement was taken up and excavation was carried on
preparatory to putting in a heavy layer of crushed rock. At one
point the excavating machine exposed a white surface which
turned out to be the top of a human skull. The workmen removed
the skull and some other bones and sent them to the University of
Minnesota. By the time these had reached Dr. Jenks, Head of the
Department of Anthropology of that institution, the road had
been rebuilt.

Dr. Jenks realized the possible importance of the discovery
and succeeded in securing permission to tear up the new road in
order to investigate further. This was done and other portions of
the skeleton were recovered, also a bone dagger and an ornament.

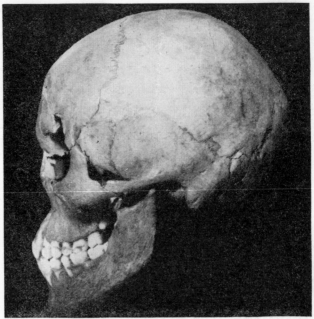

Courtesy Dr. A. E. Jenks, University of Minnesota

OLDEST KNOWN AMERICAN?
Side view of the skull of the Minnesota Woman. If this is the
skull of a woman drowned in the glacial lake, it is
that of the oldest known American.

The skeleton has caused a great deal of discussion. Some claim that we have here a skeleton of a woman who was drowned in the glacial lake. If this is true then she is the oldest known American. Others believe that this was a burial, even though it lay very deep in the soil. Unfortunately the road workers had no idea of making a discovery, and no observations were made of the earth directly above the body.

The skull resembles somewhat that of the present-day Eskimo but shows few particularly primitive characters.

Man may have been in America before the retreat of the ice, but, if so, he was in relatively small numbers. The main migrations into America began in post-glacial times and probably have continued until comparatively recent centuries. More about this invasion will be found in the pages to follow.

FRAUDS

The archaeologist must always be on guard against frauds. Some people take delight in trying to fool their fellow men; others make frauds in the hope of selling them or for gaining fame. A discovery is accepted only after the most rigid investigation, and questionable claims are discarded.

One of the most celebrated frauds to be attempted in America is that connected with the "Calaveras Skull."

In Calaveras and Tuolumne counties of California is a long winding elevation known as Table Mountain. This is really an ancient river of lava which once filled a valley in this region.

In Tertiary times—more than a million years ago—a great volcanic eruption occurred and a stream of lava poured down the mountain slopes and finally entered the valley of the Stanislaus River. When it hardened it left the river of stone filling the river bed. In the centuries which have passed, the neighboring land has been eroded away by water action leaving the hard lava as a flat top mountain winding over the land. The river cut a new channel through which it now flows.

During the days of the "gold rush" into California, free gold was found in the sands of the present river and hundreds of prospectors panned for the metal. Finally someone discovered the ancient river bed passing below the lava flow, and when he tested the sands he found them rich in gold. As a result, many tunnels were run back under Table Mountain.

In one of these tunnels the owner, upon returning from lunch, discovered a human skull, while close by were some arrow heads and stone utensils. He was quick to realize the importance of the find if it were authentic, for he knew the age of the sands in which he was working. If the skull and objects did belong to the old river bed, it meant he had found Tertiary man in America; it meant that he had carried the story of man back at least a half million years beyond any of the discoveries mentioned in the early pages of this book.

He at once summoned local scientists, and they in turn notified others. Within a short time many of the leading geologists and archaeologists of the country were at the site.

Careful study of all the surrounding sands indicated that everything fitted into the picture of the ancient river, except the skull and man-made objects. Bones of ancient animals gave clear evidence of having been carried and smoothed by water action. The skull showed no such wear; in fact, it had clay imbedded below the cheek bones. It seems certain that this would have been quickly removed, had the skull been in the waters of the river. Imbedded in the clay were some modern snails. The arrow points were lying together, a strange condition if they had been deposited by the water, and they showed no signs of wear.

The skull itself looks very modern and corresponds closely to those in the nearby Indian burial grounds, while the utensils are like those in use when the whites invaded California.

If the find is authentic it means that man and his culture have not changed in a million years. Because of its recent character, and of the fact that the objects show no sign of water action, as well as the other facts cited, it seems clear that this is a fraud.

Probably some friend or a workman attempted to play a joke on the owner of the tunnel, and, when he found how seriously everyone took the matter, he never dared tell. Calaveras man is not accepted by scientists, but his story shows how much care must be taken before accepting any claim.

THE INDIANS

We have seen that there is considerable evidence that man was in North America toward the end of the last glaciation and that he was associated with animals now extinct on this continent. It appears, however, that the important movement of peoples took place after the retreat of the ice.

Several years ago Dr. Brinton suggested that Cro-Magnon man or his close relatives may have migrated by way of Iceland and Greenland to the American shores. If the movement took place before the retreat of the glaciers, ice bridges may have provided an easy route for travel. In further substantiation of such a claim is the evidence of early man at Trenton, New Jersey, and the many likenesses of the Eskimo to Cro-Magnon and his culture.

A RELIEF MAP OF THE CONTINENT OF NORTH AMERICA, SHOWING THE GREAT RANGE OF WESTERN MOUNTAINS WHICH PROBABLY ACTED AS A BARRIER TO MIGRATION FROM THE COAST EASTWARD AND DIRECTED MOST OF THE ASIATIC INVADERS TOWARD THE SOUTH

Most students, however, believe that America was populated from Asia and that the chief route was by way of Bering Straits. They call attention to evidence that a land bridge existed there until comparatively late times. Before the Arctic Sea broke through, the effects of the Japan current were felt farther north and kept the region about the Straits free from ice. Over this route animals traveled freely and man may have done so. Even today, when the Straits are open and the climate is more severe, people travel back and forth between the American and Siberian sides. The distance is not great and islands in the channel offer convenient stepping stones.

Those who hold to this belief agree that the Eskimos resemble Cro-Magnon in some respects and that their culture has considerable in common with that of the late Ice Age people in Europe. These claims will be considered later. Now it seems desirable to sketch briefly the general picture.

A glance at a relief map of North America will show a high range of mountains along the western side of the continent. From

Alaska to Puget Sound a line of islands fringes the coast, forming an inland sea. Back from the sea is a narrow plain and then come densely wooded mountains. Invaders from Asia who found themselves on the western coast might have pressed inland, but it would have been with considerable effort. The easy way was to the south, and following this they would eventually reach California and Western Mexico.

Further study of the map shows the great range of the Rocky Mountains lying farther to the east, and between it and the coast mountains is a high plateau. Evidently some of the early peoples came in at the northern end of the plateau and pressed southward through what is now Utah, Colorado, Arizona, and New Mexico, and on into Mexico.

Beyond the Rockies opens a wide level land, unbroken until the eastern mountain range is reached. Migrants could pass southward through the Mississippi Valley and ultimately move into Mexico. Some would doubtless cross the low mountains of the east to reach the Atlantic coast.

Archaeological evidence indicates that these suggested lines of movement were those actually followed. In the Southwest conditions have been favorable for the preservation of the story. The dry climate has preserved evidences of the early inhabitants and it likewise has hindered settlement by whites; consequently many undisturbed sites remain.

The early inhabitants of this region are known as Basket Makers, because of the fact that at first they had no pottery, also because they usually covered their dead with a large basket. Evidences of these people have now been discovered in a number of caves and rock shelters, so they are quite well known. They had long, narrow heads, somewhat projecting faces, rather wide cheek bones, wide noses, and well developed chins. They are not typical Mongoloids and differ considerably from the later Indians, although evidence of intermixture with later comers is evident in many regions. This physical type, with variations, has been found in other parts of the United States, notably in the Mississippi Valley where they are locally called "Black Sand Men."

The Basket Makers lived in caves, and at first depended on seeds and game. They did not possess the bow and arrow, but

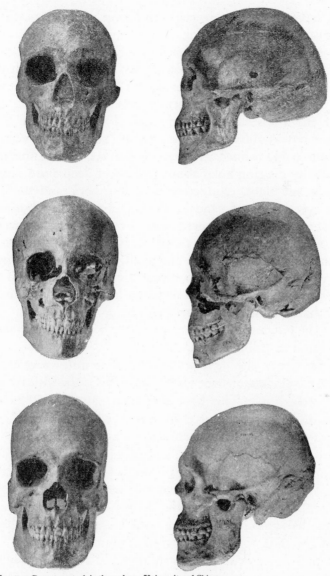

Courtesy Department of Anthropology, University of Chicago

ANCIENT AMERICANS
Above (top row): Illinois' Oldest Inhabitant—the "Black Sand Man."
Two lower rows: Typical Mound Builder Skulls.

they did have the throwing stick and long reed darts. Their one domestic animal was the dog, which apparently they brought with them from Asia. Baskets were of great importance. Evidently they used them for cooking by filling them with water and then dropping in hot stones until the water boiled. No pottery appears in their earliest settlements.

Later the knowledge of corn reached them, and we find evidence that it was cultivated to a certain extent. Corn was husked and stored in grass-lined underground cysts. These storage bins were made by digging holes about three feet deep and lining them with sandstone slabs, chinked with cedar bark and sand. Over the tops were slabs of sandstone. Sometimes they buried their dead in these cysts and covered them over so that they were preserved. With the dead or in camp refuse we find sandals, woven bags, necklaces of bone, stone and shell, and belts of woven hair. Throwing sticks and darts also appear along with corn and squash. Some graves are those of small children laid on soft cradle boards. Dress probably consisted of an apron or cloth attached to a cord.

Near the entrance of the caves were the fire places, and close by were hand grinding stones.

We can trace the development of this culture over a long period of time. Somewhere about 1000 B.C. the idea of pottery had reached them. The first specimens appear to have been moulded inside baskets and then sun dried, but later they were baked in a fire. Very little decoration was attempted, but in time they were making bowls, ladles, and other forms. Baskets, always important, were made in various ways, while the upper and lower grinding stones for breaking corn and seeds became of increased importance. About this time the people began to make circular houses on the level ground. The sides were of stone slabs set on edge, but the roof apparently was of small timbers.

This stage is known as Basket Maker III, and is important, for at its close there is evidence of a rather sudden change in population. The culture continues and develops without a break, but the long-headed Basket Makers are replaced by a round-headed people like the present day Pueblo Indians. Apparently this was a peaceful invasion, for there is evidence of intermarriage, and the newcomers borrowed the culture already established.

Courtesy Atchison, Topeka & Santa Fe Railway

DWELLINGS IN THE CLIFFS
In many places the Cliff Dwellers dug rooms back into the soft rock and then
placed a building in front. The floor and roof timbers of this outer structure
fitted into the rows of small holes.

The next step is known as Pueblo I, for at that time stone or
masonry houses appeared. These were small structures, built so
close together as to form a unit, or pueblo. Agriculture became
of greater importance, pottery was highly developed, the bow
replaced the throwing stick, and it is evident that the population
was increasing rapidly.

THE CLIFF DWELLERS

Space does not allow us to follow in detail the development of
Pueblo Indian culture, although it is well known from about the
beginning of the Christian era.

With the increase in population more and more land was
brought under cultivation, more and larger pueblos appeared, and
there was steady advance in all the arts. Then it seems that no-

Photo by Cole

MONTEZUMA'S CASTLE
The building is so protected by the overhanging cliff that it has suffered
little from the elements or weapons of enemies.

madic hunting people from the north began to press in on the
village dwellers. It is probable that these invaders were the ancestors of the Ute, Navaho, Apache, and other tribes which have
established themselves in the Southwest. Finally as a result of
this pressure the Pueblo people in many regions began to build
their homes in the caves. However, these were no longer the crude
camps of the Basket Makers.

Large houses of stone, often two or more stories in height,
filled smaller caves, while real cities—like Cliff Palace in the Mesa
Verde National Park—were constructed where the caves and rock

Paul's Photos, Chicago

CLIFF PALACE, MESA VERDE, COLORADO

With primitive tools and mere man power, these old-time builders reared enduring
monuments that have withstood the elements of centuries.

Courtesy Southwestern Monuments, National Park Service

EARLY APARTMENT HOUSE UNDER THE CLIFF

A portion of Keetsiel, a cliff dwelling in Navaho National Monument.

shelters were of sufficient size. The builders are the so-called "Cliff Dwellers." They are not a lost race as is so often claimed. They are Pueblo Indians who lived in caves and were closely related to those who built the great cities on the open land.

THE FIRST APARTMENT HOUSES

While part of the population were living as Cliff Dwellers, others were constructing towns and cities in favorable locations. At Pueblo Bonito, Aztec, Puye, and elsewhere were huge apartment houses, usually rising in steps or terraces from a central court yard. Doors and windows seldom appear on the lower floors. The people ascended to the roof by means of ladders and then entered the lower rooms through trap doors.

In the court yards, or at least close to the pueblos, were circular underground ceremonial chambers known as kivas. Judging by the use to which they are now put by the modern Pueblo Indians, we are certain that these served as places for meeting and worship for the various clans and secret societies.

Everything indicates a highly developed agricultural community with well-established religious practices. Evidently the life was much like that of the present-day Pueblos. Then a great catastrophe came upon these peaceful tillers of the soil.

THE GREAT DROUGHT

For centuries the Southwest has been semi-arid and has been subject to occasional droughts, but beginning in 1276 there occurred a period of twenty-three years with very little rainfall. Streams and springs dried up in many regions, and at this time most of the Cliff Dwellings and Pueblos of Colorado and northern Arizona were abandoned. Doubtless a considerable part of the population perished at that time while those who survived moved to the valley of the Rio Grande or into the region now occupied by the Hopi Indians.

Later we shall visit the Pueblo Indians who, as we have seen, are the modern descendants of the Cliff Dwellers.

Courtesy Southwestern Monuments, National Park Service

RUINS OF PUEBLO BONITO
The view is from the cliffs on the north side of Chaco Canyon, and shows
clearly the "D" shaped outline.

THE MOUND BUILDERS

Up to a few years ago the Mound Builders were considered as
a mysterious people who had once populated the Mississippi Valley
but had mysteriously vanished. Now their story is known, the
mystery is gone, but they still remain an interesting page in the
pre-history of America.

Probably the first inhabitants of the Mississippi Valley were
the "Black Sand People" discovered in 1930, in central Illinois,
by the University of Chicago. Here we again find a long-headed
population much like the Basket Makers. They lived in the open,
but no traces of their dwellings have yet been identified. Fortunately they buried their dead together with some of their
belongings so that we know their physical type and something of
their culture.

Courtesy Southwestern Monuments, National Park Service

CLIFF-SHELTERED HOMES
A portion of Betatakin, a cliff dwelling in Navaho National Monument.

2

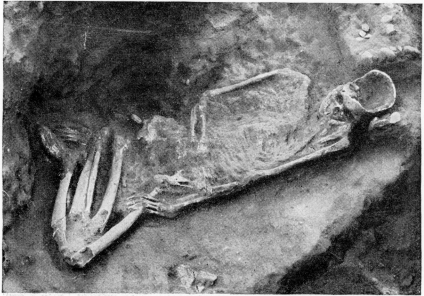

Courtesy Department of Anthropology, University of Chicago

A BLACK SAND BURIAL
An ancient long headed population was found at the lowest levels of excavation in Illinois.

Near the heads of some skeletons were crude platforms of rough stones. Stone projectile points—probably too large for the bow and arrow—drills, cutting blades, and axes were found with the bodies, also some fragments of pottery. As in the West, these people were followed by the ancestors of the modern Indians.

Some of the newcomers evidently were hunters while others devoted some time to agriculture. Later, crops became more important and with this development came larger and more permanent settlements.

The name Mound Builder was applied to these people because in many regions they erected mounds in which they buried their dead. It should be noted that the name was used for many tribes, often with quite different cultures. Perhaps this can be made clear by the statement that two great cultural patterns appear in the Mississippi Valley and that these can be subdivided into smaller and smaller groups. The first of these is known as the Woodland Pattern, the second as the Mississippi Pattern.

In general the Woodland people had some agriculture but were still quite dependent upon hunting and the gathering of wild seeds. They lived in rather small groups in round or rectangular houses made of light poles covered with reed mats, skins, and the like. They made pottery, but it was usually in the form of bowls or jars, and if decoration appeared it was in cut or incised lines. When a man died, his arms and legs were drawn close to his body, he was laid on the ground and a mound of earth heaped over him. Some groups built effigy mounds, sometimes in the shape of birds and animals, sometimes resembling snakes. In a part of these they placed burials, but others show no such use. One division, known as the Hopewell, cremated many of their dead but had a very special type of disposal for a favored few. A piece of ground was leveled and a layer of white sand was spread on it. Then a log tomb was constructed and the body laid inside with pipes, ornaments, objects of every day use, and hundreds of river pearls. Over this tomb a small mound of earth was heaped. When another burial of this type was planned, a second tomb was erected close by, and finally a huge mound, often fifteen or more feet in height, was placed over all.

This Hopewell cultural manifestation, while belonging to the Woodland pattern, was much influenced from the southeast and had also developed along its own lines. It made excellent pottery, woven fabrics sometimes in color; it had very characteristic platform pipes, ornaments of many kinds, and excellent stone and bone tools. These people had wide trade relations, and in their graves and village sites we find copper from the Lake Superior region, obsidian probably from Mexico and Colorado, sea shells from the ocean, and mica from the south. Its greatest development was in Ohio, but it extended across Indiana and Illinois to reach Iowa and Wisconsin; and it likewise spread over into New York and some other eastern states.

In contrast to the Woodland culture was the Mississippi. This is characterized by large villages with rectangular houses built of timbers and wattle work, often covered with clay. Agriculture was important and the pottery industry was highly specialized. Bowls, plates, and other dishes were often made to

Courtesy Department of Anthropology, University of Chicago

A HOPEWELL MOUND BUILT OVER THE BLACK SANDS IN ILLINOIS
Here the highly developed Hopewell is directly above the very old and
primitive Black Sand culture.

Courtesy Department of Anthropology, University of Chicago

WOODLAND POTTERY
The characteristic Woodland pottery of the Mississippi valley is bowl shape, decorated with incised lines.

Courtesy Department of Anthropology, University of Chicago

MISSISSIPPI TYPE OF POTTERY

In contrast to the Woodland wares, the Mississippi has a variety
of forms, often in colors.

represent animals and fish, and frequently were in colors. Stone work, bone, and shell were plentiful, while pipes testified to the habit of smoking.

These people also built mounds but seldom for burial. Their mounds were usually truncated pyramids on the tops of which they placed ceremonial buildings or the homes of their leaders.

Burial was in cemeteries, but since these were usually on high ground and additional earth was sometimes brought in, they frequently formed low mounds. One of the most interesting of these cemeteries is the "Dickson Mound" near Lewiston, Illinois. A permanent building has been erected over it and two hundred and thirty bodies have been exposed. They have been left in place together with all their belongings, so it is possible to observe their burial customs in detail. Sometimes the body of a warrior lay alone, with stone celt or weapon; again a woman's skeleton was surrounded with pots and shell spoons. In some cases, apparently, whole families had died at about the same time and were buried together. Always these bodies were laid stretched at full length and usually they were accompanied by burial gifts.

With varying degrees of development this Mississippi culture extends over much of the Valley and at one point enters Wisconsin.

Hundreds of bodies have been recovered from the Mounds and a study of these clearly shows that the Mound Builders were only American Indians who built mounds. Since the custom had been abandoned by most of the historic tribes, a fiction of a lost race grew up.

Near Channahon, Illinois, was a mound of the Woodland culture which was entirely of the historic period. Close to the head of the central burial was a small casket, locked with a key, inside which was a thimble, a pair of scissors, and a sleigh bell, while close to the skeleton was a silver crucifix. Evidently this mound was erected after the Indians had come into contact with white traders and missionaries.

Courtesy Department of Anthropology, University of Chicago
KINCAID MOUND, SOUTHERN ILLINOIS
This mound is a truncated pyramid, 32 feet high and covers two acres.
A ceremonial building formerly occupied the summit.

Courtesy Department of Anthropology, University of Chicago
DICKSON CEMETERY MOUND
The bodies have been left undisturbed together with their prized belongings.

UNIVERSITY OF CHICAGO STUDENTS EXCAVATING A MOUND
IN CENTRAL ILLINOIS

EXCAVATING A MOUND

Hundreds of mounds and village sites in the Mississippi Valley have been dug into and many relics obtained. Unfortunately in most cases the diggers were untrained and consequently much valuable historical material was scattered and lost. Every prehistoric site represents a page of history which can be read only by one trained for the task. Even he must keep a careful record, or his work becomes vandalism of the worst sort. Because most Americans are interested in knowing how such a record can be obtained, a brief account is given here.

Before the scientist begins his excavations he makes test pits well outside the site so that he may know what the natural conditions were until disturbed by man. Next he stakes the mound out into five-foot squares, each of which bears a number. Some little distance away he has established a plane table and a teles-

EXCAVATING AN INDIAN MOUND
The modern method of opening a pre-historic site is here illustrated.

copic alidade from which he records the different elevations of
the mound or the height and location of any object found.

When all is ready he starts a trench well outside and at right
angles to the mound and carries this down until he feels certain
it is below the disturbed soil. Using a mattock he then slices the
mound down in thin strips until a burial or object of interest is
encountered. At this stage trowels, metal pins, and orangewood
sticks are used to expose the skeleton. Nothing is moved or disturbed until every detail of the burial has been studied and each
fact recorded in a field notebook. Drawings and photographs
are made of each skeleton, and then every object is numbered before it is packed away. From such field notes the final report is
made up. It is clear, however, that unless a person is familiar with
the different cultures in a region he will miss some of the most important facts. Most foreign countries and several states prohibit
digging unless the person who wishes to excavate can prove that
he is fully qualified to obtain and preserve a full record.

Courtesy Department of Anthropology, University of Chicago

A DOUBLE WALLED HOUSE IN THE KINCAID GROUP,
SOUTHERN ILLINOIS

The Kincaid village site covers approximately one hundred acres. In addition
to houses it has four large pyramidal mounds and a cemetery.

WHAT THE TREE-RINGS TELL

Doubtless many of our readers have wondered how it is possible to say that a cliff dwelling was built in a certain year or that a great drought began in 1276 A.D. and lasted twenty-three years. Of course these occurred long before the white man reached America, and no Indian tribe north of Mexico had a written language.

Several years ago Professor Douglass, an astronomer of the University of Arizona, became interested in the effect of sun spots on our climate. It appeared that they occurred in definite cycles and if they did influence our rainfall they might have left a record which could be checked.

It is well known that many of our trees build up a growth ring each year, so that by counting the rings it is possible to tell the age of a tree.

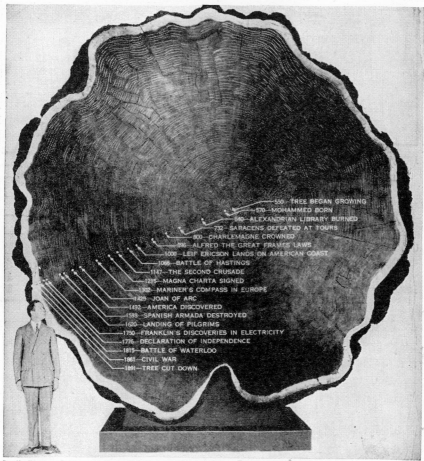

550—TREE BEGAN GROWING
570—MOHAMMED BORN
640—ALEXANDRIAN LIBRARY BURNED
732—SARACENS DEFEATED AT TOURS
800—CHARLEMAGNE CROWNED
896—ALFRED THE GREAT FRAMES LAWS
1000—LEIF ERICSON LANDS ON AMERICAN COAST
1066—BATTLE OF HASTINGS
1147—THE SECOND CRUSADE
1215—MAGNA CHARTA SIGNED
1302—MARINER'S COMPASS IN EUROPE
1429—JOAN OF ARC
1492—AMERICA DISCOVERED
1588—SPANISH ARMADA DESTROYED
1620—LANDING OF PILGRIMS
1750—FRANKLIN'S DISCOVERIES IN ELECTRICITY
1776—DECLARATION OF INDEPENDENCE
1815—BATTLE OF WATERLOO
1861—CIVIL WAR
1891—TREE CUT DOWN

Paul's Photos, Chicago

SECTION OF A GIANT SEQUOIA TREE SHOWING
ANNUAL GROWTH RINGS
This section is exhibited in the American Museum of Natural History in New York.

Dr. Douglass assumed that if there was plenty of moisture the tree would have a normal growth but should a season be very dry the growth of the tree would be retarded and consequently the ring for that year would be narrow. He tested this belief by comparing the rings of growing trees with the report of the weather bureau in that region and found that the rings and rainfall checked perfectly. When the weather record indicated heavy rainfall the ring for that year was wide and distinct; when it said scanty rainfall the ring was narrow or almost missing.

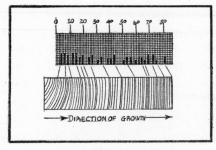

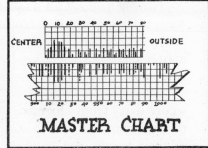

MASTER CHART

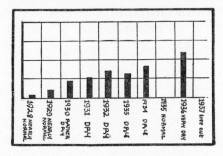

HOW THE TREE RINGS' STORY IS
OBTAINED

UPPER LEFT: Method of constructing
    individual skeleton plot.

UPPER RIGHT: Method of using skele-
    ton plots.

BELOW: The beginning of a chart with
    explanatory notes.

With this start he took samples or borings from standing
trees and by comparing many of these he was able to work out
a chart which went back of historic records. For this purpose
he used squared paper. Each square on the horizontal line indicated one year, while each square in the vertical line represented
tree-ring growth. If a year was normal no line was drawn, but
if it was a little dry a short vertical line was erected; if very dry,
a long line, and so on. Thus in the chart which begins, let us say,
in 1937, we get a vertical line in the space for 1936 indicating a
dry year; 1935 was normal, but the five preceding years ranged
from dry to very dry. Thus a chart of good and bad years is
built up.

    In the Southwest Dr. Douglass carried the record as far back
as possible on standing trees, then he went to buildings put up
by the Spaniards and took borings of the timbers they had
used. When he had made a chart of these he ran it along that of
the standing trees until they matched. Thus he was able to extend
his record back several hundred years. Next he went to the prehistoric pueblos and cliff dwellings and now he and his associates
have a master chart for that region which goes back to 11 A.D.

Now when a Cliff Dwelling is discovered in the arid Southwest, a boring is taken from a number of the timbers used in its construction. A chart is made from these and is run along the master chart until the two correspond. Then by taking the last ring on the timber it is possible to tell the year in which it was cut.

Recently Dr. Florence Hawley proved that it is possible to secure dates from charcoal, and this will probably make it possible to date many of the Indian Mounds. Most of the timbers used in their houses and log tombs are badly decayed, but quantities of charcoal from their fires have been preserved and may be dated.

This is but one of many methods used by science in recovering the story of the past.

THE ARRIVAL OF THE INDIANS

In our discussion of the first comers to America we observed the possible ways of reaching the continent and found that most scholars believe that the chief, if not the only, route was by way of Bering Straits. In this discussion it is important for us to note that the American Indian is evidently a member of the Mongoloid division of mankind. This does not mean that he is descended from the Chinese or other historic peoples of Asia, but it does indicate a common ancestry with them.

Doubtless some racial intermixture had taken place in Asia before the ancestral groups reached this continent, and in the centuries since their arrival they have undergone some change. Yet they are still remarkably alike and justify us in speaking of them as the American race. The one exception to this is the Eskimo who in many ways differs from the rest of the population. The fact that the Indians are Mongoloids further justifies the belief that they came by the easiest route from Asia.

Naturally we are anxious to know when they came. We have already seen the evidence of some very early invasions, but it is clear that the main migration must have taken place in early Neolithic times. Archaeological evidence tells us that at the time of their arrival they were still a hunting, fishing, seed-gathering people; that they had the throwing stick and quite early the bow and arrow; that they were making cords and baskets; that they had both chipped and polished stone implements; and that they

Courtesy Southwestern Monuments, National Park Service

NAVAHO CORNFIELDS
Typical southwestern lands into which early settlers came from Asia.

had domesticated the dog. This represents the very simple Neolithic, and this is apparently all the American Indian had to build on. Whatever he possessed in later times he developed through his own genius on American soil.

Had his movement into America been as late as the middle Neolithic in Eurasia, he must have learned of pottery, of domestic plants and animals. There is no good evidence that he brought pottery with him; the one domestic animal he possessed was the dog, and no domestic plant from Asia or Europe was known in North America until after the time of Columbus. This gives us a rough approximation of the time when the ancestors of the Indians began to enter the continent. Probably we shall not be far from the truth if we say this movement took place about ten thousand years ago.

It seems probable that the invaders came in relatively small numbers and slowly took possession. Through thousands of years they worked southward, developing somewhat different cultures in the different environments under which they lived. They found no hostile animals to overcome and few, if any, earlier inhabitants.

Those who made their way along the Pacific Coast ultimately reached California. There they found great groves of acorn trees which furnished an easy source of food. Some settled along the Northwest Coast where the salmon and other fish made living easy. Those early migrants who pushed in between the Coast Range and the Rocky Mountains found themselves in a semi-arid region and had to subsist on small game, seeds, and roots until, after a long period, they learned of agriculture. Their life was difficult and progress slow. On the Great Plains were immense herds of buffalo which at times could be driven over cliffs and killed or, if necessary, they could be hunted with the bow, but until the Indian obtained the horse he found buffalo hunting both difficult and dangerous.

North of the Plains was the range of the caribou, and bands of men early began to follow and live off the herds. Their life was very meager for they had to be almost constantly on the move to follow the game.

Still further north, along the Arctic Seas, were the Eskimos, a people living primarily on sea animals.

Finally came the northern and southern Woodlands. Here, until the coming of agriculture, the people lived on game and wild products and maple sugar. Over part of the area wild rice appeared in the lakes and helped furnish a steady food supply.

These were the main areas occupied by man, in which nature had offered various ways of living. Naturally the different climates and sources of food must have affected the lives and habits of the early Neolithic peoples.

In South America was a similar range of climate and wild life, for the land varies from tropical forests to grassy plains, to high mountains and plateaus.

As one approaches Mexico and Middle America, he sees the continent becoming very narrow and he also finds several environments close together. On the east coast is a low tropical coast line; this gives way to an intermediate zone as one goes up to the plateau. Then comes a highland of limited rainfall but with cool climate. Farther to the west the region is arid, and finally comes the low arid coast. Such conditions must have affected the people living there. Certainly those living in the tropical rain belt led a different life from those in the semi-arid highlands. But they were so close together that they would sometimes meet and one would influence the other, through trade, intermarriage, and warfare.

It appears that contacts are necessary for progress. Any people cut off from the rest of the world becomes conservative and unwilling to accept new ideas, but when they meet people of different cultures a certain amount of borrowing goes on.

Another point of great importance is that, as the immigrants pushed slowly southward into Mexico and Central America, they were forced close together and if they were in any great numbers they would find it difficult to live on a hunting basis. This was particularly true in the highlands of Mexico, Guatemala, and Honduras.

SECOND DISCOVERY OF AGRICULTURE

Here in these highlands, probably due to chance, the American Indian independently learned to domesticate plants. Someone learned that a wild grass, called teocentli, could be planted and would yield a crop. From this comes our maize or corn. Once this was evident, attempts were made with other plants, and we soon find the people raising corn, beans, squash, peanuts, potatoes, and other products.

In America the story of the Near East was repeated. Agriculture allowed large settlements, and these in turn led to quick development of civilization. In one respect, however, the American civilizations differed from the European, and that was in the absence of domestic animals. Except for the very limited use, in South America, of the llama and the alpaca, the only domestic animal in America was the dog.

Long before the beginning of the Christian era, a rather high culture had developed in Mexico and Middle America, and from this region influences radiated out in all directions. This is im-

Courtesy Southwestern Monuments, National Park Service

PICTURES ON THE CLIFFS
Painted pictographs at Betatakin, Navajo National Monument.

Reproduced from F. B. 1435

TEOCENTLI PLANT
The ancestor of corn, domesticated by the American Indians.

portant, for some of the developments and inventions of the region had a profound effect on the cultures to the north and south, just as in Europe the inventions of the Mediterranean region had great influence on the region of the Swiss Lakes and the North.

The idea of corn spread northward and caused great changes in the life of the people of the southern Plateau and also of the Woodlands, but it had no influence in California and never reached the caribou hunters and peoples further to the north. Pottery traveled over practically the same area as corn, but the true loom and stone house only reached the southwest.

With this general picture in mind we are now ready to see how the various Indian groups lived before their cultures were destroyed by European invaders.

CULTURE AREAS

When we place the various Indian cultures on a map it is evident that they have very definite geographic limits. The Eskimo area is confined to the lands bordering the Arctic Seas; the Buffalo Hunters were found only on the Plains, and so on. We now plan to visit some of these areas and see how the Indians lived.

THE ESKIMOS

The Eskimo is very much of a puzzle. He lives in a land where all the other people are Indians, yet he is not a typical Indian or Mongoloid. His home is in the Arctic region where winter reigns for about ten months of the year and where life is often very difficult; yet he need not have remained in the North. Never was the population in America sufficiently dense to force any people to remain under such unfavorable conditions. We must assume that the Eskimo was accustomed to this sort of life when he came and hence remained. We are also in doubt as to when he arrived. He may represent the last of the Asiatic invaders or he may have been among the first of the people who pushed in at the end of the glaciation.

Courtesy American Museum of Natural History, New York

GREENLAND ESKIMO
An idle sunny day at Umanak

Some people have claimed that the Eskimo and his culture resemble that of Cro-Magnon man, the last of the Cave Dwellers of Europe. It is true that he has a large, long and narrow head accompanied by very wide cheek bones. In this respect he does seem somewhat like Cro-Magnon, but he is short and stocky in build and in other ways does not conform. His nose is straight and long, but is large and helps to give the face a heavy appearance. In color he ranges from a saffron to reddish brown, but his hair and eyes are black.

This people extends clear across North America from Greenland to Alaska, but always they remain close to the Arctic Seas. In physical type, language, and culture they are much alike, but in the East and West they have been subjected to considerable influence. The picture which follows will apply to most of the groups.

The Eskimos do not form a tribe, nor do they live together in large bands. Usually they are in small, closely related groups who hunt and live together while game is plentiful but who break up into families whenever there is need.

Eskimo land is truly the home of ice and snow. Throughout most of the year the days are short and temperatures low, yet

Courtesy Buffalo Museum of Science, Buffalo, N. Y.

A SNOW HOUSE
Such structures are built whenever needed but in some regions they
serve as permanent residences.

ESKIMO WOMAN
AND CHILD
The garment is made
of caribou hide
trimmed with fur.

Courtesy University
Museum, Philadelphia

II—11

Courtesy Field Museum of Natural History, Chicago

ESKIMO GIRL FISHING THROUGH ICE
Fish are snagged by sudden jerking of the line. No bait is used.

during the very short summer there is almost continuous day-light, and grass and flowers appear. In spite of this the soil remains frozen just a little below the surface and hence trees cannot grow. In all the vast stretch from Greenland to Alaska the only wood is that brought in as drift by rivers which flow to the north.

In such a land there is only one method of making a living, and that is by hunting and fishing.

During the short summer months several families will go together some distance inland to hunt caribou. They have learned the usual routes followed by these animals in their annual migrations and they kill some by means of the bow and arrow and catch others with traps. The most effective way to secure the game is, however, to stampede a band and drive the animals into boggy land, or better still into shallow lakes where men in boats are waiting to dispatch them. The period of caribou hunting is brief but it is important, for at this time they secure most of the skins from which they make their winter garments.

In summer the land is visited by vast flocks of birds, particularly geese and ducks. Then the people shoot and trap them or rob their nests. Boys and men scale the cliffs in search of eggs or swing huge nets through the air to catch the birds as they fly by. This is real sport which furnishes many a meal. At this time life is easy and the people live in skin tents.

As the sun begins its journey to the south, the people go to bays, or places where the sea is protected, so that smooth ice is likely to form, and erect their camps nearby. Houses show some differences, but two types are widespread. The first is constructed by laying up side walls of stones or turf and covering them over with whale ribs or other large bones. Over this framework they place skins and turf to form the roof.

The snow house is better known. This may range from a temporary structure thrown up in a few moments, in time of need, to a rather permanent affair. Blocks of snow are cut with bone knives and are laid up in spiral fashion with each succeeding layer sloping inward to form a dome. The last block at the top serves to lock and hold the structure together. Inside is a tent-like skin so arranged as to allow an air space next to the ice. This acts like a thermos bottle and keeps the ice from melting when

Courtesy American Museum of Natural History, New York

INTERIOR OF AN ESKIMO DWELLING
The woman is cooking over a stone lamp.

fires are built within. The inventor did not take out a patent, and recently civilized man has chanced upon the same idea.

Regardless of the materials used, the main room usually is approached by a long arched entry which is closed at each end with skins. In this entry are kept sleds and other objects, and here the dogs often sleep in severe weather.

Within the room are benches along the walls. At the sides are the cooking lamps and utensils, while at the back is a wide sleeping bench piled with skins and furs. On the floor the air is cold, but at the level of the benches it becomes so warm that the people discard most of their garments. The heat, the odor of oil lamps and of perspiring human bodies is such that civilized visitors usually beat a hasty retreat.

All heat and light are furnished by small lamps. These are shallow crescent-shaped bowls of stone, filled with seal oil or blubber. Moss wicks resting along the sides furnish the flames for cooking and all other purposes. Stoves are unknown but there is no wood to burn in them if they did exist.

Over these fires are suspended rectangular dishes made out
of a soft stone known as steatite. Food is boiled in such dishes
and snow is melted. Melting snow is a hard way to obtain water
and hence bathing is practically unknown. As a matter of fact,
the Eskimo and water are scarcely acquainted. In summer the
water is too cold for bathing and in winter it is too highly prized.
Soap is an unknown luxury. When the people were given soap
by the first explorers they ate it with relish.

Aside from personal possessions, there are few additional house
furnishings. In some regions baskets and pottery are seen, while
dishes and cups of skin and bone are common.

Among the women's effects will be found bone combs, needles, and skin scrapers; while the men possess their weapons,
pipes, and bone beaters with which snow is knocked off the
garments before entering the house.

Not far from the dwellings will be one or more caches in
which surplus meat and blubber have been buried, beneath stones,
to protect them from wolves and dogs. These quickly freeze
over and the supply is preserved until a time of need. Such times
of stress may occur when blizzards or continued bad weather
make hunting impossible. Many are the stories of years when
all the supplies were exhausted and the weaker members of the
group perished.

TAILORED GARMENTS

We may think that only civilized man has tailored garments,
but here in the far north all clothing is cut according to patterns
and is made to fit. Clothing is made of skins—bear, seal or even
skins of birds for summer, caribou hide or animal fur for winter.

In cold weather both men and women wear a sort of shirt
with the fur against the body. Over this is a jacket with hair
outside. A hood is worn over the head and in some regions this
is attached to the jacket. Oftentimes the woman carries her baby
inside the jacket resting against her back and thus they keep each
other warm.

Both men and women wear trousers, but of different patterns. Siberian Eskimo women wore knickers a hundred years

ago, but styles there do not change and so they continue to wear them. Feet must be kept warm, so fur stockings are worn and these are stuffed with moss to absorb the perspiration. Over these fit high artic boots. The hands are protected with mittens.

When traveling on the ice the glare is often so bad that it would cause temporary blindness were it not for the fact that at such times the people wear goggles—not the kind worn by civilized people, but made of strips of wood or bone with a tiny slit in front of the eyes.

Two important possessions of the Eskimo are his dog sled and skin boat. Both are constructed with difficulty for they are made up of bits of wood and bone lashed together. Runners for the sleds are usually of bone, but frequently water is poured on them to make ice runners, which slip along with little friction. The dogs are driven in harness and usually spread out fan shape as they dash over the ice and snow. The leader of the pack is absolute boss, and often gives a good thrashing to dogs which fail to do their part, or insist on fighting.

The man's boat, known as the kayak, is shaped like a canoe. It is completely skin covered, except for a round opening near the center of the top. The man slips into this with his feet

Courtesy American Museum of Natural History, New York

THE MAN'S BOAT, OR KAYAK
In this the man hunts sea animals during the months when the ocean is free of ice.

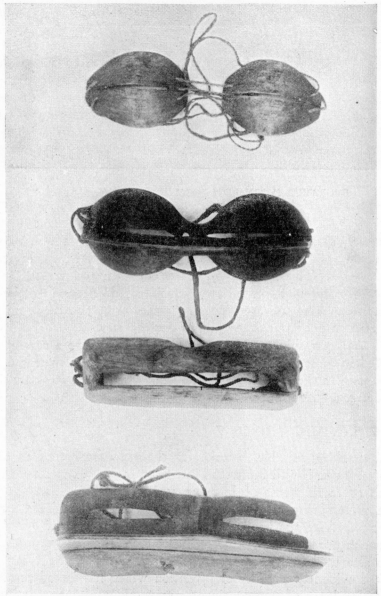

SNOW GOGGLES

The glare from the ice makes it necessary for the Eskimo to wear goggles fashioned of strips of wood in which tiny slits are cut.

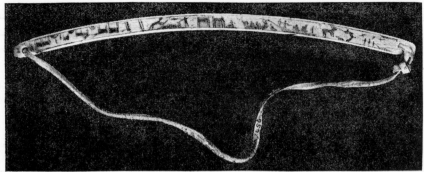

Courtesy University Museum. Philadelphia, Pa.

ENGRAVED IVORY BOW FROM NUNIVAK ISLAND, ALASKA

The bow cord encircles a wooden shaft which spins as the bow is run back and forth.
Such a device is used as a drill or in fire making.

stretched out in front of him and propels the craft with a double
paddle. Sometimes he wears a water-proof shirt made of seal
intestines. This fits tightly about the face and wrists. It also
has a wide skirt-like bottom which is tied around the central
opening. This makes everything water-tight and man and boat
can turn over and over without getting wet.

A larger skin covered boat, shaped much like a row boat, is
used in some regions, primarily by the women. These can only
be used during a portion of the year when the waters are fairly
free from jagged ice.

THE COMPOSITE BOW

Lack of suitable material for the manufacture of an object
of any size is well illustrated in the bow used here. This is made
up of small pieces of bone or wood lashed together. To give
it some spring as well as strength, a double braid of sinew is
placed along the back. With this arrows of some size and effi-
ciency are shot. It is interesting to note that this type of bow
is also used in Asia, across the steppe lands to the Near East.
It is evidently one idea or invention which has spread across the
treeless lands of two continents.

The bow and arrow are used primarily for hunting land animals and birds. For seals and other sea animals the throwing stick
and harpoon, or the harpoon alone, are employed.

2

During the winter months the ice covers all the water surface, but the seals are compelled to get air occasionally and consequently they have blow holes to which they come. Each seal may have several holes but eventually he will get back to all. The Eskimo knows the habits of his game, so provides himself with a little three-legged stool and sits down beside a hole. If the seal is slow in coming, the hunter scratches on the ice for he knows the animal is very inquisitive and, if near, will come to see what is going on. When he hears the seal coming, he stands with harpoon ready to strike. This harpoon consists of a wooden shaft into which a foreshaft of bone is fitted with a ball and socket arrangement. The two are also fastened together with sinew. Fitting into the end of the foreshaft is a bone or metal point which is attached to a line.

As the animal appears the hunter plunges the harpoon into its body, the foreshaft slips out of the handle, and this causes the point to be loosened. Such a device prevents loss and breakage of the valuable harpoon.

The animal at once dashes away but the hunter slows it up by pulling on the line. In time the seal becomes tired and must also have air, so back it comes to the hole and again it is harpooned; ultimately it is exhausted and is taken.

When the ice begins to break up toward spring the seals appear in groups. During the short period of sunshine they sleep on the ice, but always leave one of their number on guard. Every little while he will rise up and look around; then if all appears to be well he settles down for a short nap. The hunter places a sealskin over his head and back and creeps up on the sleeping animals. When the guard rises to look around, the hunter does likewise and the real seal thinks it is just another seal on guard and so is not alarmed. Finally the Eskimo gets close enough to rush in and kill one or two animals before they can escape.

After the water is sufficiently free from jagged ice fragments the men hunt in their skin kayaks. Their weapon is the throwing stick and harpoon. When an animal is sighted the hunter paddles rapidly toward where it is likely to reappear and waits for it to come up for air. As it does so, he hurls the harpoon at it. If he

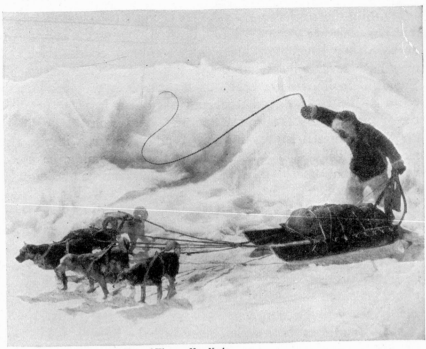

Courtesy American Museum of Natural History, New York

THE DOG SLED

During the winter months transportation is almost entirely by sleds. The
dogs are usually hitched fan shape but may be in single file.

strikes his mark the head of the harpoon will pull out and the line
attached to the shaft will unwind. As the animal swims away the
shaft is dragged crosswise through the water, thus impeding its
flight. The man in the boat follows closely, and when the game
reappears he hurls another harpoon and finally secures his game.
Even the walrus is taken by this means.

Fishing is of some importance. In the more open months large
fish are harpooned, and during the winter women and children
fish through holes cut in the ice. Little girls clad in furs sit on their
heels and keep short poles moving up and down. The ivory sinkers
act as lures, then suddenly the line is jerked and a fish is snagged.
No bait is used.

Hunting is serious business, for on it the people depend for
skins and furs for their garments, for meat, and for blubber and
oil to keep them warm. When anyone has food, all share in it

although the man who has made the kill gets the choicest pieces. The idea that one may have a surplus while another is hungry has never occurred to the Eskimo. He has no idea of barter, of sale, or of private ownership beyond the things he makes for himself. Should all food fail, the old and infirm and the children may be put to death, since they cannot aid in the struggle for existence. But such periods are rare and there is usually food enough for all.

The Eskimo is probably the world's greatest eater. All explorers in their land tell of the immense amount of meat, blood and fat he consumes. Much of this is eaten raw. Long strips of meat are forced into the mouth and, when it will hold no more, the strip is cut off at the lips.

There are no chiefs or headmen among the Eskimos. The bands or groups are usually small and made up of people closely related. A good hunter may gain some personal prestige, but he has no authority over his fellows.

RELIGION

The one man who stands out from the group is the shaman or medicine man. He is supposed to be in close communication with members of the spirit world. From them he has learned the cause and cure of sickness; he may be able to foretell the future and may at times bring injury to the living. He is both respected and feared.

When an illness appears, the shaman is called to hold a ceremony. Usually he sings and dances and then pretends to extract objects from the body of the patient either by rubbing or sucking the afflicted part.

Religious ideas are but weakly developed. It is thought that there are supernatural beings, but in general they do not greatly affect the lives of men. Spirits of dead people may linger for a time and may do evil, but ultimately they are reborn. Custom and religion are one and the same thing, and if one violates custom he sins and the sin attaches itself to the culprit as a sort of cloud or stain. This is not visible to men, but the animals can see it and will refuse to be killed until the offender makes a full confession.

The nearest approach to a deity is Sedna, a sort of sea goddess. According to one version of the Sedna myth, she and her father lived on an island. Finally she married a dog. One day while her father and husband were away, a man appeared in a boat and induced her to go away with him. The father returned and, finding his daughter gone, started in pursuit. Presently he found her on the stranger's island and started to take her back home. On the way a storm came up and, in order to save himself, Sedna's father threw her overboard. She seized the side of the boat with her fingers but her father cut off her finger joints and she sank. The tips of the fingers, however, turned to seals. Again she appeared and seized the boat. As she did so, her father cut off her second joints and each became a walrus. The third time this happened, the stumps of her fingers became whales. Then she sank to the bottom of the ocean where she still lives.

GETTING MARRIED

As a rule a man has only one wife, but polygamy does occur in some places when there is a shortage of men. It sometimes happens that nearly all the able-bodied men may be carried out to sea on an ice floe and never return. The opposite type of marriage, where a woman has more than one husband, has also been reported from some of the groups.

Marriage takes place when the young people are between sixteen and twenty years of age, and is usually a matter of their choice. Since people inside a group are closely related, the boy seeks his bride from another group. This is all arranged for in advance, but custom decrees that the young man shall appear to steal the girl. She doubtless has agreed to the match, but when the boy comes to take her she puts up a great fight and scratches and kicks.

During the winter months people of nearby villages may get together for a good time. They have wrestling and boxing bouts, tug of war, singing and dancing.

The only musical instrument is a shallow tambourine covered with skin. This is struck on the side to accompany the song and dance. Dancing is scarcely the correct word, for it consists only in swaying the body back and forth as the dancers bend the knees.

ESKIMO ANTLER BOX
FROM POINT BARROW,
ALASKA
Hunting scenes are often
carved on objects of every
day use.

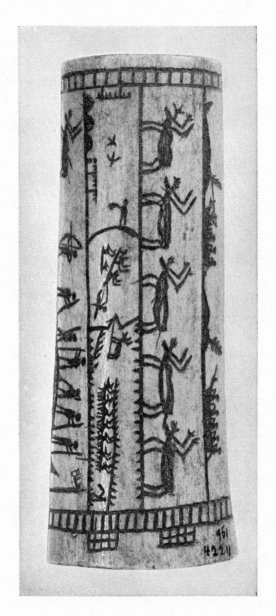

The Eskimos are not warlike although individuals do occasionally have a fight. However, the usual way to settle a dispute is to have a song contest. The man who thinks he has been injured challenges his foe. People of the neighborhood gather and then the challenger sings all the unpleasant things he can think of about his opponent. When he has finished, the foe replies, and this is kept up until one runs out of material.

Such is the life of the people of the Far North; no money, no stores, no ownership of land, no courts or lawyers, no jails, no organized religion. A life very different from ours, yet under these conditions the Eskimos have managed to survive.

THE CARIBOU HUNTERS

Just south of the Eskimos live the Caribou Hunters, typical round-headed American Indians. Their land is a dreary stretch of forest and tundra, in places dotted with lakes and bogs, and traversed by streams and rivers which flow toward the north. Hudson Bay divides this territory, but the country and people are much the same from Labrador to the borders of Alaska.

A CARIBOU INDIAN WITH TOBOGGAN

The climate is called sub-arctic, but it is quite as severe as that of the Eskimo area, while deep snows make travel difficult through much of the year.

Here the natives depend primarily on the caribou for all their needs—food, clothes, and shelter. These animals move in great herds, and the people must be ever on the march through forests or over the barren grounds, to keep in sight of their food supply.

Winter is the best hunting season and many animals are slaughtered then for use later in the year. They are skinned and the flesh is placed in caches—on high platforms or beneath piles of rock to keep it from animals.

Many methods are used in securing the caribou. All the ingenuity of the hunter is brought into play. A group of hunters will partially surround a herd and then seek to stampede it over a stretch of smooth ice. Some animals are sure to fall and be trampled by the others and thus be easily killed. Or they are driven into lakes where men in birch bark canoes lie in wait to spear and shoot them as they swim helplessly in the water.

In some regions enclosures are constructed into which the hunters try to direct part of the herd. Traps are also used, but these are of lesser importance.

This great dependence upon the caribou has had a profound effect on the people. They must be frequently shifting their camps; they can possess few things other than those absolutely necessary for maintaining life. The Eskimo can be and is an individualist, he hunts alone if he wishes; here cooperation is necessary if game is to be secured. Even here authority is weakly developed. Men recognize and follow a successful hunter, but his authority extends only over the chase and lasts only so long as his prestige.

Certain groups are quite alike in language and custom and are recognized as tribes; thus we hear of the Dog Ribs, Yellow Knives, and Carrier Indians, yet there really is no tribal organization with recognized chiefs.

As with the Eskimo the shaman or medicine man is important because of his close relationship with the spirit world, but even he must take part in all daily duties. There is no place in this culture for loafers or for those who cannot or will not work for the common good.

A CARIBOU WOMAN AND CHILD

As would be expected in a land of many lakes and streams, fishing is very important; in fact there are certain districts where it exceeds hunting. Fishnets are highly developed, but hooks and spears are often used.

Small game is taken in snares and traps, and at certain seasons berries and roots are gathered.

Houses are frail affairs of bark or skin usually built in the form of a lean-to; they are easily built and quickly deserted. No pottery is found in this area, but vessels of wood and birchbark are common. Boiling of foods is possible by heating stones in a fire and then dropping them in a bark dish filled with water. Stone work is rather weakly developed. Arrow heads are made, and stone adzes are employed in place of axes, but a man takes no special pride in this art.

In summer months birchbark canoes are of great importance in hunting and for all transportation. In winter a toboggan drawn by dogs or by women is now much used. The deep snows in the forests are usually too soft for sleds, but the flat-bottomed toboggan moves easily over this surface.

In this region we find the greatest development of the snow shoe in America. Round, wide-mesh shoes for soft snow; long thin mesh for a hard packed surface, and for speed.

Tailored garments of caribou skin are used. In general pattern they are somewhat like those of the Eskimo but are more close fitting. Frequently they are elaborately decorated with colored porcupine quills, thus giving evidence that even these lowly people have a love for design.

If we were to judge these Indians of the northern interior forests by their accomplishments, we should be compelled to place them very low in the human scale. However, we must always consider the environment under which a people live before judging their abilities. Later we shall see that the Navaho and Apache Indians of our Southwest are closely related to some of the western groups of Caribou hunters, yet they are far in advance of their northern kinsmen.

PEOPLES OF THE PLATEAU

The Plateau is a rather poorly defined area between the Rocky Mountains and the West Coast Range. In the north it fades into the interior forests, in the south it continues on into Mexico. Strong cultural influences from the Plains are found along its eastern borders while the tribes living along the Columbia, Thompson, Frazier, and other rivers have borrowed greatly in material culture from the Northwest Coast.

There is also great diversity in climate and food supply. In the north the rainfall is considerable, and roots and berries are added to fish and venison for food.

Along the rivers which empty into the Pacific, the salmon is very important, and at the time these fish are running all the Indians of the region are engaged in capturing and drying them. The meat is pulverized together with dried roots and is stored for later use. Close to the Plains, buffalo hunting was formerly of some importance and many evidences of Plains Indian culture were found.

In a large part of the plateau, particularly south of the Snake River, the land is semi-arid, often treeless with great lava flows

A DWELLING OF THE PLATEAU PEOPLE

and rocky stretches. Here plant life, except for sagebrush and cactus, is rare and animal life is scarce. No permanent lakes or rivers furnish fish or water fowl. It is a dreary, difficult land. So far as man is concerned, the natural environment offers him little either in shelter or food. Life is just a question mark between meals. Yet here men live and die with no idea of the riches the world affords.

In an earlier section we followed the slow rise of the Basket Maker out of this simple background. We saw the introduction of corn into the semi-arid regions a little to the south and witnessed the transformation of the people from primitive hunters, through the Cliff Dwellers, to the present day Pueblo Indians.

In the less advanced Indians of the Plateau area we probably have a very good picture of what the Basket Makers had to start with. A comparison of this with Pueblo life will help us to understand how greatly the latter were stimulated by contacts with Mexico.

In the desert south of the Snake River, dwellings are often only windbreaks without other protection. More commonly a dome-shaped brush shelter is found, and toward the northwest these are covered with mats or rushes. Near the Columbia River the winter house has a semi-subterranean floor above which is a conical roof with a smoke hole near the center.

Pottery is lacking or is of little importance, but coiled baskets are made, and in some regions show fine decoration. In the north bark fiber is woven or plaited and fashioned into simple garments, but deerskin cloth, still of the tailored type, is important. Blankets made of strips of rabbit skin plaited together are also much in use.

In most of the region nearly everything in the animal or insect line is used for food, even lizards and bugs are relished, while an occasional antelope or deer is a real treat. The bow and arrow, lances and clubs are the chief weapons. Tools were almost entirely of stone until recent years when metal came to these people through the white man.

CRUDE DWELLINGS OF THE PLATEAU PEOPLE

Courtesy Field Museum of Natural History, Chicago

CALIFORNIA INDIAN DANCE
Feather head dresses, strings of shell disks, and pieces of skin
around the waists make up the dance garments.

GUARDIAN SPIRITS

In this region we begin to find the idea of the guardian spirit, so important among many Indian tribes.

When a boy reaches maturity he goes alone to the mountains, and there for days he fasts and purifies his body, awaiting a vision. Usually, in his weakened condition, the vision comes. A spirit, in the form of an animal, talks to him, advises him, and may even tell him valuable secrets and songs. From this time on, this spirit is the boy's personal guardian, aiding and directing him through life.

These guardians usually reward those who follow the old customs and beliefs, and hence have a strong influence on the daily conduct of the people.

The Plateau people have no very definite bands, except as they come in contact with others along the edge of their territory. Food is too scarce to allow for the development of large groups or for the establishment of villages.

Out of this simple background came the Pueblo culture, but not until agriculture made it possible for people to remain in one locality.

South of the Snake River live the Shoshone speaking people— about the least advanced of the Plateau Indians, yet sometime in the past a group of their relatives wandered south and today are known as the Hopi, a highly developed pueblo people still speaking the Shoshone dialect.

All this seems to tell us that the environment exerts a powerful influence on the life of any people, but new elements—like corn— may be introduced which will transform the environment. It also teaches us that a people of low culture may become leaders if they move into a more favorable region or come in contact with those more advanced. The life of the Plateau is drab and colorless but out of it, in the south, came one of the most interesting of Indian peoples—the Pueblos.

THE CALIFORNIA INDIANS

California, the land of balmy climate, rich soil, and natural food supply, would seem to be the land of promise for primitive man. Here, certainly, he should have developed a high culture. But the land of promise failed, and at the time of their discovery the California Indians were among the most backward to be found in America. This is the more difficult to understand when we realize how close Southern California is to the Southwest, where Pueblo culture had begun its development at least two thousand years ago.

Let us view this land into which the first Indian invaders came and see if we can solve the riddle.

The rich coastal plain and central valley of California are separated from the Plateau by the high and abrupt Sierra Nevada mountains. This range is forested with great trees and has many valleys, lakes, and streams. Game and fish are fairly abundant. Man could and did live in the mountain valleys, but in the region of Yosemite is one of the heaviest snowfalls on the American continent, and even in the summer months the mountain dwellers were isolated from one another by abrupt cliffs and high peaks.

To the north along the coast, the typical California vegetation merges into the forests of Oregon and Washington, while to the south, it becomes drier and more inhospitable until below San Diego the waterless wastes of Lower California are found.

Central California, with its great interior valley and its rolling hill lands offered one of the greatest natural sources of food known to early man. Here were vast groves of oaks which furnished countless acorns—food for a dense population.

Judging from what we have already seen of the early Indian, we may suspect that the first comers into this earthly paradise had a very simple Stone Age culture. Doubtless they were living primarily by hunting, fishing, and gathering shell fish along the coast, but sometime they found that they could utilize the acorn.

This use of the acorn was not so simple as it sounds, for the meal is bitter, and the stomach will not retain it until it is treated. Somehow a man, or more likely a woman, learned that if she crushed the acorn into meal and put this into a hole in the sand, and then poured warm water on it, the bitter elements would be extracted.

She had no pottery, but she did possess baskets, and she made them water tight. Like other groups we have already visited, she cooked in baskets, so the next step was easy. She dropped the hot stones into the water, stirred in the meal, and she had acorn mush, food fit for any hungry Indian. That day the food problem was solved.

Man in central California did not need to plant or cultivate. All he had to do was to let Nature take its course. When the nuts were ripe, he and his fellows beat the trees with long poles, the women gathered the harvest from the ground and stored the year's supply in the village.

Of course man desired some variety. He was already a hunter and a fisherman, so game and fish were added to his menu. Many

MAN'S DRESS

Clothing is of minor importance. When well dressed the man wears a
skin loin garment and several strings of shell beads.

Courtesy Field Museum of Natural History, Chicago

FOODS WERE COOKED IN BASKETS BY THE INDIANS OF THIS REGION

BASKETS WERE ALSO USED TO STORE FOOD AND OTHER ITEMS

Courtesy Field Museum of Natural History, Chicago

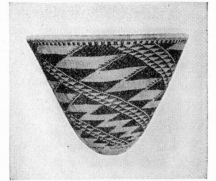

EXCEPTIONALLY WELL MADE AND
COLORFULLY DECORATED, THESE
BASKETS SERVED THE INDIANS IN
MANY WAYS

Courtesy Field Museum of Natural History, Chicago

wild plants, bulbs, and berries could be gathered in the winter and spring, while bugs, grasshoppers, and worms made a tasty relish.

An assured food supply, easily obtained, left many idle hours in which man might devote himself to developing a civilization. Just what did happen?

Clothing was of minor importance in the Valley, quite unnecessary in the summer and just a comfortable addition for the winter. Of course after a time people did establish styles of garments and ornaments and then had to possess them if they wished to be recognized as worthwhile citizens.

For the man, the proper dress finally became the breech clout, and if the weather was cold he would wear a rabbit-skin blanket draped over one shoulder. Feather belts and head-bands were worn for special events, and a head net was quite in style.

Courtesy Field Museum of Natural History, Chicago

A GIRL IN GALA DRESS

Rather elaborate skirts made of seeds, beads, grass stalks and shells
were worn for special occasions. A basket cap was also in common use.

Woman's dress consisted of a skirt made of deer skins, shredded fiber, or alternate strings of seeds and grass stalks. Ear ornaments and necklaces were worn, and, in some regions, parts of the body were tattooed.

Houses were of little importance, but several types finally appeared. In general these were simple structures of brush and reeds, perhaps only sunshades in summer. A cone-shaped device, made up of slabs of wood or bark leaning against a central pole, was a special development in one region. For ceremonial purposes the earth lodge became wide spread. This consisted of a central pole surrounded by a circle of smaller poles. Beams of the same material led from each side pole to the center, and these were lashed together with intertwining vines and reeds. A covering of grass and mud completed the roof. The floor of such a lodge was always depressed below the ground level, and the sides were built up around this.

Each village had one or more sweat lodges constructed much like the earth lodge but considerably smaller. Inside this a fire was built or hot stones were carried in and water poured on them to cause steam. Into this hot-box the men would go and stay as long as possible, then they would rush out and plunge into the stream or lake. The sense of physical well-being which followed convinced the Indian that the sweat bath had supernatural powers.

Mention already has been made of most of the foods, but the use of seeds, bulbs, and roots should be emphasized. To secure these the women used digging sticks. The legitimate way was to dig up each root separately, but the people had observed that the gophers laid up a winter's supply in their burrows, so, when they thought the animals had gathered a good store, they dug them out and not only took their food but ate the animals as well.

The baskets were made of many materials, and here the California Indians showed their greatest ability. No finer baskets were made anywhere in the world. They were of many sizes designed for many uses, and nearly all were beautifully decorated in colored designs. The chief material employed for decoration was the outer skin on the stem of the maidenhair fern, but, in some regions, shells and feathers were added to the outside.

Women often wore basket caps. They cooked in baskets; they ate out of baskets, and they harvested and stored food in baskets. In some tribes, the proper gift for a young man to give to his mother-in-law was a large basket, and after that he never spoke to her again. Perhaps even these people had their mother-in-law jokes.

The bow and arrow was the chief weapon, and a boy received careful training in its use, but it was believed that magical acts and practices were necessary to make it effective. Before a hunt, special songs were sung, and the weapons were held in the smoke of burning pepper limbs. A man might put a deer skin and head over his body and stalk the animals alone, or a group might drive the game toward concealed hunters, but always the song was necessary for success.

The fishermen also had their songs and acts which made their hooks and lines powerful. For every fish caught, they uttered words of thanks.

People had few possessions other than these mentioned, but they did have a sort of currency made of shells strung on strings. The men also had straight tubular pipes into which rolls of tobacco were thrust, thus forming glorified cigarette holders.

As the population grew, the parent village might become surrounded by several smaller settlements, and these would constitute a sort of tribe under a chief. This formed a real political unit which claimed certain land. Anyone belonging to the village had a right to hunt and fish on its grounds, but there was no private ownership of land.

For the first time we come to a new idea in social organization, one we shall meet in more elaborate form in other American tribes. The members of each group were divided into two units, called a moiety or dual division. A boy might never marry a girl in his own moiety even though she was not related to him by blood. In games the people divided themselves according to this grouping, and when a man died he was buried by the other moiety.

Great stress was laid on the proper training of the youth, and something like an initiation was given to each boy and girl at maturity. For the boy this sometimes developed into physical tor-

Courtesy Field Museum of Natural History, Chicago

A DEER HUNTER

The heads and skins of animals were often worn when stalking the game.

ture, such as being placed over an ant hill till he was well bitten in order that he might gain fortitude.

Shamanism, or practice of the medicine men, was of considerable importance and often associated with rather elaborate ceremonies.

Belief in life after death was well established, and each year some groups had a ceremony known as "the burning" during which they burned fine baskets, animal skins, and other objects for the use of the dead.

We have been following the probable course of development of California Indian culture. Of course this did not all happen in one generation, neither was it the work of one group. But all the evidence at our command indicates that the essentials of this culture were established very early and changed slowly and but little in succeeding years.

What happened when a later group of primitive Indians entered California? Did they hold a conference and decide how they should live? They did not. They looked about and saw that Indians already there had made a very satisfactory adjustment and they borrowed it without hesitation.

At the time the Spaniards arrived, they found many different tribes and at least twenty-two different language groups, but throughout the central portion of the state was one general culture. This seems to mean that, as group after group arrived, it borrowed the culture already established. This led to great uniformity. Once a tribe had been merged into the pattern, custom held it with little change. This, then, explains why we have culture areas.

From time to time, new ideas reached the California area. Thus we know that they came in contact with the Southwestern people who had corn and pottery, but the acorn and basket cultures were so well established and so satisfactory that the people refused to accept the new. After all, why plant corn when Nature furnishes acorns?

Courtesy Chicago & Northwestern Ry. Co.
PLAINS INDIAN DANCE
Drums and wild chants furnish music for the dancers.

BUFFALO HUNTERS OF THE PLAINS

The mention of "Indian" brings to most of us a picture of the man on the penny: it suggests war bonnets or human scalps: or it recalls stories of half naked savages riding furiously around a circle of covered wagons. This is the Indian of the story book and of the Wild West film. This is the Indian of the Plains, but it is only a partial and greatly distorted picture.

East of the Plateau, between the Rocky Mountains and the Mississippi River, lie the Great Plains. In general they are treeless but covered with grass. While in the west rainfall is often scanty, this area as a whole is well watered, and several large rivers traverse its wide open stretches. This was the home of the buffalo, and vast herds used it as grazing ground. Here, also, were antelope, deer, and considerable small game.

It appears that the first Indians to enter the region were hunters not far advanced beyond the Caribou people. They possessed the dog and, doubtless, used it in the chase, but many difficulties presented themselves in securing the buffalo. These animals moved in large groups, and they were dangerous and hard to kill. Consequently considerable cooperation and just the right conditions were necessary for a successful hunt.

If a herd could be found near to a cliff, a band of hunters would try to drive it toward that point and then suddenly start a stampede so that the animals would rush headlong over the edge. Thus many were killed or injured and easily taken.

In time, corrals were erected at the foot of the precipices. On the plain above, rows of brush were placed so as to form a runway which directed the animals to the desired spot. Next it was sought to entice or drive the herd into the runway. A man dressed in buffalo hide would imitate the movements of the game, and sometimes the pack would start to follow him. Once they were inside the rows of brush, Indians concealed there would begin to shout and wave objects in order to stampede them.

At other times, large numbers of men formed a great circle and attempted to drive the animals toward the enclosure. As the herd plunged over the cliff, many were killed and injured, while the others were held inside the barricade. Another method was to use fire to encircle the animals; or, in winter, they were driven into deep snow banks where they were easily killed as they floundered in the drifts.

Despite these means of hunting, it was an uncertain life, and the grass lands were but thinly populated. Even those who made their homes in the region located their permanent camps near springs and water courses. Later, knowledge of agriculture, of pottery, and the like, spread up the rivers, and more advanced peoples from the south made their settlements along the water courses. This seems to have been the condition at the time of the discovery of America.

THE COMING OF THE HORSE

With the arrival of the Europeans, all this was changed. The horse had once lived in America but, for some reason, it had died out soon after the retreat of the glaciers. Possibly man extermi-

THE INDIAN ON THE PENNY

The Plains Indian with his "war bonnet" has become the ideal Indian for most Americans.

nated it by hunting the small herds which, apparently, still existed in the Southwest.

No such fate overtook these animals in Europe and Asia. The Cave Dwellers killed and ate the horse, but the New Stone Age people domesticated it, and, by the time Columbus set sail for America, it was man's chief aid for travel by land. European explorers and settlers brought horses with them. Some were given to the Indians, some were stolen, some ran wild. In a surprisingly short time, these animals again had spread over most of the territory now included in the United States.

This new animal, "the elk-dog," appealed at once to the Indian. With it he could run down or drive the buffalo with ease; he could quickly move his camp; and in case of necessity he had a source of food at hand. Many of the agricultural peoples along the rivers gave up their fields and became horsemen. Others made a compromise, whereby they spent part of the year in villages, raising crops, and part following the game.

We shall visit the central portion of the Plains, where buffalo were most plentiful, and view the life as it was about 1800.

On the Plains were thirty-one tribes, speaking many different languages, but having a surprisingly uniform culture. On the edges of the area, the people were less typical, but through the center there was great similarity. As in earlier times, the Indian drove the buffalo over cliffs and into stockades, but now it was possible for a few men to drive the herds for considerable distances. It also became a common practice to start a great encircling movement; then, as the animals sought flight in one direction, the hunters would strive to turn them back, until thoroughly confused and frightened the buffaloes began to mill round and round, trampling each other. Then the Indians rode in close and, with lance and bow, picked off the animals. Oftentimes not a single buffalo would escape.

With the introduction of firearms began a wanton destruction of the herds. Many more animals were slaughtered than could possibly be used. Killing for fun was endangering the food supply even before the white man came in and completed the job.

How completely the Indian was dependent on the buffalo is made evident when we take stock of his culture. First of all, it furnished most of the food supply; its skin was used for making the tipi, all sorts of receptacles, clothing, and shields. Strips of hide served for ropes and lines, the strong sinews as thread. Its horns were made into spoons and ladles, and its bones into clubs and handles for implements. Part of the meat was sun dried and packed, but when storing for the future it was usual to make pemmican. This consisted of sun dried meat partially roasted and then pounded up, together with fat and berries, and made into large cakes. Quantities of this were placed in skin receptacles and buried in stone lined pits until needed. Needless to say, these pits were not refrigerated, and the odor of the meat was as penetrating as limburger at its best.

The buffalo also had much to do with the grouping of the people. Large divisions with similar language and customs constituted tribes. Usually all groups within a tribe were friendly and felt a certain unity, although there was no formal organization, political or otherwise. Within the tribes were bands, membership in which was determined by birth, and finally came the camp circle organization.

PAINTED BUFFALO
ROBE OF THE PLAINS
INDIANS
The biography of a chief is depicted in the pictures which cover this robe.

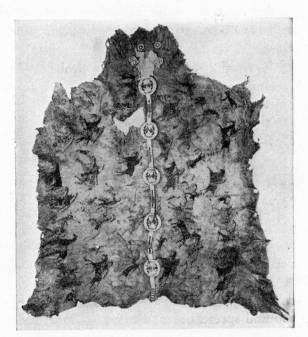

THE CAMP CIRCLE

In summer the buffalo were in large herds, and communal hunting was both possible and necessary. At this time, great camp circles were set up, sometimes with the rows of tipis three or more deep. Each band had its duties and its definite place in the circle. There were also men's societies, each with its own ceremonies, songs, and dances. All members of such groups were about the same age, and each four years, or thereabouts, they moved up into the next age-group society. Each year two or three of these societies were chosen to act as camp police. They pitched their tipis in the center of the circle, and during the encampment they kept order, but particularly they watched to see that no one attempted to do any individual hunting. This was a necessary precaution, for while a man might be successful in getting a buffalo he probably would frighten the herd, and hence injure the chances of the whole group. Should anyone break the hunting rules, he might be beaten by the camp police, or his tipi might be slashed to pieces.

Local groups had leaders, men recognized for their ability and wisdom. At the larger gatherings, the council of leaders deliberated on all necessary matters, but one usually served as head or chief.

Toward winter, the buffalo broke up into smaller herds, and the Indians likewise divided into bands or family divisions. The chief of the camp circle and the police then lost their authority for the rest of the year, hence this start toward chieftainship and a state was controlled by the game.

THE TIPI

The life of the buffalo hunters necessitated frequent movement, so that permanent houses were out of the question; likewise, only a few possessions, and these of a non-breakable type, could be carried, and agriculture was impossible.

The tipi was well adapted for the roving life. In general it consisted of a framework of four poles lashed together near the top and spread out at the bottom. Other poles were laid in be-

tween to form a circular enclosure. A half circle of tanned buffalo hide was lashed to the top, drawn tightly around the poles,
and pegged to the ground. At the top it was cut so that two flaps
or "ears" stood out on each side of an opening or smoke hole. If
it was desired to change the air current or keep out rain, these
could be turned or closed.

Oftentimes the tipi was decorated with geometric designs, or
perhaps it was covered with painted pictures, telling of the warlike exploits of the owner. Even here they found it paid to advertise.

Courtesy Buffalo Museum of Science, Buffalo, N. Y.

TIPIS OF THE SIOUX INDIANS OF THE PLAINS
These skin-covered structures were well adapted to the nomadic life of a hunting people.

A long strip of hide about four feet wide hung from the poles
to the floor inside the tipi. This served the double purpose of pre-
venting draughts and of furnishing a storage place next to the
walls. Along this curtain were couches of grass covered with buffalo robes. The place would have been fairly comfortable had it
not been for flies, bugs, and mosquitoes. A fire near the center of
the room could be made to smoke and thus help control the pests,
but it was hard on the eyes.

Few people of the Plains made use of pottery, basketry, or
wooden vessels. In their place they employed stiff skin receptacles.
The largest of these was rectangular, with ends and sides which
folded over like an envelope. Food, garments, and other articles

TIPI COVER OF THE
PLAINS INDIANS
This was a half circle of
buffalo hide, which was
drawn tightly around the
tipi poles.

Courtesy Field Museum of
Natural History, Chicago

were put inside, and it was then tied or lashed together. This was known as the parfleche. It was usually covered with squares, triangles, and lines in color. Soft skin bags, made from the pelts of small animals, were used for holding the pipe, tobacco, and personal belongings. For water buckets the women employed the stomachs of the buffalo. These were cleaned and stretched open at the top by means of willow rings. As they dried they made excellent pails. All cooking was in skins, and, as usual among those who did not have pottery, water was heated by the addition of hot stones.

When it came time to move, the tipi was taken down, the skin covering was made into a bundle and, together with the skin dishes and parfleches, was placed on the travois. This travois was really a drag frame, made up of two sticks which were fastened to a dog's back and dragged along the ground. A net or platform fitted over the top, and on this the load was placed. The dogs could not move large loads, yet were of considerable aid in traveling. Heavy packs were carried by the people, particularly the women, until the horse appeared.

When the Indian acquired the horse, he immediately began to ride him, to train him for the buffalo hunt, to transfer the travois from the dog and the heavy loads from the women to this stronger animal. The Indian man has often been charged with being lazy or even brutal for allowing his wife to do so much heavy work, particularly to serve as a beast of burden. Probably he did enjoy

PLAINS INDIANS CROSSING THE ELBOW RIVER ON THE
BLACKFOOT RESERVE

his superior position and was glad to escape such tasks, but the custom was not without reason. When the party was on the march, it was often attacked by enemies, and, unless the men were free and unhampered, the whole group might be slaughtered. It was desirable, also, that they be ready to chase game at an instant's notice.

WARFARE

All the buffalo hunters were warlike. They were great horse thieves, and raids were commonly made to secure the animals of their enemies. An honorable start for a young man was to show his skill and bravery by stealing a few horses.

Courtesy Chicago & Northwestern Ry. Co.

WARRIORS OF THE PLAINS
Until subdued by the whites, the Plains Indians devoted much
of their time to hunting and warfare.

Strangely enough a man did not steal or accumulate property in order to become wealthy, but to gain prestige. If he had animals or robes or other wealth, he gave lavishly to his friends and relatives, and he expected equal liberality in return. Thus wealth was continually changing hands. We might state the Indian viewpoint in our terms by saying, "Every man should share his possessions with others. A good citizen cannot be rich."

The desire for horses was one of the chief causes for war. Closely related to this was the value placed on military prowess. The man who killed an enemy, who brought home a scalp, who seized the weapons of his foe, or who in other ways distinguished himself gained great renown.

Upon the return of a successful war party, the people wailed for those who had been killed, but they also hung the scalps of victims on poles and held a great ceremony in which they sang and recounted the brave deeds of the warriors. Plains warfare was a strange mixture of stealth, killing of the weak and defenseless, and of reckless bravery.

When preparing for a raid, the men put on all their finery, painted their bodies, and then made sure that their weapons were ready. A round shield of stiff buffalo hide was carried on the left arm but was held by a shoulder strap, so that the man's arm was free to hold the bow. Long wooden lances were also used.

Sometimes a raid was against a single tipi: or a woman or child might be killed or captured when alone: or a strong camp might be attacked just at daybreak. Pitched battles on an open field seldom occurred.

RELIGION

Each man sought to come into close relationship with a supernatural source of power. The usual procedure was for him to go alone to some place where he fasted and prayed for a vision. He might even injure himself by cutting his flesh, or endure the torture of looking steadily at the sun until, finally, the supernatural beings took pity on him and gave him a vision. At such a time he learned songs, ceremonies, and he acquired religious equipment. Most important among these was the medicine bundle. When having his dream, he was instructed to secure a skin bag and fill it with many articles, such as feathers of birds, animal claws and bones, peculiar stones, and the like, all of which were believed to have supernatural power which they could communicate to the owner.

Some men became renowned for their power, and their medicine bags were thought to be of unusual strength. At times they would gather together for ceremonies and exchange bundles. Altars of painted earth in front of buffalo skulls were prepared in some cases, while in others the bags and their contents were spread out and treated as if they were altars. Dances and ceremonies were most common in summer, when the people were in large camp circles, and when food was ample.

THE SUN DANCE

The greatest of all ceremonies in this area was the Sun Dance. It was given for somewhat different reasons among the various tribes, but the general procedure was the same. For four or more days the people prepared the proper lodges and materials used in the dance. They fasted, went without drink, practiced self-torture, and finally danced against the sun. When evening of the final day came on, they drank, bathed, and broke their fast. Thus they gained contact with the sources of power, increased their physical well-being, and at the same time fulfilled vows they had taken during the year.

Such was the life of the Plains Indians. They were not the most advanced of our tribesmen, but they have caught the public fancy. The "war bonnet" of the Plains is thought of as the mark of an Indian, although many tribes do not use it. The Indian on our penny is a buffalo hunter, and most of the motion picture "savages" are from these tribesmen.

In times past, they have resisted with all their strength and ability the invasion of their lands by white settlers. Little by little they have been overcome, their lands taken, and they, the free hunters of the plains, have been forced to a life they neither welcome nor understand.

THE WOODLAND INDIANS

This grouping includes most of the tribes east of the Mississippi and south of the Caribou hunters. It embraces the Indians of the Atlantic Coast—the kinsmen of Pocahontas, the advanced agricultural peoples of the Southeast, the powerful League of the Iroquois, and the tribes about the Great Lakes. Within this range there are fundamental likenesses as well as great differences. For our purposes, we shall touch briefly on two groupings, the Indians around the Great Lakes and the Iroquois of New York.

Up to this time we have dealt only with hunting and food-gathering tribesmen of America. In the Indians of the Great Lakes region we meet a people in transition from this sort of

Courtesy American Museum of Natural History, New York

SAUK INDIAN (LEFT) AND FOX INDIAN (RIGHT)
Reproduced from an early drawing.

existence to that of the more settled life of the tillers of the soil. They hunt and fish throughout the year, and to accommodate themselves to this life they spend the winter months in dome-shaped dwellings made of saplings covered with mats or bark. Such structures are easily moved or built whenever scarcity of game necessitates a change. Deer, bear, and small game are sought both for food and for dress.

In summer they occupy rather substantial rectangular buildings with bark sides. Close to these are fields in which they grow corn, squash, and beans. Often villages are near lakes or marshes in which wild rice grows. These villages are much more permanent than those near the fields, for the wild rice needs no planting or fertilizer, whereas agriculture without rotation of crops or fertilization means rapid exhaustion of the soil and frequent moves. Both archaeology and history tell us that the typical Indians of this region changed the location of their settlements frequently.

Courtesy Field Museum of Natural History, Chicago

WOODLAND WIGWAM
In contrast to the pointed tipi, these dwellings are dome shaped.

From these people our ancestors learned the art of making maple sugar. They did not plant the trees, yet from them they secured an important part of their food supply. Sugar was used as regular food, as a delicacy, and, mixed with charred corn, it formed a highly concentrated food carried by hunters and warriors. A few years ago some of our manufacturers began to advertise concentrated foods as something new; the Indians had discovered them long before Columbus set sail for America.

With a more settled existence, we find a greater assortment of objects in daily use. In addition to weapons, stone axes, and similar utensils, we find pots with pointed bottoms. Birchbark receptacles of all types and sizes are plentiful; basketry is of minor importance, but matting is utilized for roof and floor coverings. Snow shoes and toboggans assist in winter travel, while birchbark canoes ply rivers and lakes. Tailored skin garments, moccasins, leggings, and skin robes are proper dress for the winter months, but during the summer the man usually wears only the breech clout and the woman a short skirt reaching from waist to knee.

In this society, class and property distinctions are but weakly developed. Chiefs are recognized, but their importance is largely dependent on personal prowess and reputation for wisdom and justice.

Nearly every family has its ceremonial bundle filled with objects supposed to possess supernatural power. This mystic force is called manitou. It is a great impersonal power which may reside in any object, or animal, or human being. A person may gain manitou by associating with objects which contain it, so heated stones with power are used in the sweat lodge, and the bathers are thus strengthened. Some objects or persons may obtain sufficient power to become almost divine.

Secret societies with considerable ritual and ceremonial procedure serve to emphasize the social and moral ideas of the group, and take the place of church and clergy in more advanced societies.

Such transitional tribes are valuable in studying the progress of people from a nomadic to a settled life.

Courtesy Logan Museum, Beloit College, Beloit, Wis.

SUMMER DWELLING OF WINNEBAGO INDIANS
While primarily hunters, these people practiced a limited agriculture.

THE IROQUOIS

Sometime in the past, a people, apparently with southeastern connections, pushed into what is now New York state. They found it occupied by Indians much like those we have just described. Endless conflict followed, with the result that the invaders became more and more closely united until, finally, they formed the famed League of the Iroquois. This League and its members have been variously described as "a democratic state in a Stone Age Society"; "a League of ruthless, blood-thirsty savages"; "the Five Civilized Nations"; and other conflicting terms.

Let us see something of this League. The first unit in the social scheme was the matrilineal family. By this we mean a family in which inheritance and descent are traced only through the mother's line.

Each Iroquois family consisted of a head woman, her daughters, and their offspring. Sons also belonged to this family but, as we shall see in a moment, their children did not. Theoretically, such a family lived in one long house. The room of importance was occupied by the head woman, the others by her sisters and daughters. When a girl married, her husband might come to live with her, but he had no rights in the house. If children were born, they belonged to the mother's family, and the father had no claim to them.

Several of these families made up the next larger unit called the clan. All people in the clan were supposed to be related, and hence were not allowed to marry. This meant that a girl must always marry a man from another clan. Thus if a girl from the Sparrow Hawk clan married a man from the Bear Clan, their children would all be Sparrow Hawks.

Each family had its representative in the clan council. This was usually the brother or son of the head woman, but the women had a veto power over his acts. Each tribe was divided into two parts, each known as a phratry, and these in turn were made up of several clans. Like the families, the clans had their representatives in the phratry, and this in the tribe. Each unit had its land, or duties, or privileges, which might roughly be

BIRCH BARK DISH

Birch bark was used in place of baskets.
From it too were made cradles, canoes, and
even house coverings.

INDIAN CRADLE

Iroquois children were strapped to cradle
boards, which could be easily carried or set
up when the mothers were engaged.

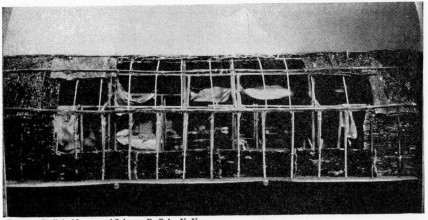

IROQUOIS LONG HOUSE

Such a dwelling was usually occupied by several families closely related in the mother's line.

compared to our precinct, ward, county, and state. When finally the League was set up, each tribe was supposed to be represented by chiefs. Actually the Tuscorora were not represented.

Most of us have read the story of the League in Longfellow's "Hiawatha," in which it was claimed that the purpose of the League was to promote peace and the unification of all the Indian tribes.

Neighboring peoples were given the opportunity of becoming junior members of the League. If they accepted, they were usually left at least semi-independent. If they refused, war was declared against them. A blood-red tomahawk was stuck in the war post of each village of the League, and the men prepared for battle. When war was declared, it was continued until all opposition was broken, even if it meant the extermination of the hostile group.

Warriors fought in close formation and made much use of the javelin and war club. The bow and arrow was used, but it was of secondary importance. When storming the walls of a fortified town, they carried their light canoes in front of them, as protection against missiles, then, when they reached the walls, they used them as ladders in their attempts to swarm over for hand to hand battle.

Courtesy Buffalo Museum of Science, Buffalo, N. Y.

IROQUOIS INDIANS, AN AGRICULTURAL PEOPLE

CEREMONIAL
MASKS

These are worn by members of False Face Societies to drive away evil spirits.

Courtesy Buffalo Museum of Science, Buffalo, N. Y.

Once peace was established, the Iroquois often incorporated into their group many of the defeated warriors together with their women and children. A family which had lost a son in battle might adopt a vanquished enemy in his stead. Thus they added to their numbers.

Chieftainship here was of great importance. The fifty Chiefs in the League all referred back to the clans and families in the tribes. A candidate was first selected by his matrilinear family, which proposed him to the clan. If the clan agreed, he was nominated to the phratry and tribe, and finally to the League.

These chiefs decided all matters of peace and war; they acted as judges; and they instructed the young. They exercised great power, yet were always subject to recall by their families. If the head woman of the family felt that the chief was acting unworthily, she went with a war chief and gave him a warning. If this failed, she gave a second notice, but on the third occasion she placed on his head the deer horns, indicative of power, and then she removed them. In this manner he was deposed, and a new chief had to be selected.

When the League was in session, a fire was kept burning in the center of the long house. To symbolize the fact that it represented all the people, the faggots for the fire were furnished by all the families.

II—14

The Iroquois had extensive fields surrounding their villages, but exhaustion of the soil caused occasional shifting even of large villages. A long rectangular house, of bark, might have as many as twenty families; and it is said that the largest towns had a population as great as three thousand people.

Around each village was a trench or moat, back of which was a log stockade. In later times, when the League had become all-powerful, these precautions were not needed and many sites were without defence.

Labor in the fields was done mostly by the women, who worked in groups or "bees." Plantings actually belonged to families, but since labor was in common and crops shared, if necessary, we can scarcely say that private ownership and use of land had arrived.

Hunting also was often cooperative and ranged from groups of four or five families, united for the purpose, to great drives. Game was a valuable addition to the food supply, but was not essential, as vegetables and maple sugar were stored in considerable quantities.

The group ideas of the elders extended to the boys, who formed gangs. These youngsters would go into the woods, hunting and playing at war. They might be absent from home for days, but in this way they learned self reliance; "playing Indian" was not only a sport with them, it was actual preparation for life.

Secret societies, usually formed to cure sickness, had their own songs and dances, and some used elaborate, grotesque masks. Many festivals attended the planting, harvesting, and storage of corn. Other gatherings of a social nature took place in connection with all the great events of life, such as marriage; but the victory dance, following a successful battle, exceeded all. Successful warriors re-enacted the fight, while others recited the brave deeds of the victors.

At times, inter-tribal councils were necessary. A belt of wampum and a notched stick, indicating the day of the meeting, were sent to each tribe. At the designated time, a great number assembled. The chiefs deliberated, and all took part in feasting, dancing, in trials of strength, and in flights of oratory.

At one time the rule of the League extended over a large part of the eastern half of the United States. Their warriors penetrated as far west as Illinois and deep into the south. But constant inter-tribal warfare, conflict with the whites, and particularly rum led to the final breakup of this power.

THE NORTHWEST COAST

A collection of plank houses set in line, close to the water's edge, totem poles with grotesque carvings, great boats cut out of cedar logs—these are the things that greet you, when you visit a settlement of the Northwest Coast Indians.

Inside the houses raised platforms line the walls, while boxes and wooden dishes of all sizes and descriptions meet the eye. This box contains clothing, ornaments, and masks; that holds food; the wooden dish carved to represent a seal is used at meal time, but that larger receptacle takes the place of pottery. These people, like many others in America, boil water and cook food by dropping in hot stones.

Courtesy Field Museum of Natural History, Chicago

TYPICAL VILLAGE OF THE NORTHWEST COAST
Near to the settlement are huge totem poles.

Courtesy Field Museum of Natural History, Chicago

FALSE LOOM USED IN WEAVING CHILCAT BLANKETS
The warp threads are suspended from a bar and the cross threads are put in with the fingers.

Boxes serve nearly every purpose which basketry and pottery serve elsewhere. They are used for storage, for cooking, for dishes to eat from, and oftentimes a person is buried in a box. Those carved spoons, made from the horn of a mountain goat, are used both as ladles and as eating utensils.

The nets, lines, and traps along the wall are employed in sea fishing, for the waters off the shore teem with fish. That long pole with comblike teeth in the side is a herring rake. When these fish are running, a man stands in the prow of his boat and sweeps it through the water. Every swing pierces one or more of the fish, and soon the bottom of the craft is covered.

That box contains knives, drills, wedges, and other utensils of the wood carver. In a community where decoration is placed on all sorts of objects, the wood carver is a man of great importance.

Courtesy Field Museum of Natural History, Chicago

A CHILCAT BLANKET

The design represents the totem animal of the owner. It is dissected and its
parts so distorted that it can only be recognized by certain symbols.

That framework is used in weaving, for the women make
blankets on a device called a false loom. Hair from the mountain
goat or from the backs of certain dogs is spun, with strands of
cedar bark, into thread. This is suspended from a bar, the weaver
puts in the cross threads with her fingers and forces them upward
to make a tight cloth. By this clumsy method, she makes really
fine blankets and other articles of dress.

No mining is done, but free copper is obtained in the region
and is beaten into ornaments and objects of daily use.

Enough has been said to indicate that we have here a culture
area radically different from any we have visited so far.

From Puget Sound northward to the coasts of Alaska are
several tribes which make up the Northwest Coast Indians. Chief
among these are the Tlingit, Haida, Tshimsian, and the Kwakiutl,
but still others are important.

Just off the coast is a line of islands forming an inland sea; deep bays and fiords cut back into the mainland. A short distance from the coast, rise densely forested mountains from which countless streams rush to the sea. During the spawning season the salmon run up these streams in unbelievable numbers. Then the Indians with nets, traps, clubs, and spears secure a large part of the year's food. When the salmon are dried and stored, the men turn their attention to ocean fishing and, to a limited extent to hunting.

The great forests which cover the islands, mountains, and coastal plain are mostly of cedar. These huge trees are used in house building, for dugout canoes, for boxes, and the bark is shredded and used in the manufacture of clothing.

So important in the lives of these people are cedar trees and salmon, that this region is often called "The Cedar and Salmon Area." This is one of the few spots on earth where a large population can live together without agriculture and domestic animals. Here we have a high culture based on fishing.

HOW THE BEAR CLAN GOT ITS NAME

In order to understand this life it is necessary to deal with the social organization. The account given here deals particularly with the Tlingit tribe, but it should be noted that there are some differences from group to group, especially from north to south

First of all is the individual family, made up of father, mother and children. A number of families make up the next unit, the clan. The clans are grouped in two or more divisions known as phratries which control marriage. No tribal organization exists but people of similar language, culture, and geographic nearness are generally called a tribe.

Each clan has a tradition that it is descended from some mythical being, usually an animal, or that the first ancestor had unusual relations with such beings. A good example of this is the myth told by the Grizzly Bear people of one tribe. They say that one day when the ancestor was hunting he came upon a bear which had been caught and pinned down by a fallen tree. The bear asked for aid. Instead of killing her, the man removed

Courtesy Denver Art Museum, Denver, Colo.

EAGLE HEADDRESS
Elaborate masks and headdresses are worn during ceremonies.

the tree. To show her gratitude, the bear took him to her home. There to his amazement, the hunter found that the bears were just like human beings with their houses, towns, songs, dances, and ceremonies. After a time he married the bear, and several children were born to them.

One day the brothers of this ancestor were hunting and they came upon the entrance to a cave. It was in this cave that they found the long lost hunter and his family. When he returned to the Indians, the bears told him all their secrets, gave him the right to their name, and allowed him to use their crest or symbol. This crest is known as the totem, and the animal is called the totem animal.

From that time, all the family and descendants of this hunter were called the Grizzly Bear clan. Now each year, the members of the clan re-enact the story, and the head of one family takes the part of the ancestor. The right to do so makes him and his family "noble," while the rest of the free born are commoners. Here we find slaves, usually prisoners of war, living much like the other people but having no ceremonial rights nor status. In former times they were sometimes sacrificed at great ceremonies, such as the building of a house, but usually they were rather well treated, although looked down upon.

2

Courtesy Canadian National Railways

SMOKING SALMON
Great quantities of salmon are secured during the yearly run.
They are smoked and dried for winter use.

Courtesy Field Museum of Natural History, Chicago

NORTHWEST COAST HOUSE AND TOTEM POLE
The carvings on the totem pole serve the Indians as a coat-of-arms or family tree.

TOTEM POLES

In front of or near the house, a huge pole is erected. On it is the figure of the totem animal and other beings who have figured in the family or clan history. This is the well-known totem pole. It is not worshipped, as was formerly believed, but is held in high esteem, for it really serves as a coat of arms.

Inheritance and descent are traced in the female line. Several clans belong to each phratry, and since no marriage is allowed inside these larger units it follows that it is barred between all people having the same totem animal. As was the case among the Iroquois, the children belong to the mother's group.

CEREMONIAL HAT

The carving shows that the wearer belongs to the Raven clan, while the disks at the top indicate that he is of high rank.

Closely patterned on the clan idea is the secret society. Each has its myth, telling how it received its name, and on certain occasions it gives dramatic representations of this legend. Young men go to the mountains, where they feast and purify their bodies until, finally, they have a vision. At that time they are visited by, or have dreams of, the guardians of the societies. By the type of vision, they know which society they are to enter. At a later time they undergo an elaborate initiation, and then they can use the society symbol in addition to that of their clan.

During ceremonies, elaborate carved masks are used. Often they are fitted with moveable parts, so that beaks of birds open and shut, eyes move, or a double mask may open and reveal a totally different figure. The initiates are supposed to become possessed; some froth at the mouth, or seek to bite flesh from the bodies of the spectators. Cannibal dancers of the Kwakuitl tribe formerly ate portions of a slave sacrificed for the event. When human sacrifice was prohibited, they substituted a corpse from the local graveyard.

Among the Northwest Coast Indians the shaman, or medicine man, is exceedingly powerful. He is supposed to overcome evil influences, to cast magic spells, or to catch the souls of enemies. He communicates with spirits which live in the earth, sky, and sea, and hence is credited with great knowledge. Actually much of his information is obtained from spies he has working for him. He has his special guardian spirits, and when he is curing the sick or taking part in other ceremonies he uses their masks and symbols.

ART

Everywhere are evidences of a highly developed art of a very special type. Many of the masks and carvings on totem poles and boxes are very lifelike, but, if the space to be filled requires the enlargement of one part and the cutting down of another, it is done. This is continued until, in many cases, it is difficult for the outsider to guess what animal is intended. To the Indian this is very simple, for certain symbols serve to identify the being. Thus, if the carving shows two large incisor teeth or cross lines on

Courtesy Field Museum of Natural History, Chicago

FRONT OF A CARVED BOX
Northwest coast art is essentially realistic, but the animal is often distorted to
fill the desired space. Here the mythical sea monster is
presented on a flat surface.

the tail, he knows it is a beaver, even though it may look more
like a man. Oftentimes the animal is dissected, and its parts are
spread on all four sides of a box, yet it is known by the symbol.

This art is applied to totem poles, houses, boxes, and to nearly
all objects of daily use. Spoons, ladles, even garments bear the
markings of the owner's family or ceremonial group.

THE POTLACH

A most peculiar use of wealth has developed here. Clans
usually control the hunting lands and much other property, but
the individual or family may lay up a store of blankets and other
valuable objects. When finally a person thinks he has enough,
he gives a cermony known as a potlach. To this he issues an
invitation, or really a challenge to someone in another phratry
who exceeds him in rank or prestige. The recipient of the challenge cannot refuse or he loses standing at once. He accepts the
invitation, although he knows that he is to be insulted and, if
possible, debased.

Courtesy Canadian National Railways

NORTHWEST COAST INDIAN IN CEREMONIAL ATTIRE

CARVED PIPE
The sea otter lying
on its back repre-
sents the ship; the
carvings on the side
the tentacles of the
octopus; the jagged
carvings on the tail
are waves, and the
bear is the pas-
senger.

Courtesy Field Museum
of Natural History,
Chicago

On the day of the party, the host awaits the guest. Beside
the trail leading up from the river, he has placed a large carved
figure. It may be that of a woman holding a child; if so, it
indicates that his visitor is as helpless before him as a child in its
mother's arms. Thus the insult begins.

When the people are assembled, the host makes a self-glorify-
ing speech, and then proceeds to destroy valuable property.
Blankets, which it has taken years to accumulate, are burned;
food is thrown on the flames, and in other ways the owner shows
his contempt for wealth and his superiority over his rival. At such
a time, valuable presents are made to the guests. They have no
choice but to accept, although at a later time they must repay
with a high rate of interest.

Within a year or two, the man who was thus challenged
must give a return party in which he destroys or distributes even
greater wealth, or he loses status, while the challenger advances
in rank.

This potlach idea extends to many aspects of daily life. In
one tribe the husband pays a large price for his wife. When a
child is born, his father-in-law must pay him one hundred per cent
interest on the purchase price; but, if the husband wishes to keep
his wife, he must then make another payment, and the process is
repeated. No greater insult can be heaped on a woman than to
have her husband refuse to make a second payment for her.

When a child is named, his family gives a potlach and distributes gifts. These are later returned with high interest, and

thus the boy is given a start in life. Very early he challenges one of his fellows by making him a gift greater than he can repay with interest. So, through life, a man seeks to outdo his rivals by huge gifts, or by conspicuous destruction of property.

This desire for prestige and position has stimulated the people to great accumulation of wealth and, doubtless, has led to the high development of their culture.

Here it should be noted that their property ideas are often quite different from ours. All the people may know a song or story, but it belongs to one person, and the right to tell it can only be acquired by purchase. Even the right to a vision is considered property.

AMERICAN HEAD HUNTERS

Warfare is carried on for the purpose of obtaining loot, for slaves, and particularly for prestige. Following the death of a relative, a chief may organize a war party in order that "others may mourn." In such a case, the heads of victims may be cut off and carried back to the village, where the victory dance causes the mourners to forget their sorrow.

Travel is always by boat, and war parties put out in great dugout canoes, sometimes as many as thirty or more men to a single craft. They use bow and arrows, spears, daggers, and paddle-shaped clubs. The idea of armor evidently has spread to them from Asia, and many warriors wear thick elk skin shirts, or a sort of corset made of slats bound together. The chiefs wear also wooden helmets.

Despite their great boasts of bravery, they usually seek to waylay small groups, or to attack from ambush. They sing taunting songs, and heap insults on their foes; but battles rarely take place between equally balanced forces.

Education of the boy is entrusted largely to his maternal uncle, that is, to the mother's brother. At about the age of ten, the boy goes to live in his uncle's house, where he is treated as a member of the family.

The people live quite different lives, according to the season of the year. When the salmon are running, temporary camps are made on the family or clan grounds, and the people devote themselves to catching and drying the fish. At such times, the villages along the coasts are almost deserted. During the winter months, the Indians occupy their great plank houses, and devote much of their time to ceremonies connected with the secret societies.

For special occasions, rather elaborate garments of skin or robes are worn. Headdress and ornaments signify the clan and rank of the wearers. Crescent-shaped ornaments are suspended from holes pierced in the septum of the nose, or bits of shell or colored cords are fastened in holes in the rims of the ears.

Among the Haida, a necessary part of woman's costume is a labret, or plug of wood inlaid with shell, which is buttoned into a hole in the lower lip. To be seen without this is considered shameless.

Throughout most of the year, dress is scanty. The warm climate, resulting from the presence of the Japan current along the coast, makes real body covering unnecessary. On the other hand, the rainfall often exceeds sixty inches, and rain capes of bark are worn. Here too, a conical hat of spruce root is used as a protection against a heavy downpour.

These Indians of the Northwest Coast of America have developed a culture unique on this continent. They have produced a highly competitive society in which wealth is sought largely for what it may bring in the way of status and prestige, rather than in material comfort. Totemic groupings are of great importance and are associated with a wealth of ceremonial, while secret societies reach a degree of prominence found nowhere else in America. Chieftainship is emphasized. There are chiefs of families, of clans, and of settlements, yet no tribal grouping has appeared. Society is definitely stratified, and one's aim in life is to gain greater status.

With the coming of the whites, a rapid decline set in. The Canadian and United States governments and the missionaries have sought to stop the potlach—the mainspring of the society—, while liquor and disease have taken heavy toll. A few thousand Indians still remain, but the culture is rapidly giving way to "civilization."

THE PUEBLOS OF THE SOUTHWEST

When the Spanish reached Mexico, they were told of powerful cities to the north, where great hordes of gold and turquois might be found. A young nobleman named Coronado started out for this fabled land, and after many adventures finally reached the seven cities of Cibola, now Zuni. He did not find the wealth he sought, but he did meet with a highly advanced people who built compact villages, who practiced dry farming, and who had a most complex religious and ceremonial life.

PUEBLO MAN
The Pueblo people of today are the direct descendants of the Cliff Dwellers.

Courtesy Field Museum of Natural History, Chicago

II—15

We have already traced the development of this culture from the Basket Makers, through the Cliff Dwellers, to the modern Pueblos. In the pages which follow, we shall attempt to see that life as it is today, for it happens that in Zuni, Acoma, Taos, the Hopi pueblos, and other settlements, the Indians are still living a life much like that of their ancestors before the Spanish invaders entered their land. Under the white man's rule, many have become nominal Christians, have adopted European dress, and make use of such conveniences as beds and stoves; but beneath this veneer the old life still continues.

Most of the existing pueblos are in the valley of the Rio Grande, but Zuni lies further west, while the Hopi pueblos are found in northeastern Arizona.

This is a semi-arid land with scant vegetation. Flat-top table-lands are separated by broad valleys where sage brush, smoke weed, and cactus grow. Along the wash, or dry-stream beds, cottonwood trees may thrive, but in general the lower land has

Courtesy Field Museum of Natural History, Chicago

ORABAI PUEBLO

A pueblo usually consists of terraced houses surrounding a court. The ladders in the foreground lead down into underground ceremonial chambers.

Courtesy Field Museum of Natural History, Chicago

THE HOPI VILLAGE OF WALPI

This pueblo is built on the top of a high table land, as protection against its enemies.

little vegetation. It is a region little suited for agriculture, yet we saw that long ago the knowledge of corn and other domestic plants came in and led to the development of a high culture.

In general a pueblo consists of blocks of terraced houses surrounding a large court. The outer walls rise without break for two or more stories, but facing the court the building recedes in steps or terraces. Thus the roof of the lower floor furnishes a front yard for the story above. In the pueblo of Taos, this step-back arrangement extends up seven floors, giving something of a pyramidal appearance on the terraced side.

Doubtless this type of construction was, first of all, connected with defense, for in most cases the entrance to the yard was through a gateway easily defended. No doors or windows were cut in the lower floor of the dwellings. The people went up to the roof by means of ladders, and then down into the rooms below through trap doors. Even should an enemy succeed in entering the court, he would still have to fight his way from floor to floor, with all the advantage of position on the side of the defenders.

2

Courtesy Atchison, Topeka & Santa Fe Ry.   Photo by Edward Kemp

PUEBLO OF TAOS
Here the upper floors rise in steps or terraces, giving the effect of a pyramid to this primitive apartment house.

Some pueblos, like Acoma, and the modern Hopi villages, are placed high on the tops of tablelands, thus establishing true fortresses. Some of the villages are made of stone slabs, others of adobe bricks, but, whatever their construction, they are kept smoothly plastered with mud, and they are whitewashed inside. Nowadays doorways and large windows are cut in the lower walls, and rooms which formerly were reserved for storage are in regular use. The courtyard, no longer needed for defense, still makes an ideal place for ceremonies and dances, with the terraced roofs furnishing space for the spectators.

Throughout the year, the people spend a great deal of time on the roofs or open terrace. In some cases "ovens" are located there as well as in the court. These are dome- or beehive-shaped devices of clay. A fire is kept burning inside until the oven is thoroughly heated, then all embers are taken out, food is put in, and the entrance is closed. In a few hours, meat can be barbecued without danger of burning, in this primitive fireless cooker.

Within the house, in the corner of one room, is a fireplace consisting of a thin stone slab or, perhaps, an iron plate set on stones. Above is a hood which catches the smoke and carries it out through a vent. These chimneys are usually made of bottomless pots and seem to belong to this land, a part of it. However, the idea was introduced by the Spaniards, for there were no chimneys in America until after the arrival of the whites.

The chief article of food cooked on these flat top stoves is piki bread. In one corner of the room is an enclosure with two or three bins. In the first is a rectangular grinding stone of rough texture; in the next is one with a much finer surface. Corn is placed on the rough stone and ground to meal by rubbing it back and forth with a hand stone of similar quality. The meal is then moved to the next bin where it is ground fine on the smoother surface. Usually two or three women grind together. They sing as they work, their bodies rising and falling in time with the chant.

THE POTTERY
MAKER

The clay, ground and worked by hand, is made into dishes by the coiling process. The potter's wheel was not known in America until introduced by the whites.

Courtesy American
Museum of Natural
History, New York

The corn meal is stirred in water containing a little wood ash, and yeast is added. When all is ready a fire is built beneath the stone slab and the batter is quickly spread over the hot surface. As it starts to bake, it is rolled on itself like a jelly cake. This is piki, a rather gritty, tasteless, but nutritious brittle. Because of the amount of grit which is in much of their food the teeth of adults are usually well worn down.

Near the fire strips of meat will be seen drying. Well-made pots and jars containing water or food line the walls or stand on the floor. The pueblo women are probably the best pottery makers in North America, and much attention is given to the form and decoration of vessels, even those intended for every day use.

Sheep skins and blankets may hang on lines during the day, but at night they serve as beds and covering. Many houses possess true looms on which garments are woven. Among the Hopi pueblos the men do the weaving, but elsewhere it is the women's task.

A section of one room is used for the storage of corn, the ears being nicely stacked along the walls much like cords of wood. In front of them lie melons, squash, and other products.

Close to each pueblo, probably within the court, are one or more underground chambers called kivas. In some districts they are round, in others rectangular. The top is roofed over, except for a central opening which serves for both entrance and ventilation. A long ladder projects high above the structure, proclaiming its existence, as a tower does a church. An elevated bench surrounds most of the room, but one section is reserved for an altar. Here also, is a fireplace in front of which is a hole covered with a board. This symbolizes the entrance to the lower world from which the ancestors came "in the first times."

The kivas serve as ceremonial chambers, yet they are also the gathering places or club houses for the men. In preparation for a wedding, Hopi men will gather in a kiva, clean and spin the cotton, and set up a loom on which they weave two garments for the bride.

Out from the villages are the fields. These Indians have learned every spot where the moisture lingers long enough to

HOPI BOWL
The Hopi Indians
make excellent pot-
tery which they dec-
orate with symbolic
designs.

Courtesy Denver Art
Museum, Denver, Colo.

produce a crop. Early in the spring, as soon as the frost is out
of the ground, the men go to the fields. Around each plot they
build a rough protection or wind-break of sage brush or other
weed. This is done to shield the young plants from the sand
which often is driven with great force by the desert winds. Next
the farmer digs a hole ten inches or so in depth and into it drops
fifteen to twenty kernels of corn. This deep planting is to assure
the roots of moisture and to develop a sturdy stock. The many
plants in each hill will form a bushy growth, affording shade and
protection to one another. It usually happens that sand and storm
destroy or injure about half the plants, but eventually the others
attain a strong growth.

Beans, squash, melons, gourds, and other products are grown,
but are not of equal importance with corn. Close to the villages
or near springs may be gardens or small peach orchards.

In this arid land, the streams range from rushing torrents to
dry washes, so there is no fishing. Hunting is engaged in as a

A CORN FIELD

The Indians of the Southwest practiced dry farming long before the conquest.

sport, but is of minor importance so far as food is concerned. The whole community is dependent on the growth of the corn for its existence. Water is all important, and so it is not surprising to find that the religious practices of this people are centered around the idea of bringing rain at the proper time and of assisting the growth of the crops.

In many ways the Pueblo people differ radically from any of the other tribes we have visited, especially those of the Northwest Coast. In most tribes it is important that the young man seek a vision and obtain a supernatural helper. Throughout life he tries by all means to increase his personal power or prestige. On the Northwest Coast the idea of status and rank dominate the activities of the group. Everywhere the shaman is important, and in many regions he is the outstanding individual.

In sharp contrast to all this, the Pueblo people are self-effacing. No man seeks office or position. If it is forced on him, he serves for the common good, but to strive for personal advancement is considered unmanly. Supernatural helpers are not sought, and the shaman does not exist.

Here we find true priesthoods, men who spend months and years learning the exact details of the rituals. Certain acts, certain formulas are powerful in themselves to compel the superior

Courtesy Field Museum of Natural History, Chicago
INTERIOR OF A PUEBLO HOUSE
In one corner is the corn bin. Nearby are the grinding stones.

Courtesy Field Museum of Natural History, Chicago
THE PLAZA AT WALPI
Here the snake dance is held in alternate years. A ladder is seen leading to an underground ceremonial chamber, or kiva.

beings to grant their favors, but errors in the ceremonies may destroy their effectiveness. The whole round of daily life is subject to the whims of the spirit world, but various priesthoods have ritualistic procedures, partially secret, partially public, to insure favorable responses. Each ceremonial group has its sacred medicine bundle and religious paraphernalia, and much of the time of the chief priests is given to their care, to contemplation, or to the affairs of their organization.

In some of the pueblos the chief priests are the actual rulers, although they may delegate some of their duties. Everywhere they are powerful in the conduct of the village, even though various chiefs may be elected for limited periods.

Each pueblo is entirely independent of all the others, but the similarity of culture and interests has led them to band together on several occasions. Nevertheless there is nothing even suggesting a tribal organization.

Rather significant differences occur in the social organization of the different pueblos, but in general we find the matrilinear family, where inheritance and descent are in the female line. These families unite to form clans which control marriage, much as we have seen in previous cases. Here the family not only possesses land and houses, but it usually owns or has the guardianship of sacred fetishes, objects powerful in the religious life of the community.

A man always belongs to the household and clan into which he was born, and he takes part in their ceremonial duties, but when he marries he labors in the fields of his wife's family. Thus his interests are divided. His family and ceremonial duties are determined by birth, but his economic life is governed by marriage. Should his wife die, however, all the products of their joint labor and all the crops go to her family. The houses belong to the women, and once the crops are stored they, likewise, are under feminine control.

Divorce is easy. A woman need only put the man's saddle or other belongings outside the door to effect a separation. In most of the pueblos, there is a shortage of women, so there is little worry about obtaining another mate.

Courtesy Field Museum of Natural History, Chicago
PUEBLO GIRL
Unmarried girls arrange their hair in circular rolls over their ears.

Pueblo life is built upon agriculture. In early times, large flocks of turkeys were kept for their eggs and for the feathers used in ceremonies. The dog has also been a member of the community since the days of the Cliff Dwellers, but for some reason he was not used as a beast of burden, as on the Plains. In modern times, a few burros, horses, pigs, sheep, and chickens have been kept, but they are of minor importance. Agriculture and the ceremonies attendant upon it dominate all aspects of the life.

Early in the year the ceremonies begin. A group of masked dancers, the kacinas, representing the deified ancestors, enter the pueblo and carry out the dance and ritual handed down from early times. From then on, until after the harvest, a series of dances and other observances take place. Two examples from the Hopi pueblos will give a good idea of these. The two chosen are the Soyal, a ceremony at the winter solstice, and the Snake Dance held in August.

THE SOYAL CEREMONY

Each winter when the sun has reached the farthermost point in its southward flight, it is necessary to hold a ceremony to compel it to return northward and thus bring the warmth required to mature the corn. After elaborate preliminary rites are over, the participants gather in an underground ceremonial chamber, or kiva. There an altar typifying rain has been erected. Close by is the seed corn to be used in the spring planting, and near this is a painting or drawing of the corn spirit.

A chant begins, and as it grows louder and stronger a priest rises on the eastern side of the kiva. On his head is the symbol of a star, in his hands is a disk representing the sun. He starts slowly toward the south, but his way is hindered by other priests who attempt to persuade him to reverse his course and go northward. Finally, when all others have failed, a warrior priest, holding a dish of sacred water and feather whip, blocks his way. A struggle

THE SOYAL
CEREMONY
A dramatic portrayal
of the sun's flight to
the south takes place
at the time of the
winter solstice.

Courtesy Field Museum
of Natural History

ensues, during which the sun-bearer is sprinkled with the sacred water, and finally is induced to retrace his steps. Thus magically, the sun is compelled to return from its southern journey and bring warmth to the barren lands. At this time, the seed corn is sprinkled with the water, and thus made fertile.

THE SNAKE DANCE

In the month of August, when the crop must have moisture and the springs must be refreshed if the people are to live, comes the most spectacular of all the ceremonies, the Snake Dance.

.At the appointed time, the snake priests begin the gathering of the reptiles. For four or more days they search for them in the four directions. Clad only in loin cloths and moccasins, carrying bags of sacred meal, bags for the snakes, and digging-sticks, they scatter out over the desert sands. If a snake is found in the open, it is picked up and put into the bag; if its trail leads to a hole, it is dug out. Always the greatest care is exercised not to injure it, and always it is sprinkled with the meal. Any kind of snake is used—bull snake, rattler, or whatever appears. When finally enough have been secured, they are taken to the kiva of the Antelope priests where the next act of the drama takes place.

An altar representing clouds, lightning, and falling rain has been erected, and in front of this is a sand painting in colors. Nearby is a vessel filled with sacred water, and beside this are feather whips. The priests gather and sit around the edge of the room. Then one enters carrying a sack or jar containing the snakes.

A song is started telling of the coming of the rain; it is steady, insistent, and compelling. At a given point in the chant, the priest puts his hand into the sack and draws out one or more snakes. He swishes them to and fro in the water and hurls them onto the sand altar. There they are met by other priests armed with feather whips with which they roll the reptiles in the sand to dry them before they are tossed to the side of the room, where they are guarded until needed. So the washing continues, until all the snakes have had their turn.

Courtesy Field Museum of Natural History, Chicago

SNAKE DANCE OF THE HOPI INDIANS
Each year the Snake Dance is held to induce the spirits to send abundant rain.

Next day a bower of leaves is erected in the court yard. In front of it a hole is dug, to symbolize the entrance to the lower world, and over it is placed a short plank. Later in the afternoon a priest bearing the snakes enters the booth. The Antelope priests issue from their kiva and march four times around the court before they line up, with their backs to the booth, to await the Snake Dancers. They come with their bodies painted a brick red, with white designs traced on them. Their loin kilts are also red and marked with the snake symbol. Like the Antelope priests, they make the circuit of the court four times, and each time, as they pass, they stamp on the board "to notify the ancestors in the lower world that the dance is in progress."

Now they line up, facing the Antelope priests, and begin to sing. The Antelope men keep time with their gourd rattles and stamping of the feet; the bodies of the Snake priests sway to and fro as the song progresses. Suddenly the line of Snake men breaks up into groups of three which move toward the bower of leaves. As a group reaches it, one of the members drops on his hands and knees, his face close to an opening in the leaves. As he rises, he is seen to have a snake in his mouth or in his hands held close to his face. A second performer throws one arm over his shoulder, and they dance away with high knee-action. This assistant holds a feather whip with which he strokes the snake, and seeks to attract its attention if it is unruly. The third man follows closely. The group makes a circuit of the plaza, and then the snake is dropped. Immediately the third man picks it up. Should it be a rattler, which seeks to coil, he waves his feather whip over it until it straightens out and attempts to escape, then he grasps it close to the head and picks it up.

Each group dances with its snake, and then returns for another, and this is kept up until all have been handled.

Now the priest emerges from the bower and draws a circle of sacred meal. Within it are six lines, representing the four directions and the upper and lower worlds. The priests gather close around, and at a given signal they throw their snakes on the drawing. For an instant the snakes lie there, a writhing mass, then the men rush in and seize all they can handle and start running with them down the steep trails. Far out into the valleys and canyons they carry their captives, finally releasing them so that they can carry the prayers of the people to the great plumed serpent who controls the rain.

Now they hurry back to the pueblo, where they take an emetic, which purifies them, and they are ready for the feast which follows.

In this way the Indians stage an elaborate prayer for rain. It is more than a prayer, for, if properly carried out, it almost compels the spirits to grant the wishes of the people. Seldom, say the priests, does the dance fail. Sometimes the rain begins before the runners are able to get back to the pueblo, but "certainly it comes within a few days."

Courtesy Field Museum of Natural History, Chicago

PUEBLO INDIAN MAN
These people still preserve the life and customs of their ancestors.

THE CULTURE AREAS

We have now seen several sharply contrasting areas of culture. Each, in a way, is dependent on or influenced by its environment. Yet it is clear that, while environment limits the activities of the group, it does not determine what they will do or what they will use within those limitations.

The Pueblo people live in a region where agriculture is difficult and where all the plants they raise have been introduced from outside, yet on these borrowed elements they have built a high culture.

The Eskimos seem to be a people perfectly adapted to their surroundings, and if we looked at them alone we might believe that they had developed their culture in response to their needs. When, however, we analyze their life in detail we find many elements shared with people far away. Their throwing stick and harpoon appear in Paleolithic Europe; they were widely distributed over America, and today are used in a land as far distant as Australia. The composite bow seems to be a direct response to a land without trees, but its use extends across the grass lands of Asia, even to the early graves of Egypt. Tailored garments are found over a large portion of northern North America, but this belt ties up with a similar area of use in Asia and Europe. So it appears that many of the things used by the Eskimo may have been invented elsewhere.

On the Northwest Coast the plank house, the great use of cedar, and the dependence on salmon seem to be a direct reflection of physical surroundings. Yet when we go to Oregon and Washington we find quite similar conditions with a very different culture.

From all this it appears that man coming into a new area may, because of his earlier history or by mere accident, develop certain of the possibilities offered. Once a culture is established, however, it is usually borrowed by newcomers into the region. Thus Culture Areas are established and are maintained. New ideas do spread to them, and if these fit their needs they may be incorporated; but, if not, they are ignored. We have a good example of this in the refusal of the California Indians or of the Buffalo Hunters to accept the cultivation of corn.

Here in America, through the study of these culture patterns and areas, we have an opportunity to see how culture grows and develops. We have traced the American Indian from a very simple New Stone Age culture to the high development of the Pueblos. Now we go to Mexico and Middle America where the Indian achieved a real civilization.

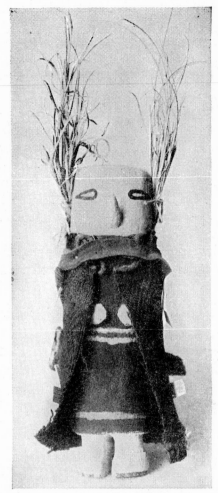

Courtesy Field Museum of Natural History, Chicago

CEREMONIAL DOLL

Figures representing the ancestors or spirits
are used at times of ceremonies.

THE CIVILIZATIONS OF MEXICO
AND SOUTH AMERICA

WHEN COLUMBUS discovered America he believed that he had succeeded in reaching the rich lands of India, despite the fact that the first people he met were little advanced in culture.

Doubtless he was strengthened in his belief that the lands of wealth and plenty were near when, in 1502, he came upon a trading canoe filled with bales of colored cotton cloth and pottery. It is said that the boat was manned by thirty paddlers, and that the merchant was clad in rich garments. Later, as the fleet cruised along the coasts of Nicaragua and Panama, came rumors of people possessing quantities of gold and jewels. The rumors grew; some of the explorers actually brought in cleverly made objects of gold and silver which they had secured in trade. But always the informants indicated that the real land of riches lay farther to the west.

AZTEC CALENDAR STONE (BRITISH MUSEUM)
At the time of the discovery, the peoples of Middle America had developed an accurate calendar.

The result was a series of expeditions, like that of Cortez to the capital of the Aztecs, or of Pizarro to the stronghold of the Inca in Peru. The Spaniards, though few in numbers, were in possession of firearms, of armor, and of horses, which made possible their conquest of an empire. They considered themselves members of a superior race, rightfully entitled to the gold and lands of the heathen, yet in many ways the people they were destroying were quite as civilized as they. Never in the world's history has there been a darker page written than that inscribed by the Spanish. Pillage, treachery, murder were all employed to destroy a people whose crime lay in possessing vast quantities of gold.

THE AZTECS

In Mexico the invaders found many tribes and cities, but dominating at that time was a warlike people known as the Aztecs. In this land the Spanish saw great cities surrounded by extensive fields in which a variety of crops was grown.

Tenochtitlan, now Mexico City, was built much like Venice, with an intricate system of canals. Causeways with drawbridges connected the city with the mainland. A great aqueduct carried water from the spring at Chahultepec to the city, whence it was distributed by smaller water mains to its various sections.

Surrounding the city were floating gardens of vegetables and flowers. Some on rafts could be poled about, while others had become fastened to the bottom of the lake by the roots of the trees

TURQUOIS MASK
The Aztecs and other Mexican peoples used quantities of gold and turquois in their ceremonial and art objects.

Courtesy Field Museum
of Natural History

Courtesy Illinois Central Railroad, Chicago

AN AMERICAN PYRAMID

Here is shown the Temple of the Sun near Mexico City. Unlike Egyptian pyramids this
was used as the foundation for a temple.

that grew on them. Lighthouses stood on high walls along the
water front, while fires in braziers illuminated the streets at night.
Even the Spaniards were dazzled by this fairyland which excelled
in splendor their wildest dreams.

Narrow paved roads, lined by low thatch and adobe houses,
led to the great square. Here were the homes of the nobles, structures of stone surrounding pleasant courts where fountains played
and flowers bloomed. Most elaborate of all were the temples and
the home of Montezuma, the supreme ruler.

Bancroft, the historian, describes one of the temples which
stood on the summit of a flat-top pyramid. This pyramid rose in
five terraces to the height of eighty-six feet. On the upper platform were sanctuaries housing gigantic images of the War God
and his half brother. Before them was a green block of stone on
which human beings were offered to the idols, for the sacrifice of
captives was a part of Aztec religion. Close by was a small chapel
where girls and priests kept a fire continually burning.

AMERICAN PYRAMIDS

Pyramids were common in Middle America, but unlike those of Egypt they served only as foundations for temples and palaces. One which still stands near Mexico City is three times in bulk the size of the largest ever built in the Valley of the Nile.

The palace of Montezuma had many rooms and courts. Rare animals and birds, beautiful roof gardens, and swimming pools were provided for his pleasure. Soft mats and elaborate feather robes served as beds; beautifully carved tables and low stools stood at convenient places; incense burners and torch holders, braziers for fires, screens for privacy, were all at hand. No potentate of Europe at that time lived in greater luxury than this Indian ruler.

Within the city was the great public square and the market place where artisans carried on their crafts and venders offered goods. No coins were used. In their place bags of cacao, gold-dust, copper axe blades, and other objects were used in barter.

NO WHEELS IN AMERICA

Merchants were held in high esteem, for they not only supplied local needs and kept up trade over a wide territory, but they also acted as spies and contact men with distant peoples. Often they traveled in caravans large enough to withstand attack. To aid this trade, as well as to allow quick movement to the army, an elaborate system of roads was constructed. But over these roads no vehicle passed, for the wheel was unknown in America until after the arrival of the whites.

The Spaniards found much more than great cities, a powerful ruler, and elaborate temples. They found a people with great armies, with extensive farms, with metal workers, weavers, sculptors, and potters. They found courts, judges, and a well established code of laws. They saw schools for boys and girls. They found a system of writing, of the rebus type, in which pictures might represent objects, syllables, or sounds. In the same way that an American child might draw a picture of an eye and of waves to express the idea "I see" (eye-sea), so the Aztec worked out a system of writing without an alphabet. Closely related to the religious and agricultural interests of the people was an elaborate system of mathematics and astronomy.

DESTRUCTION OF THE SACRED WRITINGS

On parchment or on fiber paper the scribes wrote the history of the nation; they gave lists of tribute exacted from conquered tribes; they made records of the laws; they wrote poetry; they traced the movements of the planets. Unfortunately they wrote also of the gods, and glorified the sacrifices made to them. Thus they doomed their writings to destruction, for the Spanish priests sought to destroy all such works of the devil. Bonfires were lighted in the public squares, and priests and soldiers vied with each other in piling on the heathen books. They nearly succeeded in destroying the history of a people, but fortunately a few writings escaped and are now safely lodged in museums.

In every sphere of life the Aztecs showed great organizing ability. Most men served at some time in the army, and, if they distinguished themselves, were allowed to wear distinctive garments and to be known by high-sounding titles. Chiefs were usu-

FIGURES FROM THE CODICES
Aztec writing was placed on parchment or fiber paper. Only a few of these manuscripts have survived.

Photo by Evans

CITY OF MITLA

The Ruins of Mitla are among the most interesting and most accessible of the Mexican ruined cities. They lie about 25 miles from the city of Oaxaca.

Courtesy Field Museum of Natural History, Chicago   Photo by Cole

TOLTEC SCULPTURE

This is a portion of the stone wall recently uncovered at the ancient Toltec city of Teotihuacan, 30 miles from the present city of Mexico. The Aztec invaders secured most of the elements of their culture from these Toltec peoples.

ally elected from among such warriors, although there was a strong tendency to keep the major offices within certain families.

A city was divided into wards, which had title to lands and distributed them among their members for the period of use. Each unit had its head, but above all were war and peace chiefs. Ordinary matters were settled by a council of the chiefs, but in times of trouble or war, the war chief was supreme.

Many lesser tribes or nations of equally high culture were found in the highlands of Mexico, but most of them owed at least nominal allegiance to the Aztecs.

THE CAPTURE OF MONTEZUMA

The conquest of these hardy warriors by a handful of Spanish adventurers is an amazing story. Montezuma, the ruler, was not certain whether the Europeans were men or gods. Their skin was white; they wore helmets much like that of one of the gods and made of iron, a metal unknown to the Aztecs. They had staffs which spurted fire and caused death; they rode great animals unlike any known in America. Surely they were superhuman. Yet Montezuma was suspicious and sought to prevent their entry into his city by sending them rich gifts.

Far from being satisfied with these presents, the Spanish were fired with the desire to possess this land of gold. They boldly entered the city, they seized the ruler, they desecrated the temples. Finally the people, driven to frenzy, attacked the invaders, destroyed the drawbridges, and appeared to have the Spaniards at their mercy.

Cortez attempted to escape under cover of darkness, and had almost succeeded when a woman gave the alarm. A battle followed in which the Spanish met defeat, but the Indians failed to follow up their victory and allowed the survivors to escape.

A few months later, Cortez led a new army against the capital, and this time he succeeded in breaking the power of the Aztecs.

THE MAYAS

Farther to the south was a people who had passed the zenith of their power before the arrival of the white man. They are known to us as the Mayas. Unlike the Aztecs, they lacked a genius

Courtesy Illinois Central Railroad

A MAYA CITY

Beyond Merida, rising out of the jungle that has hidden them for centuries, are the magnificent ruins of the last of the great Maya capitals, Chichen Itza.

Courtesy Field Museum of Natural History, Chicago

GOVERNOR'S PALACE AT UXMAL, YUCATAN
This great structure stands on a truncated pyramid.

for organization and never developed anything approaching a state. Apparently each city or district was independent, although we do know of certain leagues which had been set up late in their history.

Their first stronghold was in Guatemala and Honduras where they built powerful cities. These were later abandoned, and most of the population migrated to Yucatan, where they entered upon a new period of glory. The cause of this wholesale migration is not known, but it is thought that exhaustion of the soil probably forced the move.

As one travels through the interior of Guatemala, he seems to be in a virgin forest. Yet many of the great trees are growing above the ruins of ancient cities or in fields which, a few centuries ago, were waving fields of corn.

Today we know this culture primarily from its magnificent ruins, despite the fact that more than a half million Maya Indians are still living.

Apparently, in ancient times most of the people lived in thatched huts and practiced agriculture, as do their descendants today. But at favorable localities the priesthood built great religious centers, and it is to them that we turn for our story.

Courtesy Field Museum of Natural History, Chicago

THE MAYA ARCH
The true arch was unknown in prehistoric America, hence the walls had to be very thick
to support any superstructure.

Photo by Fairchild Aerial Surveys, New York
THE TEMPLE AT UXMAL
The temple stands on a high pyramid. Nearby was the nunnery where the girls lived
who tended the sacred fires.

Most of the ruined cities have courts around which cluster the principal structures. The buildings usually, the temples always, stand on high terraces or flat-top pyramids. Such a pyramid is made of rubble, faced with cut stone or cement. Steep stairways lead to the elaborately sculptured temples.

Larger structures, called palaces or nunneries, occupy lower elevations. It is said that the maidens who tended the sacred fires in the temples lived in some of these structures, while others were the dwellings of the priests, who were also the nobles.

Maya architecture is peculiar in that the buildings are mostly walls. The architects did not understand the principle of the true arch, and so they resorted to long, vaulted chambers. Facing stones were smooth on the outside, but long and rough, extending back into the cement. When an arch was attempted, each facing stone was beveled and extended a little beyond the one below. This

Courtesy Illinois Central Railroad, Chicago

A MAYA MONOLITH
These markers were raised each ten years and on them was inscribed the chief events of that period.

**STONE CORNER
MASKS**

Corners of buildings
were frequently
adorned with masks
representing various
deities.

Courtesy Field Museum
of Natural History,
Chicago

continued until the two sides nearly met, then a cap stone was
added and cement placed over all. If a second story was to be added, it was situated over a central wall or set back over a solid
section.

Several cities had observatories with round towers, through
openings in which the priests could watch the movements of the
planets. They had no telescopes, yet the Maya had gone far in the
development of astronomy. They had a Lunar, Solar, and Venu-
sian calendar and had worked out a year of three hundred and
sixty-five days. They also had a numerical system based on zero.
Counting was by twenties, rather than by our decimal system.

The count to ten was kept by dots up to five, when a bar was
used; six was a bar with a dot above; seven a bar with two dots;

twelve was two bars and two dots; and so on. The oldest dated object from the culture is a small figurine bearing a year mark corresponding to 98 B. C. Thus it appears that this people had a zero system and accurate astronomy centuries before our own came into existence in the Near East.

A highly developed form of hieroglyphic writing had been devised, in which conventionalized pictures had become true symbols. This was placed on buildings, on stone pillars, and in books. The Spanish clergy took delight in destroying these books, since they were related to the heathen religion. One priest, writing to his superior, boasted of the fact that he had that day burned hundreds of these works of the evil one.

So thoroughly did they carry out the destruction that, aside from three codices, we have left only inscriptions in stone, most of which deal with dates and deities. The date and names of some of the gods can be read, but most of the glyphs still remain a mystery. Some day the key may be found. Perhaps some friar, more intelligent than the others, may have sent a description of this writing to Spain. All that is needed to open this sealed volume of history is an accurate translation of a few lines, just as Egyptian history was revealed by the discovery of the Rosetta stone. It is possible that some obscure monastery in Spain or a forgotten file of records in the Vatican may hold the key.

BASKET BALL

A striking feature of nearly every ceremonial center was the ball count. This consisted of a rectangular floor with high side walls and a temple at each end. On each side near the center a stone ring was set vertically near the top of the wall. Play was much like that of modern basket ball, the contestants seeking to drive a rubber ball through the rings. Rivalry was intense, and so excited did the spectators become that they often showered the victors with robes and jewels. If they did not, the successful players had a right to seize all they could.

Spanish writers tell us of the audiences taking to their heels following a successful shot in order to save their garments.

RUBBER IS DISCOVERED

It is interesting to note that in connection with this game we have the first mention of rubber in the world's history. Spanish writers tell of hard, heavy balls which bounded as they struck "as though alive." These balls, they say, were made of the gum of trees.

Nearly all stone buildings were elaborately decorated. Certain portions were covered with colored stucco, but corner portions facing the court were adorned with masks or realistic figures of men and serpents. Geometric designs were used to fill in the spaces between the more elaborate figures. Such work was done in high or low relief, either modeled in stucco or carved in stone. In some cases several figures depict scenes, such as priests standing with their feet on captives, or great persons making offerings or receiving homage. We see gods or priests wearing rich garments, feather mosaic head-dresses, armlets, leglets, or breast ornaments.

While different in spirit and execution from Asiatic and European art, the products of the Maya, it must be agreed, should be ranked with the best the world has produced.

Perhaps the ideal of beauty is shown in figures in which the front of the head is flattened so that it is in line with the bridge of a long thin nose. While speaking of beauty, it is of interest to learn that mothers attempted to make their children squint or have cross eyes by hanging an object from the hair so that it dangled between the eyes.

RELIGION

Maya religion is far too complicated to discuss in detail. Some of the gods are depicted as part human and part animal; most are in human form, but with identifying characters. The maize god is a youth wearing a head-dress representing an ear of corn. A grotesque figure with fleshy ears attached to a skull, or with bare backbone and ribs, is the god of death. The plumed serpent, Kukulcan, which is the dominant figure in most of the later art, is depicted as a ruler, a culture hero, or as a god. Usually a benevolent

deity, who aids and protects man, has his counterpart bent on injury. Thus the forces of good and evil are ever in conflict.

The priests formed the ruling class. They, likewise, were the
astronomers and directors of ceremonies.

HUMAN SACRIFICE

Certain months were sacred to particular industries, but agriculture overshadowed all others. Human sacrifice, while of less
importance than in Aztec religion, still played an important part.
A Spanish writer gives a vivid description of the sacrifice. After
telling of the actual killing, he describes how the priests threw the
heart against the face of the idol and then kicked the body of the
victim down the steep flight of stairs.

Another form of sacrifice took place at the sacred wells. Yucatan is a low limestone peninsula without rivers. However, below the surface are underground streams, and here and there the
crust breaks through to expose large pools. Such openings, known
as cenotes, were the sources of water for the towns and hence
were sacred to the Rain God.

Courtesy University Museum, Philadelphia

MAYA ART

This carved lintel from Guatemala is an exceptional example of Maya art. The central
figures are in relief. The border is made up of glyphs.

The most renowned of these pools was the one at Chichen Itza, where the water lies more than seventy feet below the surface of the ground. Here, at certain festivals, maidens laden with offerings were thrown from a platform into the green waters. Several years ago, when this cenote was dredged, it yielded the bones of many young girls, as well as ornaments of gold, jade, and precious stones.

Trade was important to the Maya, and stone roads were constructed from city to city. These highways also served the pilgrims who came in great numbers to the ceremonial centers.

In warfare these people were inferior to the Aztecs; in massive architecture and road building they did not compare with the Incas of Peru; but in art, sculpture, mathematics, and religion they surpassed all the other native peoples of America.

THE INCAS

In the highlands of South America and especially in Peru, we find still other evidences of a highly civilized people. They are generally known in history as the Incas, although that term really applied to the ruling class.

Here was a graded system which began with clans, each with its allotment of land. Ten clans formed a phratry; ten phratries made up a tribe; and four tribes constituted a province. Each unit had its officers, but the rulers of provinces were men of great importance who served as counselors to the court. At the top was the Inca, child of the Sun, a divine ruler.

Everything throughout the empire was regulated according to strict rules. The clans furnished a certain amount of produce for the support of the state; another portion was for the support of the local temples, while a third and larger portion was retained for the maintenance of its people. No group was allowed to accumulate beyond its needs, for the government placed all surpluses in warehouses. It is said that there was always sufficient food stored to support the nation for several years. Hoarding was impossible, for an elaborate spy system kept the government informed of the acts of commoners and petty rulers. Everyone was assured of food, cloth, and assistance when needed, but his life was governed with an iron hand.

RUINS OF MACHU PICCHU
A great Inca city in the Andes.

INCA MASONRY
Carefully fitted stones, laid without mortar, have withstood the ravages of time.

Courtesy University Museum, Philadelphia

GOLDEN BREASTPLATE

Ornaments of gold and precious stones were possessed by the rulers, while quantities of gold were kept in the temples.

Able-bodied men gave a portion of their time to pubilc works and to mining, a fact which may account for the stupendous building accomplishments and for the gold in the possession of the court. Every male also served a certain number of years in the army, so that at all times one-tenth of the men were enlisted.

No people of ancient times, not even the Romans, equalled the Incas as builders of highways. The Incas constructed more than two thousand miles of roads, which traversed high snow-clad mountains and the desert lowlands along the ocean. Suspension bridges with massive abutments spanned rivers and gorges.

Steep mountain sides were terraced to supply additional farming lands, and canals and aqueducts carried water to them, as well as to the lower lands.

Palaces and public buildings were built of huge stones so carefully prepared and fitted that they have withstood the ravages of time as well as the violent earthquakes which have destroyed the later buildings of the Spaniards. Because of earthquakes, even temples and palaces were low structures, but what they lacked in outward display was more than made up by the richness of the interiors. Ornaments of gold, silver, and precious stones adorned the walls, while rich fabrics and cleverly made furnishings were in profusion.

EMBROIDERED
FABRIC
FROM PERU

A Spanish visitor describing the Temple of the Sun at Cuzco
said that the inner walls were of solid gold. On the western wall
was a golden disk set with precious stones, representing the sun.
This was so placed that the first morning rays would fall upon it,
and then the whole chamber was illuminated with its yellow glow.
On either side were the mummified bodies of dead kings seated on
golden chairs. Even the water pipes which entered the temple

Courtesy Field Museum of Natural History, Chicago
PERUVIAN POTTERY
Many of the vessels were made to represent vegetables or human beings. Maize, with
human heads, is shown above.

were of gold, while gardens with artificial flowers, birds, and animals were constructed of the precious metal. Little wonder that
the gold-mad Spaniards broke all pledges, desecrated temples, and
even murdered the ruler to obtain the metal.

Commoners, of course, did not share in this wealth, but they
did live in substantial adobe or stone houses and were well fed and
cared for. Perhaps the whole system can be summarized in the
burial customs. Today an American farmer cares for his horses
because they are valuable to him, but when they die he disposes
of them without ceremony. So it was in Peru. The rulers lived
in luxury, and, when they died, the finest products of the land
were placed in their graves. The body of the commoner, on the
other hand, was thrust into a crevice of the rocks, or was thrown
into a hole dug in the sands. No rich objects were prepared for

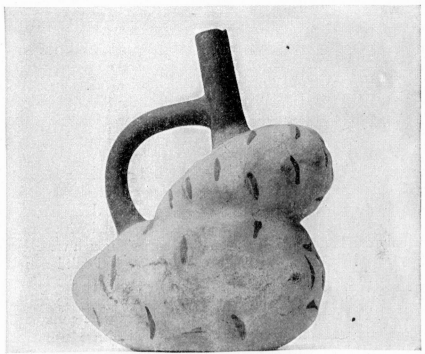

VEGETABLES IN POTTERY

Pottery in vegetable form is found in many Peruvian ruins. The potato was a popular subject with these artisans.

his use in the future life; at best he was supplied with coarse garments, an ear or two of corn, and a water container.

Great progress had been made in the industries. Most tools were of stone, but metal working was far advanced. Bronze and other alloys had been discovered, and casting was beautifully executed.

In textile arts the Peruvians were unequaled by any other people either of ancient or modern times. With all our modern equipment we fall far short of the products of Inca land. The visitor to any of our great museums will find practically every type of weaving and decoration known to man produced by this people. Even the tapestries and tie and dye work of Europe and Asia were equaled here. The dyes, after a lapse of centuries, are as fast and perfect as though of recent production.

Pottery also was brought to a high state of perfection. Some of the finer pieces were made in the form of vegetables, or of fully dressed people, so lifelike as to suggest portraits. Even the large storage vessels were often covered with intricate designs in color.

North American cultures were without domestic animals, except the dog, but in the highlands of Peru the llama and alpaca were used as beasts of burden, and their wool was spun for weaving.

In many ways the Incas were more advanced than the Aztecs or Mayas; yet, strange to say, they had no written language and only a rudimentary system of keeping count.

Their wealth of gold was the first cause of their downfall. The Spanish adventurer Pizarro invaded their land with a force of only one hundred and eighty-three men. Through treachery, they seized the ruler and, when his subjects had filled a large room with gold as a ranson, the Spaniards killed him.

Deprived of leadership, the Indians fell easy prey to the invaders. Their principal men were slain, many were enslaved in the mines, while the white man's vices and disease assisted in breaking their morale. Thus perished another American civilization.

THE MIDDLE AMERICAN CULTURES

We have now passed in quick review three of the outstanding cultural achievements of Middle and South America. Other tribes might have been mentioned, but these furnish a wide range. All have much in common, but, where one shows great organizing skill and military prowess, another has specialized in art and religious practices, while the third has shown what stupendous works can be achieved in a socialistic state, provided a powerful ruler can order the lives of his subjects as though they were dumb beasts of burden.

What is the history of these very diverse developments? All these people are Indians; all have developed their cultures on American soil; all had much the same background on which to build. Why, then, these differences?

Courtesy Field Museum of Natural History, Chicago

PERUVIAN BURIAL
In the lowlands burial chambers were dug in the desert sands, some distance from the rivers.

Doubtless the first comers into Middle America were primitive Stone Age hunters, similar to those we first met in our discussion of America. Like the people of the North, they certainly made some adjustments to their environment, and we may suspect at least a start toward culture patterns and areas. But the very nature of the country forced these people close together. The life and habits of the residents of the tropical lowlands must have become known to the nearby dwellers in the temperate highlands. They, in turn, were not far distant from the dwellers in the more arid lands to the west. Later, people pushing in from the north were forced into a sort of funnel, made by the ever narrowing shore lines, as the Isthmus was approached. Thus one group learned from another, and conservatism must have been broken to the extent that considerable borrowing took place.

Perhaps even more important was the fact that the concentration of population made it impossible to live by hunting and seed-gathering alone. Here agriculture was developed a second time in the world's history. First came corn, then many other domestic plants. A settled life began, and with it came an accumulation of goods, and other discoveries. Pottery was made, weaving was invented, permanent houses appeared, trade sprang up.

Recent excavations show that several quite different cultures were developing, but ultimately they became so much alike that we speak of an Archaic Horizon. By this we mean that, despite differences in tribes and languages, the people had so much in common that we can class them as a unit.

Perhaps the best picture of this early life is afforded us at a place not far from Mexico City. Here an ancient lava flow spread out over a village site. A few years ago, material for road building was being taken from this area, and in the debris appeared many fragments of pottery, clay heads, and figurines typical of the Archaic culture. Investigation showed that the lava had covered fertile fields, once the home of man. Tunnels, run below the ancient rivers of stone, encountered roadways, sites of dwellings, and even the graves of the inhabitants.

The figurines, made much like gingerbread men, tell us of dress and ornaments, of weaving and of weapons. Stone work and pottery were well advanced, and agriculture developed. At one point, the lava had spread around the base of a pyramid which really was not a pyramid at all. In shape it was much more like an ice-cream cone set upside down, with its top third cut off to form a platform for a structure.

PERUVIAN MUMMY

The bodies of important persons were wrapped in fine cloths and were buried with objects needed in their future life.

The Archaic culture was wide spread, and it appears that all the high cultures of Mexico, Central America, and western South America go back to it.

Perhaps because of its early history, one group developed war-like pursuits; the agricultural interests of another may have led it to devote its energies to religious practices; while the difficult surroundings of the third might emphasize the need of communal effort. Once started on their paths, they would become more specialized as they developed. If we turn back to our culture areas, we find a similar story. There succeeding generations built on foundations laid far back in the early days of the settlement.

Other factors are always at work. The picture never is simple. Trade often is a powerful force in spreading ideas and objects far beyond the land of their origin. In some regions the new ideas are not appreciated, but in others they are borrowed and fitted into the local pattern.

Out of Middle America many inventions spread north and south. Agriculture, pottery, weaving, the stone house, and many other elements of culture reached the Southwest and there developed into Pueblo Indian life. Many of the same ideas entered the Southeast and there underwent quite different development. A minor number of these traits penetrated to the region of the Great Lakes, yet even the few which were adopted served to separate the life of the Woodland Indians from that of the neighboring hunting tribes.

America has furnished us with a variety of cultures. In some regions it has given us a long story of development; in others it has shown the quickening effects of trade or introduction of new ideas. We have learned a great deal about the living peoples of this continent. Now we turn our attention to other lands, and to people of other races.

PYGMIES AND GIANTS have appeared in stories since very early times. People wanted to believe that there were exceedingly small folk and enormously large ones; and early writers created them as heroes or demons of weird tales.

It was not until adventurers pressed far into unknown parts of the world that it became known that pygmies really did exist. Explorers into the Congo found people smaller than ever had been seen before. Spice traders, daring the unknown in their quest for riches, pushed farther and farther eastward, to India, the Malay Peninsula, the East Indies, and among the strange peoples they discovered were pygmies.

Eventually more were found, and today we know of groups living in the Congo, the Andaman Islands, the Malay Peninsula, the Philippine Islands, and New Guinea. The little people who had been merely mythical are now known to exist in the flesh and blood; and in many ways they are as interesting as those appearing in fiction.

[271]

GOVERNOR
BERKELEY AND
TWO PYGMY
MEN OF THE
MALAY STATES

Photo by Cole

They are the most primitive of any people living today, and possibly are leading much the same lives as early palaeolithic man. They do not have stone tools, for bamboo serves most purposes for which stone might be used, and bamboo grows in abundance in the jungles which they inhabit. They have no iron except the little they acquire in trade with other tribes, and they have little of anything to offer in trade.

These various groups of pygmies are so separated that they do not even know of one another's existence, still they are so much alike in looks and certain customs that it is probable they are closely related.

In height they reach about to the shoulders of the average European. The men are rarely more than four feet and nine inches, and often they are much shorter. Their heads are bullet-shaped with low sloping foreheads; their noses are broad and their lips thick. These characteristics, together with their dark skin and tightly curled hair, caused the Spaniards, when they came to the Philippines, to call them Negritos, or little blacks.

It is believed that the pygmies were the aboriginal inhabitants of all this island world, and that their Golden Age was when they held complete possession of mountain and valley, stream and jungle. Being nomads, they made no plantings, but wandered fancy free, depending for food on jungle products or on the game and fish they could catch.

Then came invaders, tribes with iron knives and spears, and they wanted some of the rich lands that the pygmies possessed. The little people, having no iron, could not cope with the new-comers. They were killed, enslaved, or driven back into the more inaccessible and worthless places. Dark times came for the little blacks, as wave after wave of the more advanced tribes arrived and robbed them of their lands.

The newcomers possessed domesticated animals. They culti-vated the soil, built granaries for their rice and substantial houses in communities, so that they could better protect themselves. They increased in numbers, while the little blacks grew more and more shy, retreated farther into the jungle, and diminished in numbers.

They even lost their own language, if they ever had one. To-day, except in the Andaman Islands where they are the only in-habitants, they speak the language of their neighbors.

In the Philippine Islands about twenty thousand pygmies still live in the most worthless sections; but they are only a remnant of the larger numbers who are believed to have held these lands at one time.

How they ever reached these isolated islands in the first place has long been a puzzle, and, of course, the pygmies themselves know nothing of their past. They are no seafarers, and today it seems quite impossible that they ever could have made the trip by water. Yet it is unlikely that they at any time possessed a higher culture than now.

It seems most likely that the pygmies came to these sections when the islands were a part of the Asiatic mainland, perhaps during the last Ice Age.

This seems even more probable because of the presence of certain plants and animals in the Islands. In the northern Philippines are trees like those of China, yet they never could have made their way across the water. And in the south both the plants and animals are closely related to those of Java, Sumatra, and the Malay Peninsula, making it quite evident that they came to these islands when a land bridge connected them with the islands to the south and to the mainland.

Quite probably, then, the far-back ancestors of the pygmies wandered to these parts, and, as geologic changes took place and the islands were separated from the mainland, their connection with others of their kind was cut off.

In the mountains across the bay from Manila, lives a small group of these little nomads which is quite typical, and we shall now pay a visit to them. They may have been there forever so far as they know or care. Sufficient unto the day is their worry. They show no concern whatever for the past nor the future.

It is a lively game of hide and seek for the white man to find these slippery little blacks. They have no fixed habitations, but wander about from place to place as fancy calls them, and they never leave a forwarding address. Moreover, their ears are keen to strange noises, and their knowledge of the jungle enables them to hide like birds in the trees. Unless the pygmies are convinced of friendly intentions, many pairs of black eyes may watch a white man cut his way through their thick jungle and across their rocky streams without giving him any knowledge of their presence.

In seeking a new habitation, they look for a clearing in the jungle where the sun penetrates each day, for otherwise the leeches, which live on damp leaves and underbrush, make life almost unendurable. Even small clearings are rare, however, for jungle rapidly devours open spaces, and usually the pygmy is compelled to cut down the smaller trees and shrubs and burn them in order to find a place for his frail shelter.

Courtesy Field Museum of Natural History, Chicago

PYGMY MAN AND CHILD
A man is never too busy to devote time to the youngsters.

Photo by I. H. N. Evans

PYGMY HOUSE IN THE MALAY STATES

Forked sticks are driven into the ground and on these cross sticks are laid. Over this framework a covering of palm leaves is placed, and the dwelling is complete.

If he has learned something of farming from his Filipino neighbors, he may even clear enough land so that he puts in a planting of corn, rice, or sweet potatoes, but this does not prevent him from changing his location if fancy calls. He does not bother to wait till his crop is ripe, if he takes a notion to move. He merely picks up his few possessions, bows and arrows, and a musical instrument or two, and goes. He has no furniture, no extra clothes, and no culinary utensils.

The jungle soon encroaches, and in a season the labor he has put into preparing the ground is obliterated. Until he feels the urge for another clearing, the pygmy and his family, or perhaps two or three families together, may live on wild tubers, fruit, and game which they kill with their bows and arrows.

Houses are quickly built wherever the pygmies stop. Forked saplings driven into the ground hold smaller sticks which support the leaf roof. They are mere shelters, sometimes five or six feet square, with neither sides nor floor. Some of the better ones may have a raised platform of bamboo covering about half the space, and this is used as a sleeping place for various members of the family or families who occupy the house.

The pygmies have no blankets, but they do like to feel warm at night, so a fire is often built under the platform. If there are too many in the family to sleep on the platform, some rake out the coals and curl up in the warm ashes. The pygmy is dark in color, but sleeping in the fireplace often gives him a peculiar ashy appearance. He never takes a bath for fear he will take cold, and indeed he would feel the loss of the layers of dirt and ashes which cover his skin.

Courtesy Field Museum of Natural History, Chicago

PYGMIES OF THE PHILIPPINES
The Pygmies, tiny blacks, were the first inhabitants of the Philippines.

Clothes give them little concern. The sole article of dress of the man is a bark clout, and in cases of extreme prosperity a hat or cast-off blanket secured in trade from some other tribe. The woman rarely possesses more than one article of clothing, and that is a "skirt," a strip from the inner bark of a tree, fastened around her waist and extending to her knees. This bark, taken from certain trees, is beaten with a wooden mallet until it is soft and pliable, then it is dried in the sun and is ready for use. It is never washed, and if a pygmy woman is offered some cotton cloth, she will invariably select black since that does not change color so quickly as other hues.

Children wear nothing at all with the exception, perhaps, of a string of berries about their necks. They never are subjected to commands from their parents to keep their clothes clean, wash their faces, or comb their hair. They play in the mud and water, and then eat their food or go to sleep, as carefree as puppies.

The pygmy's hair, which is black and kinky, is never combed. Some of them shave a round spot on the top of the head "to let the heat out," but as a rule the thick woolly mass stands out all over their heads. It is allowed to grow until it becomes troublesome and then it is chopped off with the bolo, or long knife, a laborious and painful process. Bamboo combs are sometimes worn by the women, but only as ornaments. They are never used.

Since the pygmy in his simple manner of living does not see the necessity of taking thought for the morrow, he has a hard time to get enough to eat. There is scarcely anything in the animal or vegetable kingdom of his country with which his stomach is not acquainted. Fish, eels, wild boar, deer, wild chickens, lizards, crows, hawks, and vultures are all on his regular menu, while large pythons furnish especially toothsome steaks.

When necessity compels him to become a vegetarian, he eats any kind of fruit or tuber which can be found, even some which in the raw state are deadly poison. One particularly poisonous vegetable is a yellow tuber called ca-lot. This the pygmy woman cuts in thin slices which she soaks in water for two days. Then she boils it in several waters till it loses its yellow color, when the

Photo by Cole

WOMAN'S DRESS

Garments give little concern. The woman's dress is a strip of beaten bark.

Courtesy Field Museum of Natural History, Chicago   Photo by Cole

PYGMY WOMEN OF THE MALAY STATES

poison is believed to be gone. To make sure, however, she feeds some to a dog and, if the dog does not die, she feeds it to the family.

Their manner of eating is simple. They never have more than two regular meals a day and usually only one. They have no dishes. When they are hungry, they put some rice or tubers in a joint of green bamboo and place it in the coals and hot ashes to cook. If there is meat, small pieces are strung on a strip of cane and hung over the fire; or, if a fowl is to be cooked, it is wrapped in banana leaves and slowly roasted over the coals. When it is done, the members of the family and any others who are around sit down on the ground near the fire, turn out the food onto a banana leaf and eat ravenously. There are no plates, no knives and forks; no table to be cleared, no dishes to be washed. When they have eaten all they can hold or all there is, they tip up a bamboo tube of water which stands near and take a drink. Then it is time to sleep. The monkeys in the trees are not more carefree.

A necklace of dried berries is often worn about the necks of both men and women, but it is not so much for ornamentation as for convenience, since the pygmies have no pockets. These berries are said to be effective in relieving the pangs of indigestion, so when a pygmy feels a pain he pulls off a berry and eats it. It is not uncommon to find these necklaces on which very few berries are left.

Most of the ingenuity which the pygmies possess is devoted to the making of bows and arrows, traps and snares. The bows are cut from palma brava and are highly polished. The strings are of twisted bark, made soft and pliable, and the arrows are cleverly fashioned.

BLOW GUNS

In regions where the upas tree grows, as in the island of Palawan just north of Borneo, and in the Malay Peninsula, the pygmies use poisoned darts. The poisonous sap of the upas boiled down to a thick, sticky substance is kept in a tube hanging from a tree or a house-post ready for use. The blow-guns are long tubes through which the men blow darts about six inches in length. At one end of the missile is a cone of pith which collects the air; at the other is a tiny point covered with the deadly poison. The upas sap is an alkaloid which, once it enters the blood stream, causes the death of the victim but does not injure the meat for food purposes. The pygmy simply cuts away the flesh from around the wound and eats the animal without any ill effects.

Although so much of their sustenance depends on the chase, they are not very accurate shots except on large game. Wild chickens and birds are generally caught with spring traps in a primitive but effective manner.

Deer are hunted by bands of pygmies, sometimes as many as thirty at a time, each man carrying a bow longer than he is tall and a handful of arrows, while half starved dogs accompany them to chase the animal after it had been wounded.

They know that the deer go to graze only at night, and that

PYGMIES WITH BLOW
GUNS
Poisoned darts are blown
through these tubes.

in the daytime they lie in cool, sheltered places, so the pygmies hunt for a thickly wooded ravine through which a little stream flows. Several men plunge through the thicket, yelling and beating the underbrush, while the others wait on the outside, watching till a frightened deer appears. Then they shoot at him with their arrows, and the dogs take up the chase. Sometimes a long net of rattan is stretched in front of the place where the deer is likely to run, and he is thus trapped.

Notwithstanding their antipathy for work in general, the pygmies are tireless in the chase and will hunt all day without eating unless they happen to find some wild fruit. If dogs are scarce, women frequently take part in a hunt, running through the brush, yelping like dogs; but they are never permitted to carry bows and arrows.

A successful hunt brings great rejoicing, for often it ends

a period of fasting. Bad luck, bad weather, or poor marksmanship means no food for the pygmy.

After the animal has been skinned, the most influential man present takes a part of the entrails or heart, cuts it into small pieces and scatters it in all directions, chanting as he does so a prayer of thanks to the spirits for aiding in the chase. When the spirits have been thus appeased, the body is cut up and divided, the head and breast going to the man who first wounded the deer, and the backbone to the one who sent the final shot. One hind quarter goes to the man whose dog started up the animal and the rest is equally divided among the hunters.

A pygmy man is prepared to cook his game wherever he may be, for he always wears his fire making apparatus. When in need of heat he tears a piece from his bark clout and lays it beneath a dry stick on the ground. Then, unwinding the rattan that ornaments his arm, he saws it rapidly up and down between the bark cloth and the stick till the friction produces a spark which he blows into a flame. Or he may use the common fire-saw method.

Courtesy Field Museum of Natural History, Chicago

MAKING FIRE
A fire saw is made out of two pieces of bamboo.

Courtesy Field Museum of Natural History, Chicago

PYGMY BEAUTY TREATMENT

This Pygmy woman uses a piece of sharp bamboo to produce a scar on the chest of the
Pygmy man. These scars are highly regarded as marks of beauty.

He takes two pieces of bamboo and runs the sharpened edge of one rapidly back and forth in a groove of the other till the friction produces enough heat to ignite the tinder. Either method is almost as quick as a match.

Simple as the life of these people seems, style plays an important part in it, and both men and women are willing to suffer physical pain in order to be beautiful. Many of their neighbors tattoo their bodies, but the pygmies' skin is so dark that this method does not show up well, so they scarify their bodies. Incisions are made with a piece of sharp bamboo, and dirt is rubbed in to cause infection. As a result the pygmies wear great scars on their breasts, arms, and backs.

They also file or break their teeth into points, and make holes in their ears in which they wear fresh leaves and flowers. They are particular, too, about the care of their skin, rubbing themselves all over with pig grease. The shinier they are, the more they are admired.

Courtesy Field Museum of Natural History, Chicago

PYGMY WOMAN SCARIFYING HER HUSBAND

Cuts are made with a bamboo knife and soot is rubbed into the wounds. When they heal
up they leave large raised scars.

Even the way a pygmy smokes a cigar is different from any
other. Tobacco may have come to him, in the first place, through
the white man, but his way of using it is original. He rolls his
cigar, usually green tobacco, and places the lighted end in his
mouth. When after a few puffs the fire is extinguished, he re-
lights the cigar in the coals and repeats the process. Men, women,
and children all smoke if they can beg, borrow, or trade for
tobacco, or for a few puffs from someone's cigar.

A girl is a valuable asset in a pygmy family, and she is not
parted with until a satisfactory price has been paid for her. She
is allowed little choice in the selection of her husband, for the
momentary worldly possessions of a prospective son-in-law have
much to do in gaining parental consent.

When a boy has chosen a girl he wishes to marry, he consults
his relatives as to how much they are willing to contribute for
her purchase. This settled, he, or one of his relatives, consults the
parents of the girl. If the amount offered sufficiently compensates

Courtesy Field Museum of Natural History, Chicago

A PYGMY WEDDING
The bride and groom feed each other rice, smoke of the same cigar, and drink together,
and the ceremony is complete.

them, they give their consent, and presents of tobacco, corn, rattan, or whatever may be on hand, are turned over. This completed, the rest is simple. A feast is held at which all the relatives assemble. A mat is spread on the ground, and some food is placed in the center of it. The bride and groom squat on the ground on opposite sides of the mat. The boy places some of the food in the mouth of the girl, and she does the same to him. They drink from the same coconut shell and take a few puffs from the same cigar. The people give a great shout, and the ceremony is over.

The pygmies of Palawan are one of the few groups in the world where both polygamy and polyandry are practiced. A man may have as many wives as he can secure, and a woman may have two or more husbands if she desires.

Their method of naming is confusing to a white person, but they appear to have no difficulty. There is no difference between the names of men and women. A child is usually called after some striking object which is near at hand at the time of its birth. If he is born under a tree, he may be called by the name of that tree; if a monkey is playing in the tree, he may be called Barac (monkey); or if he is born during a storm, he may be called

Layos (flood). If he is sickly, it is known that the spirits are not pleased, and his name is changed.

The pygmies are exceedingly fond of music and dancing; and the sounds from a bamboo jew's-harp, a four-hole flute made from mountain cane, or a bamboo violin is sweet and inspiring to their ears. They have only four notes, but the time is good, and that is all that is necessary since their chief amusement is dancing. Sometimes the bark is removed from a small log which then is suspended from a frame by rattan cords. The women line up in front of the log and with short sticks beat out a rhythmical tattoo.

They have many dances, the most popular being pantomimes. These are quite clever interpretations. As a preliminary the pygmies sit in a circle clapping their hands until finally one man leaps into the open space and dances around in a circle, clapping, as if warming up. He then gets into step with the music and starts the acting.

In one called "The Sweet Potato Dance" the performer hunts around until he pretends to find a potato patch. He appears greatly pleased, bounds high in the air, and claps his hands for joy. He goes through the motions of digging the potatoes and putting them into an imaginary sack which he swings over his shoulder. There is a change in the rhythm, and he dances in a circle with the sack on his back, keeping close watch that he is not caught in the act of stealing. Finally he pretends to come to a brush fence built around the patch to keep out deer and wild hogs, and with his long knife he cuts an opening and passes through. He goes on, stepping high over obstacles in the path, till he comes to the river. He tests the depth of the water with a long stick, but, in doing so, he slips and drops the imaginary sack into the imaginary current which carries it away. This is the climax of the dance, and the spectators give a great shout as the performer resumes his place in the circle. All the time that he has been acting, the feet, arms, and body of the little black man have been in perfect accompaniment to the music.

Though they have a number of dances, the pygmies know but few songs. These, however, they make appropriate for all occasions. One is a love song and has countless verses, but it so embarrasses the singer that it is difficult to get anyone to render it for an outsider.

Another is sung on any occasion, and while the tune is always the same, the words are made to fit the need. When sung for a white man, it is usually a suggestion that a gift be made.

This song, like their dances, has an introduction which must be given before the words can be sung. Several men, each with one hand over his mouth, walk around in a circle, their bodies stooped. The leader strikes a note which he holds as long as he has breath, and then the others take it up. They move increasingly faster, then abruptly stop, go back a few steps, and begin over again. After a few minutes of this, they are in condition to start the words of the song. Though only one sentence may be used, it is sung over and over till the desired length is reached, or more likely till the gift is forthcoming.

Nothing could be more simple than the religious life of the pygmy, unencumbered as it is by creed or dogma. Pygmies believe that there are beings stronger than themselves, and that these live in the sky, streams, certain rocks, and trees. All adverse circumstances such as sickness, failure of food supplies, and unsuccessful ventures are attributed to these spirits. At times of special stress such as an epidemic, earthquake, or typhoon, they even make offerings and pray to them; but so long as all goes well, the spirits are not much considered. There is a certain large black bowlder which is the home of the most powerful immortal, and into this all spirits of the dead seem to go. No pygmy passes this rock without leaving some article of food, lest bad luck should follow him; but, this offering made, his responsibility ceases and he has no fear.

Each group has a sort of medicine man, one who is thought to have power to talk with the members of the spirit world, and in times of sickness, he may go into a trance to learn the kind of dance or the herbs necessary to make a cure.

When all remedies fail and a person dies, there is great wailing and weeping among the pygmies. They dress the deceased in fresh bark cloth and lay him in his house for two or three days with a fire burning nearby, and a man armed with bow and arrow stands guard to prevent evil spirits from injuring the body. When the period of mourning is over, the body is buried in a shallow grave.

Courtesy Field Museum of Natural History, Chicago   Photo by Cole

PYGMIES OF THE MALAY PENINSULA
These people lead the simple life with very little toil or care.

The pygmies immediately desert the place and seek new abodes.

However monotonous the existence of the living pygmy may be, as soon as one is dead, they tell us, he starts on an eventful journey. He first travels over an easy plain at the end of which is a tall banana tree from which he attempts to pick fruit. If he fails he must return to the body; but if he succeeds in securing the fruit he continues traveling till he reaches the edge of the world. He advances from one stage to another until at last he becomes almost as powerful as one of the great spirits. But this cannot last forever. After he has enjoyed this blessedness for a time, he becomes a mosquito or a gnat which may be killed by his own descendants. And this is the end.

The folklore of the pygmy is very meager and unorganized. The group on Palawan believe that a giant crab lives in a hole in

GOVERNOR PACK AND PYGMY MEN

Drawn up to their full stature, the Pygmies still seem very tiny when standing beside a
tall American.

the sea. When he comes out of the hole, the waters rush in, resulting in low tide on shore. When he returns to his hole, the water is
forced out and we have high tide once more. This crab, they say,
is the son of the moon.

An eclipse of the moon is one of the most terrifying things
that can happen in the world, according to these little people. It
is this giant crab trying to swallow his mother, and if he succeeds
the greatest of all calamities will fall upon the people.

At the first indication of the eclipse, the medicine man is im-
plored to come to the rescue, for he alone has any influence with
the crab. He orders the people to shout and beat on drums, to
which they respond with great vigor. Above the din, the high
pitched, terrorized voice of the medicine man can be heard beseeching the great snake spirit to avert the calamity.

Amid the frenzied beating of drums and shouts of the people,
the monster slowly devours his prey. Just as they reach the depths
of despair, they behold the prayer of their medicine man being
answered. They see the moon slowly emerging from the mouth of
the giant captor, and they cease shouting. They are convinced
that the world has been saved because of their medicine man and
the fact that they have followed the custom of their ancestors.

Thus we find these little people, the pygmies, living the simple
life. They have few possessions of any kind, and unencumbered
they move about from place to place as they please. They take
no thought for the morrow; their only real concern seeming to be
food enough for today. They are leading much the same life, perhaps, as early Stone Age man. But even stone plays little part in
their existence, since bamboo serves most purposes for which stone
might be used.

If some great catastrophe should suddenly wipe out all the
pygmies, there would be little left, after a few years, to tell of
their life. We should have even less than we now have of the early
Stone Age in Europe.

Courtesy Field Museum of Natural History, Chicago　　　　　　　　Photo by Cole

THE BAGOBO DENTIST
All adults have their teeth cut or filed to points to add to their beauty.

PHILIPPINES

MANY OF THE MALAYAN TRIBES who invaded the Philippines and took lands away from the little blacks can still be found in the mountain regions. They are much more advanced in culture than the pygmies, but they are apparently leading much the same sort of lives, following the same customs that they have for hundreds of years.

In many ways these tribes resemble the Lake Dwellers of the Neolithic Age, except that they use iron in place of stone utensils, and they are casters of brass. But they are still savage and primitive, and their entire lives are governed by pagan beliefs.

For long periods these Malayan tribes probably occupied the lowlands and rich river valleys of the Philippine Islands. Then some three hundred and fifty years ago, the Spaniards came, and many of the tribes fell under the rule of Spain and adopted the dress and certain customs of their conquerors. They gave up their pagan beliefs and savage practices and became converts of Catholicism.

Courtesy Field Museum of Natural History, Chicago   Photo by Cole
NOISY OUTFITS
The women wear bells attached to their belts and rattles around their arms and ankles.

The more conservative tribes, however, refused to change their customs and beliefs and they, in turn, withdrew into the mountains and more inaccessible places. Here, in isolated spots, they established themselves, each tribe according to the customs of their ancestors.

High mountains and swift rivers discouraged much trade between them, and they seldom had contact with one another save through warfare. Because they knew little of one another, each tribe feared all the others, and each believed that those just beyond their territory were "bad people."

Since the coming of the Americans, schools have come into the edge of the "wild" country; roads have been built, and many of these tribes are beginning to know more of their neighbors and to fear them less. Head-hunting and human sacrifice, to a large extent, are being supplanted by less savage sports. But in their mountain homes they still carry on the customs and beliefs of their ancestors and lead much the same lives as they have for generations.

THE LAND OF HUMAN SACRIFICE

Perhaps the most interesting, the most savage, and the best dressed of all these pagan peoples are the Bagobos, far famed for their custom of human sacrifice.

They live on the slopes of Mt. Apo, the highest peak in the Philippines, and this, they tell us, is the original home of the human race.

Mt. Apo towers ten thousand feet above the sea on the Gulf of Davao, in southeastern Mindanao. Back of the coast line, along the Gulf, rise densely timbered mountain peaks, some ending in abrupt cliffs which overlook the sea, some in grass covered plains sloping gently down nearly to the water's edge. Deep river canyons cut between these mountains and across the plains. If the mountain chains and river courses are followed back, it is found that they all radiate from one stupendous mass, the center of which is Mt. Apo.

Near its summit is a deep fissure from which, on clear mornings, columns of smoke or steam can be seen rising; and the first rays of the sun turn into gold the fields of sulphur that surround its cone. Only for a short time each morning is this visible. Later in the day it is hidden in a thick veil; and the Bagobos know that Mandarangan and Darago, two mysterious spirits who dwell in its crater, would guard from human eyes their secrets. All Bagobo traditions, religious observances, and daily life are closely related to the hidden power in the old volcano.

Cibolan, the home of Datu Tongkaling, the head man of the Bagobos, is about seven miles back from the coast on the slopes of Mt. Apo. Tongkaling traces his genealogy back through ten generations to the time when the Spaniards first came to the Philippines.

Salingolop was then ruler. He is said to have been a powerful man "as tall as the highest tree in the forest." When the Spaniards heard of this giant, say the Bagobos, they sent a battalion of soldiers who fired on him, but the bullets made no impression. It was not until they dropped their rifles and struck his legs with bars of iron that he was conquered. As he fell, they say that he struck on his side in the sea, causing the waves to make such a great noise that it reached to the Cape of San Augustin.

Salingolop was succeeded by his son, Bato, who was powerful also; and under him and those who came after him, the Bagobos grew into a great and powerful people, making frequent forays into neighboring districts where they secured many slaves and rich loot. Finally came a datu who was not a great warrior, and in matters of dispute his decisions were not always wise and just. Under him dissensions arose among the people, and petty rulers of other districts sprang up.

This was the condition when Tongkaling became datu, but he proved to be a great warrior, and the people prospered under his rule. With the coming of the Americans, Tongkaling was officially recognized as head of all the Bagobos, and he finally succeeded in gaining recognition from most of the petty chiefs.

When his reign began, he made a great feast according to long established custom. Seven hundred of his people came, and for six days they feasted, danced, and made merry. Then, going to a great tree in the forest, they sacrificed a decrepit slave whom the Datu had bought; and they prayed to the spirits to make his reign one of prosperity, without defeat in battle. His prayers appear to have been answered. He is subject to the laws and customs handed down by his ancestors, but he is supreme judge in all matters concerning his people.

NOISY DRESSERS

The Bagobos are of slight build but somewhat taller than the pygmies. They are a light reddish brown in color, with dark wavy hair and dark eyes.

They are very dressy. In fact they weight themselves down with clothes heavily beaded and with many brass anklets, bracelets, and bells.

The Bagobo man wears hemp cloth trousers scarcely reaching to his knees, the bottom of each leg finished with a beaded band. His coat is heavily beaded and embroidered, and since he has no pockets a hemp bag is worn on his back. This is often completely covered with beads in beautiful designs. In his belt,

Courtesy Field Museum of Natural History, Chicago

Courtesy Field Museum of Natural History, Chicago

A BAGOBO MAN OF THE SOUTHERN
PHILIPPINES
The Bagobo people are the most elaborately
dressed of any of the pagan tribes.

BAGOBO WOMAN OF THE
PHILIPPINES
Quantities of beads, bells and other orna-
ments are attached to their garments.

whence he can quickly draw it, he always wears his long knife
in an ornamented scabbard. Another article often worn is a sort
of belt known as anting-anting. This may consist of some peculiarly shaped stones, a tooth, a shell, or any simple object
wrapped in an old cloth. It may not impress us, but to the Bagobo it is a charm which may save his life. It may protect him in
battle, ward off evil spirits, cause trouble or even death to an
enemy. Or, he will tell you, a little dust gathered from the foot-
print of an enemy and placed in one of these belts will immediately cause the foe to fall ill.

The woman's cotton jacket, which reaches to the waist, is
decorated with appliqué, embroidery, and intricate designs in
shell disks or beads. Her narrow tube skirt of hemp cloth is made
like a sack open at both ends. Many strands of beads and carved
seeds are worn by both men and women around their necks, while
just above the calf of the leg they wear plaited leglets which have
magical power.

The women are always busy. When they are not working in the fields or cooking the meals, they sit down with their work baskets. Often far into the night they sew on beads, take fine stitches in embroidery, or tie together hemp fibers for their cloth.

In nearly every house is a hand loom on which the women weave hemp by the intricate tie and dye process. The realistic and conventional designs of crocodiles, rice mortars, humans, and other objects are made in the warp by overtying parts with waxed thread before it is dyed. The accuracy and fineness of their work is amazing. Everything worn or used by the Bagobos is carved or decorated in some way.

They are not bad-looking when they keep their mouths shut. Both men and women chew betel-nut prepared with lime and a leaf which makes the spittle a bright red. Their teeth are cut into points and blackened. The red stain of the betel-nut on teeth and lips, together with the pointed and blackened teeth, presents an amazing sight when a Bagobo opens his mouth in a broad smile —which he often does.

Courtesy Field Museum of Natural History, Chicago   Photo by Cole

MEN'S BAGS
These beaded bags take the place of pockets.

Courtesy Field Museum of Natural History, Chicago   Photo by Cole

BEADED BAGS OF BEAUTIFUL DESIGN
Bagobo women are expert in the making of these beaded handbags.

They have many industries. The brass casters, clever artisans, melt up old copper gongs to make the bells, bracelets, and betel boxes so essential to their happiness. Their forge consists of two bamboo cylinders in which feathered plungers work up and down forcing air through a tube into a charcoal fire, the Malayan type of bellows. The copper is melted in a small crucible made of burned rice straw. The bells are first moulded in beeswax over damp ashes, and when thoroughly hardened they are covered with several layers of the ashes. The molten metal is poured through an opening in the cleverly fashioned mould, and as the wax melts its place is taken by the hot copper. When thoroughly cold, the mould is broken open, and quite perfect little bells appear. Fine betel-nut boxes, bracelets, and anklets are made in the same fashion, and great pride is taken in this work. The caster is held in high esteem by the people and is under the care and guidance of a certain spirit to whom they make yearly sacrifices.

Of even greater importance to the Bagobo are the smiths who make the fine spear-heads and knives used in warfare. Their forges are hidden deep in the hemp fields, and no woman is ever permitted to see a smith at work. These forges are similar to those of the brass casters, except that hollowed-out logs take the place of the bamboo tubes, and a metal anvil and iron hammer are used.

The smiths cleverly inlay steel edges in their weapons. When an iron knife or spear-head has been roughly shaped, the smith splits the edge slightly and inserts a band of steel. The iron is pounded down on the harder metal and brought to a white heat in the charcoal fire. Placing it on the anvil, the smith gives it several light blows, reheats and repeats the blows until, finally, the iron and steel are welded together. It is heated again and held over a trough of water until the glowing metal becomes a yellowish green. It is then plunged into the water, and the process is repeated till a fair temper is obtained.

The smiths are believed to be under the care of certain spirits, and they are held in the highest esteem by the people, for on their skill may depend much of a man's success in battle and, hence, his standing in the community.

RED SUITED WARRIORS

One cannot be long among the Bagobos without noticing that the strongest and most powerful men of the tribe are distinguished by a certain costume which they always wear. While it is ornamented like that of the others, it is of a distinct blood-red color. This is a mark of membership in the order known as magani, an order to which no man may belong until he has gained distinction among his people for bravery and prowess.

When a man has taken two human lives, he is permitted to wear a peculiar chocolate-colored headband. When he has taken four, he may put on the blood-red trousers; and when he has six lives to his credit, he is a full member of the order and is allowed to wear a complete red suit with a bag of the same color on his back. It is the chief aim in the life of a man to become a magani, and this desire, as much as to gain loot and slaves, causes many raids to be made on his enemies.

BAGOBO METAL WORKERS
Women are not allowed to be present when the iron worker is at his task, but they assist in brass casting and other metal work.

2

Sometimes they go out in parties of sixty or more men, making their way through the jungle in the dark to some hostile village. There they lie in wait till dawn when, as the people come out singly and unarmed to go about their regular tasks, the warriors make an attack. They seize a few victims and depart, carrying the women and children home with them as slaves.

At times, however, the invaded village has had lookouts and is prepared. Then they meet the attackers in real battle and at close quarters. While fighting with their spears or long fighting knives in their right hands, they try to ward off blows with the wooden shields they carry in the left, using all their skill and ingenuity as they dart from side to side in their attempts to pierce the foe or cut him fatally.

Finally, when the Bagobo has made a lucky strike which gives him the advantage, he quickly ends the battle. He cuts open the body of his victim and takes out the heart and liver which he holds above his head, shouting to his companions to see that the strength and valor of a brave foe are now in his possession. Each of the successful warriors does likewise, and a grewsome feast is held when later they devour the hearts and livers of their victims.

They are not cannibals, as they have been reported to be. They do not eat this for food, or because they like the taste, but because to them it means adding to their own bravery that of their foes. Datu Tongkaling proudly admits that he has eaten of the hearts and livers of more than thirty victims he took in fair fight, and to that fact he gives much credit for his success in governing his people.

THE SPIRIT WORLD

Though the Bagobos are cruel in their warfare and savage in their practices, they are faithful in following the customs and beliefs of their ancestors. They believe in many spirits, powerful beings who make their homes in the sky above, in the space under the earth, or in the sea, cliffs, streams, mountains, and trees.

Manama, the greatest of these, and the creator of all things, lives in the sky whence he can observe all that goes on in the world. Offerings for him, the Bagobo says, should be white and should always be placed above and in the center of offerings intended for other immortals. There are many good spirits, and there are evil ones who eat people and have power to injure the living.

Stars, thunder, lightning, and similar phenomena are considered signs or signals from the spirits, and one common method by which they communicate with mortals is through the call of a bird known as limokon. All the people know the meaning of its calls, and all respect its warning. If a person is starting on a journey, building a house, or planting a field, and hears the bird call, he stops immediately and makes offerings or even gives up, for a time, whatever he is doing.

There is a certain class of individuals called mabalian who know better than anyone else the wishes of the spirits. The mabalian are usually old or middle aged women, though men are not barred from the profession. They may live the greater part of their lives as ordinary individuals, and then suddenly be warned in dreams or visions that they have been chosen by the spirits.

They then go to an older mabalian and study for months the duties of the office, the correct medicines to use at certain times, the way to build shrines and conduct ceremonies, and the prayers that must be used in addressing spirits. Sometimes at ceremonies the mabalian is believed to be possessed and to talk with the people not as a mortal but as the spirit itself.

A mabalian is the chief official at a marriage. The parents of a boy usually select a wife for him, and it is unusual for either a boy or girl to object to the choice their parents make. Going to the home of the girl, the parents, together with other relatives and the datu, discuss the price to be paid for the bride. Gongs, skirts, betel-nut boxes, sometimes a horse, are among the articles that may be given in payment; but, whatever it is, the parents of the girl return half of it to the family of the boy "so that they do not sell their daughter like a slave." For about a year the boy must work for his future father-in-law, and then the marriage takes place. Relatives and friends assemble and feast and make merry for two or three days. Then the mabalian spreads a mat on the floor, and on it she places many valuable articles which she offers to the spirits in order that they will be willing to give the couple a long and prosperous life together. Finally she places a dish of rice on the mat between the boy and girl as they sit on the floor. The girl takes a handful of the rice and feeds the boy and he, in turn, feeds her; and the ceremony is complete.

A man may have as many wives as he can afford. For his second wife a husband must not only pay her parents, but he must give a like amount to his first wife. For his third, he must pay her parents and both of his other mates, and so on, so that wives become increasingly expensive. But each new one understands that she must work for and obey those before her, and this, perhaps, is the reason that they all seem to live together in harmony.

Almost everything edible in their country is included in the diet of the Bagobos. While rice is the main dish, they nearly always have sweet potatoes, corn, bananas, sago, and coconuts. For meat they eat deer, pigs, chickens, monkeys, fish, eels, crabs, and grasshoppers.

Courtesy Field Museum of Natural History, Chicago   Photo by Cole

INTERIOR OF DATU TONGKALING'S HOUSE
A fighting man of the Bagobo tribe playing on the copper gongs.

PRIMITIVE AGRICULTURISTS

They are not such good agriculturists as the Malay tribes of the northern Philippines who raise their rice in splendid terraced fields on the mountain sides, still they are much better farmers than the pygmies. They make small clearings on the mountain slopes where they plant rice, sweet potatoes, and corn, but the cogon grass invades the fields so persistently that it is necessary to make some new clearings each year.

Nothing is more important in the life of the Bagobo than his care of the rice. Not only does he depend on it for the greater part of his food supply, but by its growth he can tell with what favor he is looked upon by the spirits.

When each year in the month of December the constellation of seven stars known as Balatik (pig trap) appears in the sky, the Bagobos know that it is placed there by the spirits to remind them that it is time to prepare their fields. Those who are going to make new clearings gather at the forge of the local smith, taking their weapons and working tools, and offerings of rice and chickens. They perform a ceremony for the patron spirit of the forge, that he may make the tools do good work and protect the users from injury and from enemies. The food is placed on a rice winnower near the forge, and on it the men deposit their weapons and knives. The smith in a droning voice invites the spirit to come and eat of the food and to accept the gifts. From this time on, these tools belong to the immortal, and while the former owners may use them in the fields, they cannot dispose of them without first making it right with the spirit.

For three days the men do not work, and the forge stands idle. Then, when the fire is again lighted, the first knife made is the property of the patron spirit. When work is about to begin, offerings are made in the fields to Manama to insure the good health of the workers and abundant crops.

Everything is put in readiness but nothing is planted till the spirits give a further signal by placing the constellation marara in the sky early in April. Then great care is taken that everything is done according to the customs of their ancestors. Mabalians build the spirit houses and make offerings; gifts pleasing to the various spirits are made; and Tarabume, the spirit who cares for the growing grain, is begged to protect the rice from all animals, blight, and drought. Manama is besought to control the sun and the winds, so that they will be favorable to the growing rice, and to see that everything is done to insure an abundant crop.

No chance is taken of any spirit feeling slighted, and when all obligations are fulfilled, the men start work. Even the planting sticks have bamboo plumes and clappers at the ends of the long shafts, that the flapping of the plumes may be a pleasing sight to Tarabume and the rattle, music to his ears.

The men move in a long row, digging shallow holes in the ground with the planters. A row of women follow close behind the men, dropping a few kernels of rice into each hole and pushing the soil over it with their feet.

Ceremonies are made when the crop is harvested, and a great thanksgiving feast is held. At this time the knives and other implements used in the fields are laid on a large basket filled with rice "so that they, too, may eat and have no cause to injure their owners." All inanimate objects have souls, according to Bagobo belief, and they must be treated accordingly.

The Bagobos have always raised some hemp, and now, when large plantations have been developed on the coast by the Americans and Japanese, the Bagobo in the mountains has increased his plantings. When he needs brass wire, cloth, beads or, perhaps, a new gong, he goes to his patch and strips some hemp. When it is dry he makes bundles which he loads on to the backs of his wives, and perhaps some slaves, and they start for the coast. They tramp, single file, over the narrow mountain trails, the husband in the lead, well armed with spear and long knife, and always on the alert for enemies or for omens.

Small individual houses of the Bagobos are usually near the fields or in little settlements, but for festivities or in time of danger the people gather at the large home of the Datu. His house, like the smaller ones, is made of bamboo and is raised on piles high above the ground. It has but one door and no windows, only peep holes in the walls.

HOUSE OF DATU TONGKALING
The building is large enough to house more than 200 people.

This great house has but one room, a vast room capable of holding more than two hundred people; and here live the Datu, his wives, children, and slaves, together with some forty fighting men. A raised platform across one end of the room is reserved for the warriors, while bamboo cages built high against the walls are the sleeping places of the Datu's wives and children. The remainder of the men, women, children, and dogs occupy the floor.

The room looks almost like a museum. On the low sides hang dozens of copper gongs, drums, ancient Chinese plates, looms, shields, spears, knives, and pieces of beautiful bead work, while hanging altars hold spirit offerings. Near the center stand two decorated poles around which the warriors relate their brave deeds after a human sacrifice.

At the far end of the room is the "kitchen." Here women cook over little fires, balancing pots on three stones sunk in a bed of ashes. When the food is prepared, two long rows of plates are set on the floor, and the household prepares to eat. The warriors take their places first, followed by the other men, then by the women and children, all squatting on their heels and diving in with their hands.

The Datu squats off to one side all by himself, using a special bowl and plate, for his prestige will not permit him to eat with any save one of his own rank. He mingles freely with his people; does not hesitate to work in the fields or do any other kind of labor, but he must maintain a certain dignity, and eating alone is part of it.

Festive evenings at the Datu's are gay affairs. The various trails leading to the house resound with the tinkling of bells and clatter of brass anklets as the people hasten along. They climb the bamboo ladder into the house and squat about on the floor, moving over to make room as more arrive in the doorway. The gorgeous garments and shining brass lose none of their beauty in the flickering light of torches and burning nuts, but the air is heavy with the smell of coconut oil, for many have had their long hair freshly oiled for the occasion.

For a time the men talk and tell stories, while the women ply their needles or tie hemp threads. Then some musician steps up to the gongs, a dozen or more of different sizes suspended from the rafters. He begins to strike them with a padded stick, and one or more other musicians join him. Faster and faster the music grows till it becames a compelling rhythm which starts several dancers to their feet. They rise on their heels and toes, bending the knees and twisting the body till finally they are in step, when they dance off, encircling the gongs and gliding around the room.

The music continues, inviting; others join the dancers. They grow more and more animated, performing fancy steps, sometimes grabbing a stick from the musicians to beat on the gongs. It is a wild though merry time.

Red suits gleam in the flickering lights. The clatter of bells and brass adds to the din of the gongs, and the air is stifling with the odor of hot bodies and coconut oil.

Near the center of the room the two decorated poles dedicated to Mandarangan and Darago are unheeded. So sacred are they that they are touched but once a year, following a sacrifice, and then only by members of the magani.

HUMAN SACRIFICE

Those two mysterious spirits, Mandarangan and Darago, who live in the smoking mountain, are greatly revered and greatly feared by the Bagobos. They give special protection to the warriors; they grant them success in battle and give them loot and slaves, but in return for these favors they demand offerings, and, at certain times, the sacrifice of a human being.

Each year in December, when the constellation, Balatik, appears in the sky, it not only tells the people that it is time to prepare new fields, but it also reminds them that they must make a sacrifice to thank the spirits in the mountain for the good year that they have had, and to secure their favor for the coming season.

It has been difficult for the Bagobos to explain to these two beings why the United States government insists on the use of a pig in place of a human being for this sacrifice. In fact, there is some doubt as to whether, in the more remote regions, the spirits have accepted the substitute.

When the sign appears in the sky, all who have had trouble or death in the family during the year are invited to join in and to share in the expense of the ceremony. People come from near and far, and for several days they feast and dance at the house of the Datu. On the morning of the last day, they go to a great tree in the forest and make offerings of clothes, weapons, food, and betelnuts. When a human being was sacrificed, he was bound to a tree with his hands above his head, and all who shared in the ceremony took hold of the shaft of the spear which killed him. "It was always a decrepit slave, not good for anything else," the Bagobos say, and it is plain to see that they think the ways of Americans are strange.

But death is not a thing to be feared by the Bagobos. It is merely the passing of the soul down through the earth to another world directly below this. On its way it comes to a black river where its head and joints are bathed in the water. This takes away all desire to return to earth, and the soul is filled with peace and contentment.

In this Land of the Dead there is light when we have darkness on earth, and darkness when we have light. Life goes on much as it does on earth, and they use the clothes, weapons, and tools which the Bagobos bury with their dead. They plant and reap, work and play, only things are reversed, for it is in the darkness that the dead are active.

As soon as it becomes night on earth, and the sun goes down to shine on the place of the dead, they cease their activities. Each soul selects a broad leaf which he shapes something like a boat. Then he sits down on the leaf and waits till the hot rays of the sun cause him to melt and the leaf boat is full of water. Not until our day begins, and the Land of the Dead is enveloped in darkness, do the ghosts take up their activities again. When the sun rises on earth, each soul takes on his former shape, and life goes on as though there had been no interruption. While the Bagobos are not, as a rule, unkind to their slaves, they do not feel that killing one and sending him to a place like the Land of the Dead is cruel, especially if he is old and useless.

Nearly all peoples consider themselves the original ones, and the Bagobos are no exception. In the following tale, which is evidently very old, they account for their own origin and for that of their neighbors, and they have even added to the story to account for the white people.

In the beginning, the story goes, there lived one man and one woman, Toglai and Toglibon. Their first boy and girl went far away across the waters to live, and nothing more was heard of them till their descendants, the Spaniards and Americans, came back.

The other children remained with their parents at Cibolan on Mt. Apo till Toglai and Toglibon died and became spirits.

Soon after this a great drought came which lasted for three years. All the rivers dried up, and no plants could live. The children thought that the great spirit, Manama, was punishing them and they must seek other places to live. Two of them went toward the sunset till they reached a place of broad fields and abundant water, and there they made their home. Their children still live there. They are called Magindanau because of stones which the couple carried from Cibolan.

Two by two, the children of the first couple left the land of their birth, and in each place that they settled a new people arose. And so it happened that all the people on earth received their names from the things that the couples carried out of Cibolan, or from places were they settled.

All the children left Mt. Apo save two, a boy and a girl, who were too weak to travel. One day when they were just about to die from hunger and thirst, the boy crawled out and to his great surprise found a stalk of sugar-cane growing lustily. He cut it, and enough water came out to refresh him and his sister until the rains came. Because of this their children are called Bagobos.

And so it happens, according to these people, that all the people in the world are related to the Bagobos.

HORN OF THE FABLED CARABAO
This is said to be the horn of the animal for which the tribe is named.

ONE OF THE MOST ADVANCED of the primitive groups is the Menangkabau, a Malayan tribe living in Sumatra in the Dutch East Indies. Here is a place where woman actually has the last word. Here are a million and a half people living under a form of government where all descent and inheritance are through the mother.

The women are said to have equal rights with the men; they actually have a little more. In matters of state they have the same vote; but, in regard to the home, the lands, and the children, their word is almost absolute. In fact, the men are sometimes called homeless husbands because they are only visitors in the houses of their wives.

Partly because of their successful form of government, and partly because of the rich lands they inhabit, the Menangkabau have become a prosperous and happy people. They say that it is all due to the fact that they have followed the adat, or customs, of their ancestors.

Courtesy Field Museum of Natural History, Chicago

MENANGKABAU VILLAGE OF CENTRAL SUMATRA
Reproduction in Field Museum of Natural History.

These people occupy the Padang Highlands, a tableland in the western part of Sumatra; and, although the equator runs through their country, they are some three thousand feet above the sea, and the air is cool and bracing.

Three volcanoes surround their lands, Merapi, Singalang and Mt. Ophir, all teeming with tales of romance and adventure. It is from Mt. Ophir that Solomon is said to have secured the gold for his temple. Sailors of old, seeing its peak in the light of the setting sun, might well have believed it to be a mountain of gold.

It is smoking, restless Merapi, however, that is dearest to the hearts of the Menangkabau. According to their history, it was on this mountain, right after the flood, when only its smoking top rose out of the sea, that the ancestors of the Menangkabau first landed. Their leader, Seri Maharaja di Raja, was a very strong man who gave his people many good laws. As the waters subsided, the people moved farther and farther down the mountain sides. They cultivated the rich lands, followed the precepts of their ancestors, increased in numbers and became prosperous. They always remembered that Seri Maharaja had said, "To change the custom is like reaching for one grain of fallen rice and losing the whole plateful."

The country of the Menangkabau is not only one of the richest, but also one of the loveliest sections of the Indies. Rain falls almost every day the year around, and this means plenty of water for their rice. The little valleys are covered with a mosaic of fields which extend far up the mountain sides, and tiny waterfalls drop from one flooded area to another. The rice is in all stages of growth: the tender green shoots, newly transplanted, the rich green of the growing stalks, and the golden yellow of ripened grain.

In the midst of the rice fields, half hidden by clumps of coconut palms and banana trees, are groups of grass-roofed houses, their ridge poles turned up at the ends like the horns of the carabao. Near the houses are rice granaries with the same sort of curved roofs, and the fronts of these, as well as the fronts of some of the houses, are beautifully carved and painted in colors of red and yellow and black.

Courtesy Field Museum of Natural History, Chicago   Photo by Cole

TYPICAL SCENE IN THE LAND OF THE MENANGKABAU
These people live in the cool highlands of Central Sumatra.

Near the houses are fish ponds, some mere holes with earth embankments, some fine cement basins twenty feet square. Each family must have its fish, and the ponds are drained and restocked from time to time. They are much more than mere fish ponds, however. They are always in use. Women sit on the edges, vigorously rubbing wet garments on stone wash-boards, or scrubbing dishes with sand, and men, women, and children are taking baths with their clothes on. Water for cooking and drinking is also taken from these ponds.

In nearly every settlement the white minaret of a mosque rises among the palms, for these people are Mohammedan. Every Friday morning the men go to the mosque to worship, but the women, having no souls, are not allowed to enter.

The Menangkabau, like the Bagobos, are Malays, but, because their home in Sumatra was on the main route between India and the Spice Islands, they have been subject for centuries to outside

Courtesy Field Museum of Natural History, Chicago   Photo by Cole

RICE FIELDS
All rice is transplanted from seed beds into flooded fields.

MENANGKABAU FISH POND AND HOUSES
Fish ponds are found in every settlement where they serve also as the local water supply.

influences. As early as the second century A. D., Indian rulers had begun to extend their power to the coast of Sumatra, and by the eighth century they were exceedingly powerful. Later came Arabian traders who introduced Mohammedanism, writing, and many other elements of Arabian culture. Still later, European colonizers brought more ideas and products.

The Menangkabau, unlike the pygmy and the Bagobo, were willing to adopt many of the new ideas. Still they have retained many of their old customs and beliefs, some of which are directly opposed to Hinduism, Buddhism, and Mohammedanism. Influences from India, Arabia, and Europe are evident in much of their material culture, and account to a great extent for their high development, especially in some of the arts such as weaving and work in the precious metals.

Photo by Nieuwenhuis

MENANGKABAU VILLAGE ON A CRATER LAKE IN SUMATRA

Imported cotton cloth, purchased from Chinese merchants, is used for the everyday clothes of the Menangkabau, and, since it is washed in the fish ponds, it never looks very clean. But folded away in ancestral chests in their houses are exquisite cloths woven in silk and gold and silver threads, fine spun fibres of the goldsmith's art. On festive occasions, when the women are clad in these rich garments and their beautifully wrought jewelry, they present a gorgeous appearance. In fact, they give evidence of being a wealthy people.

Aside from land, cattle, and carabao, most of their riches are worn, since they have no banks. Many United States twenty-dollar gold pieces and English sovereigns hang on gold chains about their necks, and considerable amounts of gold are wrought into the bracelets, earrings, necklaces, and rings that adorn them. These riches, like the land, do not belong to individuals but to families, and they are handed down from one generation to another, through the mothers.

The inside of the Menangkabau house is as interesting as the outside. Across the front is one long living room, a common room used by all the members of the family. Opening off this, is a row of tiny bedrooms, one of which is occupied by the mother or head woman, while the others are given one to each daughter as

Photo by Nieuwenhuis

CARVED HOUSE
Menangkabau houses are often elaborately carved and painted. The curved roofs represent
the horns of a mythical buffalo.

she marries. So the mother and her daughters and their children
occupy the house, and here the husbands and fathers visit their
families, but they have no ownership in the house and nothing
to say about its management.

In the rear is a small, windowless kitchen containing a "stove,"
three stones sunk in a bed of ashes; and here the various families
cook their meals. Sometimes, if the family is too large, an addition
is built on to each end of the long house. A one-horn roof covers
each addition, and consequently there may be houses with eight
or ten horns on the roof.

Occasionally one of the daughters occupies a house next door.
Then the Menangkabau, who love maxims, explain, "The pot
and the spoon had a fight, so we built this daughter a house for
herself."

The sons of the family are allowed to sleep in the long living room of their mother's house if they care to, but unless they are ill or in bad repute they usually stay at the house of one of their wives.

WOMEN'S RIGHTS

Mohammedan law allows a man four wives, but Menangkabau law requires him to treat them all alike. He must never spend more time nor give more labor to one than he does to all the others. If one wife feels that she has been cheated, she gives her husband such a scolding when he comes to her for a meal that he never repeats the offense. She not only scolds him and tells him all the faults of his mother and sisters, but she does it in a voice which can be heard plainly through the thin walls of all the neighboring houses. A man truly eats from his wife's hand.

Division of labor is very pronounced by the Menangkabau. Both the men and the women know exactly what is required of

Courtesy Field Museum of Natural History, Chicago   Photo by Cole

CARABAO CART
In recent years roads have been constructed and wheeled vehicles introduced.

A MENANGKABAU RICE FIELD
The field is flooded and carabao are driven round and round until the soil is a soft mud.

them, and neither thinks of helping the other in his or her tasks. A man must prepare the fields, repair the fences, and help build or repair the houses of each of his wives. When this is done he has much leisure for rest or to take his bird for a walk. He does not even have worries over his own children. In fact, when a woman needs advice or help in the rearing of her children, she consults her eldest brother or her mother's brother, never her husband. A father's relationship to his children is belittled, for, as the proverbs say, "A rooster can lay no eggs," and "A mother is to her children as a hen to her chickens."

Woman's word is absolute in everything concerning the house and the family. In matters of government she has equal rights. Each house selects a man, usually the brother or eldest son of the mother, to act as adviser and father to the house and to represent it in a clan council. Several families, bound by blood ties, make up a clan which is governed by the various representatives of these houses. They, in turn, select one of their number to represent them in the council of the clans or phratry. The women attend the meetings and freely discuss the various questions that arise. All matters are settled according to the adat or custom.

They are an independent people. They have preserved for centuries their matriarchial form of government, and they will not be subservient to a ruler who disregards their custom. The Dutch have ruled them for about a hundred years, but even now the white brother is accepted as an equal, never a superior.

The carabao (kabau), or water buffalo, is a most important animal among the Menangkabau. Their very name is derived from it: the ridge poles of their houses curving up at the ends are symbolic of its horns: and their daily food is dependent largely on its strength.

AN ANCIENT BULL FIGHT

Many years ago, they tell you, a strong man came to their land in a boat, and he brought a carabao with him. When the animal had grown very large and powerful and had long pointed horns, the man said to the people, "I will wager that you have not a carabao in this land that can defeat mine. If you have I will give you all the contents of my boat; but, if yours is defeated, I shall henceforth be your ruler." The people were very much concerned, but they accepted the challenge and asked for seven days time. They took a baby carabao away from its mother and shut it up, so that it could not get any milk; and they made a spear with nine sharp points of iron.

On the morning of the contest they tied the spear in the mouth of the baby carabao and turned it loose. The half starved little creature, looking for food, ran as hard as he could and thrust the spear into the stomach of the strong man's great beast. The animal ran away in great agony, and the strong man was so ashamed that he fled, leaving his boat and all its contents for the winners. Since then they have been called Menangkabau (winning carabao).

In the little village of Menangkabau is a shiny, black horn which is kept carefully encased in a red velvet bag. This, the people say, is the horn of the carabao which gave them their name. The right to be custodian of this relic is hereditary and is the duty of a man, but his successor is always a nephew, never a son.

The carabao is the most awkward, sluggish creature imaginable, but it has the redeeming quality of being equally at home on land or in the water.

When it comes time to prepare a field for rice, the man repairs the embankments between the plots so that they will hold water, then he breaks the ground. Often he does this by driving from fifteen to twenty great carabao around and around over the flooded fields, their heavy feet sinking deeper and deeper into the soft ooze till finally the ground is broken and soft.

Then he plows. A great beast yoked to a crude plow moves at a snail's pace, while the man following guides it by a rope through

TAKING HIS
BIRD FOR A
WALK

Fighting pigeons are treated with great consideration, and men frequently are seen giving their birds a walk, carrying them around in a cage.

Photo by Nieuwenhuis

its nose and taps it with a small stick at every step. When this is done the man can rest and watch the women work.

This land of the Menangkabau gives the highest yield of rice of any in the East Indies, due partly to the volcanic soil and partly to their methods of farming. The women bring the young rice from the seed beds and stand knee-deep in the mud and water as they set it out spear by spear.

There are always women in the fields, for after the rice is transplanted the weeds must be kept out. When it begins to mature, the birds are a constant pest, and the women beat here and there with long poles to scare them away. In some fields are bamboo clappers connected by strings which radiate from a little bamboo house built high above the grain. A boy who sits and sings in the house occasionally gives the strings a jerk, and flocks of frightened birds rise up and fly to more quiet spots.

Still other fields look like fourth of July celebrations with flags of many colored cloths attached to bamboo poles floating in the breeze; and the hungry birds have no place to light.

The women cut the ripened grain by hand and stamp it with their bare feet to loosen the kernels from the straw. But they have one labor-saving device. While most Malay women pound out their rice by hand, the Menangkabau does it by water power. Huge wooden and bamboo wheels in streams are turned by the running water, and they raise heavy pestles which drop into long troughs of grain, loosening the husks. Then the grain is winnowed and is ready to cook.

The women work hard but nothing gives them more pleasure than to go to market with baskets of fine white rice. Growing rice, however, is only a part of their labors. They also raise tapioca and many vegetables which they gather and take to market. They do the family cooking, care for their children, and spend long hours at the loom. Yet they rarely appear weary, and they always have time to visit with their friends.

The men appear to have much leisure for visiting and bird fights, their favorite sport. Often they are seen on the roads or the narrow trails carrying their fighting pigeons in flat round cages of bamboo. Beautifully embroidered gold cloths, weighted

Photo by Nieuwenhuis

A SUGAR MILL
The cane is crushed between the heavy wooden cylinders and the juice pressed out.

down with silver tassels, cover the cages to protect the birds from the hot sun, and the men handle them with great care.

Sometimes they are merely taking the birds for a walk; sometimes they are going for a practice fight, but on Thursdays they are all headed in one direction. They are seeking a certain narrow trail which leads over the embankments between rice fields far out to a tightly enclosed bamboo shelter where regular fights take place.

These contests are not exciting. Sometimes the birds refuse to fight at all and then the betting is on the number of coos they give in a certain time. Still, pigeon and cock fights appear to be the most enjoyable things in life to the men. Like most Malays, they love to bet, and, win or lose, they have a good time. Fortunately they cannot risk the family property, since that is in the hands of the women; and if a man wishes to risk his weekly allowance on the coos of a bird, that is his affair.

While, in general, the men appear to have much leisure, many of them are fine artisans and, aside from the cloth, most of the things of beauty in their culture are the results of their ingenuity. Goldsmiths spin the fine threads of gold and silver that are woven into cloth; they manufacture by hand the beautiful rings, bracelets, earrings, and other ornaments worn. Brass casters make the elaborate betel-nut boxes and bowls, as well as brass pots for cooking rice. Blacksmiths pound out iron and fashion long work knives and axes, cleverly inlaying edges of tempered steel. Wood carvers sit long hours working with gouges and dies, making the beautiful panels that adorn their rooms or form the fronts of houses and rice granaries.

It is the men, too, who raise the tobacco. This plant so exhausts the soil that it can be planted in the same field only once in seven years, and the tobacco beds are far up the mountain side where rice will not grow. Tobacco factories are found in little bamboo sheds near the fields. Boys rip out the center spine and roll the leaves into small bundles which are allowed to cure for a few days. The bundles are spread on bamboo frames and set out in the dew and the sun for two days and two nights before they are ready for sale. Much of their tobacco is shipped to Java, Singapore, and the Straits Settlements.

Men also gather cinnamon bark. The lovely touches of color scattered throughout the country are the tops of cinnamon trees. The green leaves of the lower branches shade into lighter green, then pink, and the tops are a brilliant red giving them the appearance of giant poinsettia plants. Every settlement has some; and the housewife, when she wishes a bit of flavoring, runs out and cuts a chunk from the bark of a tree. The bark for sale is stripped off and curls as it dries in the sun. The sticks, a meter long, are bound into large bundles which the women carry to market on their heads. Export buyers take it to the coast whence it is shipped to Holland and other countries. It is not the finest quality and is used in soaps and to adulterate better grades of cinnamon.

THE MONKEY WORKS

The work of gathering coconuts is done by monkeys. Men, to be sure, aid and abet these creatures, but the actual work is done by these trained animals. Not every family possesses a monkey, so a man owning one goes about hiring him out.

Threatened and urged by his master on the ground, the monkey, attached to a rope, climbs a tall tree, and when he reaches the top he sits down on a leaf and surveys the landscape. After much urging from the ground he paws the various nuts, and when a desired one is touched, the cord is jerked, whereupon the monkey twists and chews till the nut drops to the ground. It is a slow process, but time means little to a Menangkabau, and it is an easy

MONKEY
CLIMBING A
COCONUT
TREE

Monkeys are trained to gather the ripe nuts.

Photo by Cole

Courtesy Field Museum of Natural History, Chicago   Photo by Cole

COCONUT GATHERERS
The monkey climbs the tree and throws down the nuts, while the man rests in the shade
below and gives directions.

way of harvesting nuts. The owner of the monkey receives one out of every ten he gathers, and the monkey is rewarded with a choice bit of food.

Menangkabau men are courageous hunters. They go out, sometimes a hundred or more at a time, to an open spot on the mountain side. Dogs hunt about in a ravine below till they scare up a wild boar, and the men and dogs join in the chase up the mountain. Finally a man stabs the beast with a short spear, but often it has already killed several of the dogs and wounded some of the men with its huge tusks.

AN OPEN-AIR DEPARTMENT STORE

Saturday is the great day in Menangkabau land. It is the time of the big market at Bukid Tinggi which is in the center of their country. Smaller markets are held on different days in various places, but on Saturday is the "big market" when people come from near and far. Often from fifty to sixty thousand people attend this one event, gathering like swarms of ants from all directions. From daylight on, the roads and trails are alive with people. Balancing great loads on their heads, women take strong, quick strides as they make their way over mountain trails from other valleys, along the narrow embankments between flooded fields, by wagon road and river ford.

There are men, too, moving more slowly, as a rule. Some have bundles, some have bark baskets of tiny fish suspended from poles across their shoulders. If they stop to rest on the way, they constantly rock the baskets of water, lest the little fish die for want of oxygen.

Men, women, and children make their way to the great open-air department store which is somewhat protected from the sun by the open sheds and spreading waringin trees. Everything that the Menangkabau heart could wish is to be found at this market.

There are bananas, coconuts, papayas, oranges, limes, mangosteens. There are vegetables and meat, tapioca and cakes of brown sugar, betel-nut and leaves to roll it in. There are fish, tiny dried ones, thin as paper, large ones cut in chunks, and middle-sized, lying on mats out in the sun. There are the evil-smelling duriens.

In the spice department are nutmegs, cloves, mace, and cinnamon besides ground pepper black, white, and red. Twenty or thirty women sit on the ground behind cloths spread with peppers —red, green, short, and long. Bunches of pepper plants are for sale, for the Menangkabau love highly seasoned concoctions to eat on their rice. Clean, smooth banana leaves are used for wrapping paper. Coffee is sold in the berry, either roasted or green; and the leaves are for sale strung on sticks, for the Menangkabau use coffee leaves steeped like tea.

There are brass, iron, gold and silver departments, baskets, and carved wood. Cotton cloth of every hue occupies a large department. Tailors with hand-power sewing machines wait to make it up, with no respect for fit or hang. Gay pantaloons, held by a single string, dangle about the legs of the men, effecting a garment midway between shirt and trousers.

The tobacco department is very popular. Tobacco is sold either in the leaf or rolled into match-size cigars. Great care is exercised in the selection of smokes. Some packages contain one or

Courtesy Field Museum of Natural History, Chicago

TIGER TRAP

Tigers are held in high regard but if they begin to prey on the villages they are caught in traps and killed.

Photo by Cole

THE GREAT MARKET IN CENTRAL SUMATRA
As many as fifty thousand people sometimes attend this market.

two more pieces than others, and when a man is allowed only fifty cents a week spending money by each wife, he cannot afford to be careless, especially if he has only two or three wives.

These thousands of men and women spend the day in this market, buying and selling, but mostly bartering and gossiping. "How much?" is the invariable question when a customer approaches a saleswoman. A figure is named, and however reasonable it may be it brings forth a battle of words. Half the fun of going to market would be spoiled if the first price were paid.

A short section of bamboo is used to measure out the rice, but no two measures seem the same size. Many women have two, one for buying and a smaller one for selling. Evidences of civilization are seen in the condensed-milk cans used by some for measures. These are particularly desirable, since the bottom is easily bent.

Those used for selling have the bottom bent up, while in those for buying it is pushed down. These little devices are not deceits, for everybody knows them, and they only add zest to the day's bargaining.

Cattle and carabao are sold for slaughtering or for work, and this sale takes place in an open space near the market. Prospective buyers examine the animals and argue long and vehemently. All offers are made in secret, the owner holding a cloth beneath which he grasps the hand of the buyer, and bystanders may not know what price is paid. It is a slow process, for they are keen traders.

MENANGKABAU WOMEN GOING TO MARKET
Amongst this group, all loads are carried on the head.

Photo by Cole

Photo by Cole

MENANGKABAU MEN CARRYING BASKETS OF FISH
Minnows for restocking the fish ponds are sold at market.

At night they all straggle home. They have sold their produce and acquired full baskets. Live chickens and ducks lie peacefully on the top of baskets on beds of pepper plants, bananas, fried grasshoppers, sugar cakes, and fish. Men and women know that they have made good bargains; they are happy and contented, looking forward to the next Saturday.

THE WOMAN PROPOSES

When a girl has reached a marriageable age, her family selects a husband for her. They make the proposal to his family and offer a dowry which consists, usually, of about six guilders and a sarong. If he accepts, the bride's family arranges the wedding which may last for a week or more, according to their wealth. The Mohammedan service takes place first, when the religious man reads from the Koran and asks both parties if they are agreeable to the marriage. After this formality, the bridegroom is not much in evi-

dence. In fact he stays much of the time at the home of his mother, while the bride and her bridesmaids have the party. Many relatives and friends gather, and there is feasting, dancing, and general festivity. If the bride's family owns rich rice lands, they may
kill a carabao for the occasion, and there are fried bananas, coconut concoctions, and fancy cakes.

The bride and her bridesmaids are dressed in all the family
jewels, exquisite old cloths of gold and silver, heavy gold bracelets

A
MENANG-
KABAU BRIDE
Gold cloth and jew-
els adorn the bride
and bridesmaids.

Photo by Nieuwenhuis

2

Photo by Nieuwenhuis
HEADMEN DANCING AT A WEDDING
Instead of dancing girls the Menangkabau have dancing men at their great festivals.

Courtesy Field Museum of Natural History, Chicago

A CHICKEN FIGHT
This is the favorite sport of the men.

and necklaces, while their fingers are covered with huge rings. The bride wears a gorgeous gold crown, while her maids have gold headbands folded to represent the horns of the carabao.

At all the festivities the women sit on one side of the room and the men on the other. All the gold cloth and ornaments belonging to any of the families represented are worn, even the men having gold cloth sashes. The headmen appear in formal attire—huge black sateen trousers, black crepe caps, betel-nut bags of gold embroidery, and silver-headed canes. According to custom they sit on the floor at the left of the door at all functions. Dancing men, instead of dancing girls, entertain the guests, their performances being mostly rhythmic stepping about and graceful posturing with the arms. A bridegroom sometimes looks very bored, for marriage may occur quite a number of times in his life.

Divorce is easier than marriage in Menangkabau land. A husband may say to his wife in the presence of two headmen, "I divorce you," and the marriage is annulled. If within three months and ten days the couple wish to be remarried, they have the privilege. A second time a man may divorce his wife and she may remarry him in the same way; but the third time she cannot remarry him until she has first been wedded to another.

For more than three centuries the Menangkabau have been Mohammedans, but they still have a strong belief in magic. They make offerings to ward off evil spirits and to please those who are able to bring abundant crops and good health. They believe in certain charms of combined pagan and Mohammedan power, and they pay big sums for tiny cloth bags containing passages from the Koran which they wear about their necks to ward off illness.

A sickly child is believed to be disliked by the spirits, and, to fool them and pretend that she does not care for the child, a mother may change his name to some such derogatory term as "Horse's Tail." Then, they say, he is sure to grow well and strong.

Earthquakes are a bad sign. They cause illness and fire, and they also prevent eggs from hatching. So the people do all they can to prevent them. The earth, they say, is like an egg resting on the horns of a bull. When he is tired he shakes his head and

that causes the earth to tremble. If the people run out of their
houses and beat loudly on brass trays, the bull will soon become
quiet, and the earth will cease to shake.

There are magicians among the Menangkabau who are believed to be very powerful. They control certain spirits, and they
can make it rain or shine. They can cure illness caused by magic,
or they can make a person lame by saying a charm over his footprints. They can go to unfriendly towns and make the enemies
go out and cut down their banana trees, because the trees look like
wild pigs to them.

Certain of the people are trained to do torture dances under
the direction of a magician. They put red-hot chains about their
necks without being burned, and drive knives into their bodies
without drawing blood. The people are very credulous and have
a very wholesome respect for the magicians.

It is not uncommon, the Menangkabau say, for a man to turn
into a tiger. Sometimes tigers protect the people, especially if they
are fed, but at other places they are to be greatly feared. They

Photo by Cole

BEAUTIFULLY CARVED RICE GRANARIES OF THE MENANGKABAU
IN SUMATRA

tell, with great alarm, of a tiger-man who came to a village on the slopes of Mt. Merapi and killed ten people. Magic words, if said quickly, will save a man's life at such a time. But they must be said very quickly.

Men may turn into wild pigs when they die. Whenever hunters kill a pig which has teeth sharpened like those of the Menangkabau they know that formerly he was a man.

So the Menangkabau, far advanced in some ways, are very primitive in others. Their great numbers are all well fed and cared for, and through their industry they are able to export some of their produce. Through their own initiative and their contacts with others, they have become a prosperous and happy people.

To them there is but one explanation for this well-being. It is due to the fact that they have followed the adat, the customs laid down by their forefathers. "When we stand, we stand together; and when we sit down, we sit down together," say the Menangkabau, which means that all are equal.

T HE HAIRY AINU OF JAPAN is one of the strangest groups in the world. They are not like any other people and no one knows where they came from nor when.

In the earliest Japanese writing, telling how the Japanese conquered and subjugated the first inhabitants of the Islands, we read, "When our august ancestors came down from Heaven in a boat, they found the Ainu."

So far as the Ainu themselves are concerned, they have been in Japan since the beginning of time. They have no records. They have no form of writing whatever, not even picture writing. They have a tradition, however, of a race of dwarfs who used to live in their country, whom their ancestors finally drove out. These dwarfs, they say, belonged in the Stone Age and occupied the pits which archaeologists have investigated all over northern Japan. These people were so small, the Ainu claim, that as many as ten of them could be sheltered under one burdock leaf during a shower. Burdock leaves in this country are large, some of them measuring four feet across, but even so the pit dwellers must have been small.

It is thought that the Ainu at one time may have occupied all Japan, for geographic names in the Ainu language are found from the south to the Kurile Islands in the far north. Even the sacred mountain, Fujiyama, an extinct volcano, derives its name from the Ainu "Fuchi," Goddess of Fire.

The Japanese, through a long period of warfare, exterminated, absorbed, or drove back the aborigines till today less than twenty thousand of them remain, and they are mostly in the island of Yezo which is north of Honshu, the main island of the Empire.

The language of the Ainu is no help in trying to solve their origin, for it shows no relationship to any other known speech. Nor do they look like anyone else. The Japanese called them dog-men because their bodies are covered with hair, and because of a myth that their mother was a maiden and their father was a dog.

Ainu men are only about five feet and three inches in height, and the women are shorter still, but both are extremely stocky with thick, heavy ribs. Their eyes are brown or hazel in color and not at all the shape of the Mongolians. Their skin is lighter than that of the northern Chinese and the Japanese. In fact it is more the color of a tanned white man.

Their thick, coarse hair is usually black and quite wavy, and as the men grow old their beards become very curly.

But the thing which distinguishes them from all their neighbors is the hairiness of their bodies. Besides heavy beards and mustaches, the men have a quantity of black hair all over their bodies, while the women have short black hair on their limbs. The beards of the men are coarse, matted, and far from clean, but by the use of a finely carved bamboo "lifter" at meal time they are able to keep their mustaches out of the soup.

WOMEN LOOK LIKE MEN

The women, having no hair on the face, tattoo bluish-black marks around the mouth to resemble mustaches. Tattooing is a painful process and is accomplished little by little. The center of the upper lip is done first, then the lower, and this is extended from time to time till it reaches almost to the ears. Gashes are cut

AN AINU MAN OF NORTHERN JAPAN

AN AINU GROUP

The Ainu are the aborigines of Japan. Although they possess some Mongoloid features, they differ radically from all other people of Eastern Asia.

in the flesh and soot, scraped from a kettle hung over a birch-bark fire, is rubbed in to give the bluish-black color.

The women tattoo their arms, also, to frighten away the demons of disease. They learned this custom from the sister of Aioina, their culture hero, who came down from the sky with her brother and told them that the wives of all the supernatural beings were decorated in this way. Now, they say, when the demons come and find the Ainu women tattooed, they mistake them for immortals and flee.

Both men and women have their hair cut just above their shoulders and wear metal or strips of colored cloth in slits in their ears. Their dress is similar also. Ankle length coats with wide sleeves are worn by both, but the designs embroidered on them differ, those of the men being more elaborate. These coats are held at the waist by embroidered girdles.

2

The cloth, which is made on primitive looms, is woven from bark fiber and is a dirty brown in color. The bark is peeled off the elm trees and soaked in water for about ten days, till it becomes soft and the threads can be separated. They are dried in the sun, tied together, and wound into balls for future use. The cloth is very strong when damp but becomes brittle when dry. Thread for sewing is bark fiber chewed until it is round and pliable, but for embroidery Japanese material is used.

Snow covers the country of the Ainu for about half the year, but the summers are extremely hot, and a heavy rainfall creates excessive humidity. During this season children go about quite naked, and adults remove part of their clothes because of the heat, though they never take them off for cleaning purposes. In winter the skins or furs of birds, seals, bears, and other animals are sewed together into sleeveless garments which are worn over the coats; and underwear of deer skin is often worn. They go barefoot in summer or, if they are going on a journey, wear sandals of walnut bark; but in winter they have moccasins or boots of leather or salmon skin stuffed with straw to keep their feet warm. Leggings of bark or skins protect their legs from insects in summer and cold in winter.

Snow shoes are in common use and are of two kinds, one of wood, resembling a ski five or six feet long, the other of woven bear skin thongs on an oval wooden frame, for use when the snow is very loose.

The country of the Ainu is mountainous and has a number of volcanoes, some of which are still active. Earthquakes are frequent, caused, they say, by the movements of a giant fish on whose back the earth rests.

The rich volcanic soil is covered with forests of evergreen and deciduous trees such as the willow, oak, walnut, elm, birch, chestnut, and many others, while in places there is a thick undergrowth of scrub bamboo. The Ainu live mostly in villages along the seacoast and on the banks of the larger rivers. Viewed from a distance, the clusters of thatched huts are quite picturesque.

AN AINU GENTLEMAN

The Ainu are the most hairy of human beings. Men wear heavy beards, and their bodies are well covered with short black hairs.

HOUSES HAVE FEELINGS

They are very particular to have all their houses of one type, for the first hut was brought from the sky by the Goddess of Fire as a pattern. Moreover, each house has its own individual life, and it would not like to be different. When it ceases to exist in this world it will live in the next and be for the use of those who occupied it on earth.

The average hut is about ten by twelve feet. The roof is always built first, both men and women working diligently. When it is completed, they raise it to rest on posts standing six or seven feet above the ground. Then they cover both roof and sides with thatch, and make covers for the windows of rushes or reeds. Entrance to the house is through an anteroom or shed where the tools, firewood, and dogs are kept. This is always on the west, while on the east, which is sacred, must be a window.

In the center of the room is a rectangular hearth, slightly depressed, sacred to the Goddess of Fire who came down from the sky to watch over mankind. She gives warmth and oversees the cooking. Fire, sacred to her, is saluted before and after meals, and the first thing in the morning. One must be careful neither to spit in the fire, nor drop a hair or nail parings in it, nor should one point a sharp stick at it, for these acts would be disrespectful to the Goddess.

There is no chimney in the house, and the smoke, or part of it at least, escapes through a hole in the roof. On a wicker platform above the fire, fish, meat, and vegetables are dried or smoked. The floor is covered with mats woven of grass or reeds, and near the door are the water buckets and household utensils.

Crude benches made of planks along the side walls serve as beds. The people have no bedding, so they sleep with their clothes on. In winter, with the wind whistling through the frail structures, they must huddle close together for warmth. Fleas infest the beds but are tolerated because of their divine origin. Snakes glide along the rafters in search of mice. In summer the place swarms with insects.

AN AINU DWELLING
The thatch houses are all of one type and are under the protection of special spirits.

Still each house seems attractive not only to the Goddess of Fire but also to her husband, a guardian spirit known as the Ancestral Governor of the House who resides in the sacred northeast corner. In this corner are kept the family treasures, heirlooms, sacred objects, bows and arrows, fishing implements, all decorated with fetishes.

The east window is peculiarly sacred. Prayers to supernatural beings or to ancestors must be offered through this window. Birds, bears or deer killed must be taken into the hut through it. Care is taken that nothing is carelessly thrown through it, and one never should look through it into a house. Just outside this window, several feet from the hut, is the "sacred hedge," a picket-like structure made of inao and the skulls of animals.

Inao, found near the hearth, on the seashore, by the roadside, are a peculiar type of fetish, a link between man and the gods. They are whittled from willow wands two or three feet long, and

THE AINU MAN
WEARS EAR
RINGS

Courtesy American
Museum of Natural
History, New York

the shavings are left attached to curl up in clusters. Sometimes they are crude representations of the human figure, the one to the Ancestral Governor of the House having a slit for a mouth and a coal from the hearth for a heart.

When a new house is completed it is the time for a great house-warming and worship of the ancestors. Women prepare food while men whittle inao and bring saké, the fermented drink made by the Japanese from rice, for no religious observance can take place without quantities of millet beer and saké, of which they are all too fond.

Supernatural beings, inside and out, are worshipped and propitiated. Inao are hung by the fireside, near the sleeping benches, in the northeast corner, at the doorway, for they are the "house pulse" preserving life in every part of the dwelling. No spirit may be left out lest he be jealous or angry and take vengeance by bringing disease and death, misfortune or famine. The spirit of the water spring may take away all the water, or the one who watches over the beds might prevent the family from sleeping.

The men go about from place to place—to the shrines of the Goddess of Fire, the spirit of the treasures, the pots, water tubes,

AN AINU HOUSE

doors and windows, the east and west ends of the hut, to the out-side, to the spring, the garden plot, to trees, and at each spot they dip their mustache lifters into the wine and let fall three double drops to the guardian spirit. When all have been propitiated the men return to the hut to eat and drink, and they give a little wine to the women. When the supernatural beings have been rightly treated, they are supposed to do their part, but if they fail they are often scolded and even threatened with having no more liba-tions offered them.

Women are never allowed to pray, for the men fear their power with the supernatural beings. Men know that their lazi-ness causes the work of their wives to be harder, that their inveter-ate love for saké and millet beer brings ruin to their families, and they do not want the women to tell this to the spirits. As for the ancestors, that is different. People who have died still live in spirit, and unless they are treated well they may harm the living, so the women are free to offer food and drink to those deceased.

The regular meals of the Ainu consist of a light breakfast at dawn and a heavy meal at night. Salmon is sometimes smoked over the hearth fire or dried, and occasionally fish is roasted on spits, but for the most part they eat stew. Fish, roots, seeds, game, seaweed, the flesh of surplus dogs are all dumped, from time to time, into the large iron kettle which hangs over the fire.

When it is time to eat all the members of the family, together with any guests, bring their wooden cups and sit around the hearth. The housewife ladles up the stew into the individual cups, and they eat. When they have finished each person wipes out his cup with his index finger and licks it off, then he replaces the cup near his bed until the next meal. The kettle is rarely cleaned, just more ingredients added to what remains. Housekeeping is simple.

They do not make pottery. The iron knives which they secure from the Japanese make carving possible, and they have ladles, mustache lifters, mortars and pestles, and some utensils carved from wood. Buckets and dippers are made of bark stitched into shape.

They have little need of water, for, though they may wash their hands on ceremonial occasions, they never do it for cleanliness. In fact, they consider washing an admission of filth, and, since they do not consider themselves dirty, why wash? The inside of their houses smells of the fish drying or decomposing in the rafters, of the refuse near the door, of smoke, of clothing perspiration and fish stained, of unwashed bodies. A traveler to an Ainu village wrote, "I poked my nose into several of the huts along the beach. This was a mistake on my part, for in Ainu country the nose is the last thing one ought to poke in anywhere."

To the Ainu, however, his odor partakes somewhat of his personality. Aioina, their first ancestor and culture hero, is believed to have come down from the sky to teach them how to make utensils, how to hunt and fish, and to perform religious rites and ceremonies. By some his name is interpreted as "a person smelling of the Ainu," and this story is told. It seems that, when Aioina was on earth teaching the people all they now know, he lived as the Ainu do, slept in their houses, wore the same clothes, ate the same food. After he had completed his task on earth he went

Courtesy Field Museum of Natural History, Chicago

INTERIOR OF AN AINU DWELLING
Note the mustaches tattooed on the lips of the women.

back to the sky, but he forgot to take off his earthly clothes. Soon all the supernatural beings came near him, sniffing their noses and inquiring where the smell of Ainu (man) came from. Finally they discovered that it came from Aioina, and he was requested to go back to earth and remove his garments. After he had done so, he returned to the sky and was once more well received.

It was Aioina, too, they say, who dissuaded them from being cannibals. Formerly they ate all flesh raw—bears, deer, fish, and even their own people. But when Aioina came and taught them how to make bows and arrows, fish spears, and other useful things, he told them that they must cook all kinds of flesh before eating it, and they must never again eat human flesh.

EVEN THE DOGS GO FISHING

The Ainu have always been great fish and meat eaters. They gather clams, crabs, oysters, and lobsters along the shore. They build dams and set traps in the streams. They go out in boats, dragging bait along the bottom, or setting crude decoys. These boats are dugouts of oak with planks added to increase their height. The sides are lashed in place through holes burnt in the wood, and the cracks are calked with moss, making them sturdy in rough weather; while the sterns are carved and painted, making them pleasing to the gods of the sea and the souls of the fish. Anchors of wood are weighted with stones.

With harpoons and clever spears having detachable heads, they obtain large fish, even sharks, seals, and whales, the prongs of the spears being poisoned for the latter. At night they carry torches which attract fish within reach of their spears; and in winter they fish with hook and line through the ice. Every device is employed and every religious requirement fulfilled to secure fish, their main food.

Until the Japanese came, dogs were the only domesticated animals known to the Ainu, and they trained them to assist men in fishing and hunting. Trained dogs will swim out into the water in two rows several hundred feet apart, and at a certain call from the men they will turn and swim toward one another and in the direction of the shore, driving the fish by their splashing. When they reach shallow water, each dog seizes a fish and carries it to his master who gives him its head as his reward.

Upon the capture of certain fish, feasts are held and inao used. Prayers are offered and thanks given to the sea-god for his assistance and to the fish for being caught. The soul of the fish is also begged to come again, for if well treated it may return to animate other fish.

The great god of the sea sometimes allows himself to be seen by man in the form of the very largest of whales. He is greatly revered and offered inao and much saké, especially during the fishing season. He has two servants who appear in the form of the tortoise and the albatross, and who act as messengers between the people and their master. During the fishing season, particularly, inao are presented and quantities of saké are offered and drunk for them. These messengers may be caught and eaten, their souls transferring into other bodies, but the heads are dried and kept in the house where they are taken out and worshipped before each fishing trip.

Salmon is the most prized of all fish having come, originally, directly from the sky; and the favorite of all pursuits is salmon fishing. Boys begin when very young to practice with fish spears, and one of the few games played by the Ainu is believed to train the eye for this work. A hoop about six inches in diameter is rolled between two rows of men. With imitation spears they attempt to pierce the hoop as it passes, and when a man on one side succeeds, that side demands a man from the other row. This they achieve quickness and accuracy.

When the salmon run, men go out in groups and stand along the banks of the river in the water, watching, and when a fish swims up, they throw their spears. They also use traps and nets. When they go after salmon they always carry thick willow sticks for killing them, for they claim that salmon do not like to be killed with a stone or any wood other than the willow. But these fish, they say, are very fond of being killed with a willow stick. When a certain kind of salmon is killed, its head is placed on a tray before the fire and worshipped.

Since the life of the Ainu centers so much around fishing, the fact that they are being deprived of it more and more is given as one reason for their decrease in numbers and the loss of much of their vitality. The Japanese use herring and even salmon for fertilizer on their soil, and as the export trade in fish increases, they have established more and more canning factories along the coasts. The Ainu, they find, have the most choice fishing areas, and, in order to secure these grounds, the Japanese try to interest the primitive people in agriculture, even sending in experts to teach them the methods of raising vegetables. "Eat your spinach," say the Japanese. But the Ainu do not like spinach: they want fish.

Nearly a hundred different kinds of wild plants add variety to their diet—fruits, berries, nuts, seeds, and roots. Chestnuts boiled and pounded into a paste are mixed with fish roe for a delicacy.

The roots of the dog-tooth violet are boiled, dried, and pounded into flour for cakes.

Meat, however, stands next to fish in importance, and hunting provides them with much of their food. The bow and arrow is their chief weapon, and for larger game the points are poisoned. The arrow heads, which are fitted into notched and feathered shafts, may be of bamboo, bone, or iron, the bamboo being so hard that it will penetrate wooden planks. The ancestors of the Ainu used stone arrowheads, adzes, and hammers, but for the past two centuries, since iron has been available, the art of stone work has been forgotten.

They do not know how to work in iron, but they trade their fish, furs, and stag horns with the Japanese for ironware, as well as for ornaments and saké. Measuring and counting are simple with them. Distance is reckoned by steps, quantity by handfuls. Their numerical system is based on twenty instead of ten, and eight hundred is the highest number they know. They have no money or other medium of exchange, but they do know how to barter.

Deer are becoming scarce since the Japanese have been hunting them with guns, and the Ainu are finding them more and more difficult to secure. Both deer and bear are sometimes caught in traps so constructed that when the animal touches a string a bow is released and a poisoned dart is shot. Also deer are hunted with the aid of trained dogs, or sometimes the hunters lure them within arrow reach by imitating their calls on a clever instrument made of wood and skin. Pitfalls, well concealed, sometimes catch large animals.

BEAR HUNTING

Killing a bear in his den is, perhaps, the most dangerous thing the Ainu do, and it requires great courage on the part of the hunters. Before setting out on such an expedition, the chief and elders meet together with offerings and prayers to propitiate the supernatural beings. They appeal to the spirits of the mountains, of the rivers, the spring, and the fire, all to aid and protect the hunters and to grant them success.

The hunters set out in the early spring, while the bears are still hibernating. They search till they locate a den, then try to tempt the bear out. If they are not successful in this, a hunter binds up his head and face, enters the den, and jabs the bear with his knife until he drives him outside. Often the man is badly scratched or injured in doing this. As the angry bear emerges, the other hunters pelt him with poisoned arrows. Then comes the most dangerous time, for, before the poison takes effect, the enraged beast fights and claws at the hunters who strike with knives and spears. When it finally succumbs, the heart and regions affected by the poison are buried to keep them from the dogs. Inao are offered and thanks given for the successful kill. The meat is divided among the hunters, the head, breast, and viscera going to the one who has most distinguished himself. When the men return to the village, a feast is held, and, if any of the party have been killed, the feast becomes a mourning affair.

Each village has its recognized fishing and hunting grounds. Formerly many feuds developed over these, and the chief led his warriors into battle, the women accompanying them and proving especially valuable in fighting the women of the enemy. In addition to bows and arrows, in these battles, they used daggers, and war clubs made of hard wood weighted with stones.

ETIQUETTE

Though crude and barbarous in many of their practices, the Ainu are very particular about their social etiquette. A woman meeting a man uncovers her head, puts her right hand over her mouth, and looks at the ground in silence. Women always back out of the presence of men, for it is bad manners to turn one's back, and men leave their hosts by walking sideways. When a man greets a male guest, the two sit cross-legged on the floor facing each other for an hour or so, each rubbing his palms together and stroking his beard, while he makes rumbling noises in his throat and asks polite questions. Finally they relax into ordinary conversation. A woman greets a visitor by drawing the index finger of her right hand up the left arm to the shoulder and thence across the upper lip, ending by stroking the hair behind her ear.

AN AINU SALUTATION
Though rude in many of their practices, the Ainu are very particular about their
social etiquette.

An Ainu doesn't even use his head to say yes and no. Instead
of nodding when he means "yes" he brings both hands to his chest
and waves them downward. To say "no" he passes the right hand
back and forth across his chest.

The father is the authority in the household, and property
descends from father to son, with the exception of household
utensils and clothes which go to the daughters.

Each village is ruled by a chief whose position is hereditary,
provided his son or brother possesses the necessary qualifications
of courage, strength, and intelligence. If not, the elders elect another man to fill the position. The chief lives in a large hut, has
several wives, and enjoys considerable prestige. He takes the lead
in hunting, fishing, and warfare, presides at ceremonies, settles
disputes, and judges crimes, but his decisions are not absolute. A

council of elders has the right to veto his judgments. Women are allowed to attend the council meetings but they have no power.

Blood feuds never arise among the Ainu; in fact, serious crimes are rare, and individuals usually settle their disputes themselves. When an offense is serious enough to arouse the village, a public trial is held at the home of the chief. For several days they discuss the matter, and finally the chief with the advice of the elders pronounces judgment and fixes the penalty.

TRIAL BY ORDEAL

Ordeals are sometimes resorted to in order to determine guilt, or in case a person is proven guilty but refuses to confess. The death penalty is never inflicted, for death is not considered a punishment. Pain and disgrace are much worse than death. In fact, a criminal will sometimes commit suicide rather than go through an ordeal. To determine guilt, a suspect may be required to thrust his arm into a kettle of boiling water or to hold a hot stone in his hand. If he is not burned, he is innocent. Or he may be ordered to drink a cup of water and throw the cup over his shoulder. If it lights right side up, he is innocent; if not, he is guilty.

In case of theft the culprit must return the value of the stolen goods and receive a flogging. If he repeats the offense, he may be ostracized from the community and have the tip of his nose cut off. This is in case he steals from another Ainu; theft from a foreigner is considered praiseworthy. A murderer may be crippled for life by having the tendons of his feet cut, or he may be deprived of an ear or his nose. An ordeal for women is to make them smoke several pipes of tobacco, emptying the ashes into a cup of water which they must drink without becoming sick.

It is said that the Ainu never laugh. Even their games take on something of the aspect of an ordeal. The men may amuse themselves for a half a day at a time, beating one another on the bare back with war clubs. The man who can stand the most blows wins the contest.

The people have little in the way of song or dance. Sometimes they sing to drive off evil spirits, or when they are doing a monotonous task like rowing a boat or pounding grain, or an account of one's exploits may be given in a sort of chant, but they have no real songs nor any idea of tunes. There are no musical instruments except the shaman's drum and a bamboo jew's-harp used by the children.

Dancing among the Ainu also lacks gaiety and consists mostly of imitating the calls and movements of some bird and bending the body forward and backward as far as possible.

FIRST DUTIES OF A FATHER

The Ainu have a peculiar custom when a child is born. The mother must remain quiet for six days and the father must do likewise for twelve. For the first six days he may go to the hut of some friend and rest by the fireplace; he must not drink wine or call upon the supernatural beings. At the end of this period he returns home, but he must remain quiet by his own hearth for six days more. The child is believed to acquire its body strength from the mother, but the spirit life and intellect come from the father during the twelve days after birth. Following the first six days many inao are made and offered to the gods of the west doorway, who are the ones that look after the birth of children.

When man was first created, according to their lore, his body was made of earth, his hair of chickweed, and his spine of a stick of willow; and the life of each person has its seat in his spine or willow. As soon as a child is born, his grandfather goes to the river bank and cuts a green stick of willow which he cuts and shaves into an inao. This he worships, beseeching it to watch over the child while he is growing up and to give him strength and long life. With great reverence he stands the willow by the bedside of the baby whose guardian spirit it is. This inao is worshipped all through life, particularly at times of sickness.

Naming a child is extremely difficult, for the title must not be like that of anyone living or dead. A name is a living thing, identified so closely with the person possessing it that when a person dies, his name dies with him, and it must never be spoken again. A woman never speaks her husband's name, for to the Ainu it would be equal to killing him. She speaks of him as "my man" or "my person at the upper end of the hearth."

A child must not be called after a living person, for that would be theft. A name brings good luck or ill to a person, and if a child is sickly or unfortunate they know that the name was not a happy choice, and it is changed. This, they say, outwits the evil spirits, for when they come inquiring for the person called so-and-so, no one can be found by that name, and the spirit leaves. After they are fed, babies are kept much of the time in wooden cradles suspended from beams near the fire. When they cry they are ignored, for, say the Ainu, "Babies are like talkative men and women, they must have their say."

BITES INSTEAD OF KISSES

Young people do their own courting, and, strange as it may seem, they never kiss, but bite as a sign of affection. They marry whom they please, in spite of the fact that they may have been betrothed by their parents in childhood. Either the boy or the girl may propose, and the parents of the one proposing arrange the marriage ceremony.

The fathers of the two meet, worship the Goddess of Fire, exchange a Japanese sword, and drink saké, while relatives and friends gather for the feast. The bride gives millet cakes to the groom, and he provides saké which they both drink. Presents are exchanged and the feast held. The young people usually build themselves a hut near that of the girl's parents, if she offered herself to him, or near his, if he was the one who proposed. A short time after the marriage ceremony, to show that they are satisfied, the groom makes a loom, a shuttle, a knife sheath, and a spoon which he presents to the bride, and she makes an exchange gift of a girdle, a necklace, a pair of leggings, and a cap.

The Ainu do not fear death, but they are very careful to keep away from a grave and never to speak the name of one deceased.

The soul of a person may return after death and give aid to the living or it may injure them greatly, according to its treatment. These souls cannot be seen by men but dogs scent them and give notice of their presence by howling.

When a person dies, a bright fire is built on the hearth; the children gash their foreheads, and the husband or wife shaves his or her head with a sharp shell. The body is laid beside the hearth, dressed in its best clothes, but these are always cut or torn in places. In this way the clothes are "killed," and their souls thus released will be able to clothe the deceased in the next world. Tools, weapons, utensils, whatever the dead may need in the future world, are placed by the body and buried with it, but all are broken, chipped, or torn. Offerings of food and drink are made and messages given to the dead to carry to those who have gone before. The mourners, carrying the various objects, follow the corpse in single file as it is carried to the grave. After the burial they wash their hands, brush their clothes with grass, and return to the village where they burn the hut. In this way the ghost of the deceased is assured of a house in the other world, for there they live exactly as people on earth.

In like manner it is only the essence which the ancestors take of the food and drink offered them, so that after the offerings the people consume the food and drink itself, just as they drink the great quantities of saké and millet beer used as offerings to the supernatural beings.

THE BEAR FESTIVAL

Perhaps the most enjoyable event in all the life of the Ainu is the bear festival, a feast believed by some to be a survival of totemism. A bear is cruelly sacrificed and his flesh eaten, but the feast is not for the people alone. It is for the bear also. He is fed his own flesh, is requested to take some to his ancestors, to go back to his home in the mountains, and to return, clothed in a new body, in order to give food to the people and to be sacrificed again.

When a hunter is lucky enough to capture a young cub, there is great rejoicing. He takes it home and keeps it in the house where

it is a playmate for the children. If it is too young to eat
it is suckled by the women, and sleeps in the warm embrace of the
father. When it has grown too large to be a pleasant house companion, it is placed in a strong cage outside where it is fed and
cared for.

When it is two or three years of age, the bear is ready to be
sacrificed. The owner sends word to all the people in his village
and to some from a distance, and they all come, for there is sure
to be plenty of saké and millet beer. Their best clothes and all
their ornaments are worn to these feasts.

The men make many inao, and, after worshipping the various
spirits, place them in the "sacred hedge" outside. The women
dance, shout, and clap their hands around the cage of the bear in
order to excite him. Then a chosen man sits down by the cage
and reminds the beast how honored he is to be the object of all
this celebration. He tells him that they are about to send him to
his ancestors, but that there will be plenty of cakes and wine for
him to take to them, and he begs him to tell them how kind the
people are. The speaker ends by asking the bear to come again
that they may honor and sacrifice him. The bear is then roped and
led out of the cage amid shouting and clapping of the people who
also begin pelting it with blunt arrows.

The bear, frightened and furious, struggles and rages till it is
near exhaustion. Then men rush out and seize its legs while a
piece of wood is forced into its mouth, and it is strangled between
two poles. An arrow shot into its heart ends its agony. The warm
blood of the bear is drunk by some of the men and smeared on
their beards, that its virtues may go to them and make them successful in hunting. The head and skin of the bear are placed by
the east window, and offerings made for him to take to his parents
—inao, dried fish, cakes, and a cup of his own flesh boiled. The
remainder of the meat is cooked for the general feast which follows, but each one present must partake of the cup from which
the bear has enjoyed the essence.

Eventually the bear's head is added to those already on the
"sacred hedge" outside the east window. The festival is a wild
affair ending in much drunkenness, but it is one of the few great
occasions in the life of the Ainu.

WHITE HOUSE
A cliff dwelling in Canyon De Chelly.

A NAVAHO INDIAN SUMMER HOME IN CANYON DE CHELLY

THE KAZAKS, HERDERS AND HORSEMEN OF CENTRAL ASIA

OUT OF THE GRASS covered steppe lands and deserts of Central Asia hordes of horsemen, from time to time, have descended on the rich lands of Persia; they have swept northward and eastward into Russia and have overrun China.

In the 12th century the roving herders were welded into the semblance of an empire by Genghis Khan, one of the greatest military leaders of all time. Knowing full well that his tribesmen could be kept content only when warfare promised adventure, fame, and loot, he led his armies from conquest to conquest.

Under his leadership they penetrated beyond the great wall of China, they scaled the lofty mountain ranges of the East and poured down upon Persia and Afghanistan. The rich and powerful cities of Bokhara, Samarkand, and Kiva fell, but the raiders, not content with their conquests, soon were pushing northward to the shores of the Black Sea.

A KAZAK WOMAN

Following the death of the great Khan the raids subsided, although several expeditions were undertaken to subdue rebellious or troublesome leaders. Then in 1236 the tribesmen were again on the march, this time toward Russia.

The horde surged north to the Volga River and then swept southward to destroy and loot the city of Kiev. With Russia conquered, the invading armies ravaged Poland and Hungary, and it is possible that they would have pushed into Germany had it not been for the sudden death of the ruling Khan.

For two hundred years Russia paid tribute. Wealth poured in upon the conquerors, but without the activity and excitement of warfare their unity began to break. New conquests were ordered. This time Bagdad, the stronghold of the Mohammedans, was the goal. Again the tribesmen triumphed, and the Caliph and all his subjects were slain, while the city was looted. On into Syria they moved. Aleppo and Damascus fell. Then again the scourge was stayed by the death of the Khan.

A KAZAK AND HIS GOLDEN EAGLE

So the story runs. The new Khan, the Kublai Khan described by Marco Polo, turned his attention to China and to the rich lands of Burma. In the East he established a court of dazzling brilliance. No longer was he the savage warrior, for, conqueror, though he was, he and his court were won over to the civilized life of the conquered. But the wild tribesmen of the grass lands had no desire to settle in cities and lead a life of luxury. In 1294 Kublai Khan died, and shortly afterwards the kingdom began to fall to pieces.

In the steppes of central Asia the old life still went on much as it had before Genghis Khan started his warriors on the road to empire, and quickly it reverted to its old ways when once that power was broken.

Today in the grass lands live herders and horsemen who closely repeat the life of the past. It is the Kazaks, the most powerful of these, to whom we now turn our attention.

CONSTRUCTING A KAZAK TENT

THE KAZAKS

The Kazaks are said to number over three million people scattered over the vast territory between European Russia and China. In general this land is a high semi-arid plateau with few permanent rivers or lakes. Part is desert but most of it is covered with grass following the spring rains. Extremely cold in winter it is correspondingly hot in summer and hence is unfitted to produce anything except grass and quick growing plants.

In spring the country is green, but soon the heat of summer so parches the soil that pasturage is scanty. Then the people must be often on the move to find feed for their herds and flocks. In some favored regions the melting snows of the mountains furnish moisture to the valleys, while in the northern portion midsummer rains make life easier. Autumn storms again revive the grass, and for a few weeks feed is plentiful.

Courtesy American Museum of Natural History, New York

MONGOL SHEEP HERDERS

Finally comes the long winter. Then the people seek sheltered places near such rivers and water courses as exist. Here there is usually sufficient dried grass to carry the animals through the severe months when high winds sweep endlessly over the uplands. This winter supply of feed is preserved against foraging until after the frosts by vast swarms of flies, bugs, and mosquitoes which make life impossible for man or beast. Thus the life of the people is governed largely by their environment. When feed is scanty, they must scatter over a wide territory in small groups; when winter sets in, they are forced to a settled life.

What is left of the great organization which welded these people into one of the greatest fighting forces the world has known? Practically nothing. Theoretically the Kazaks are still organized into three great divisions or hordes. In the days of the Empire these were political and territorial units, but today they have little significance of any kind.

KAZAKS AND THEIR TENT

One remnant of ancient days still plays an important part. Those families who claim descent from Genghis Khan and those whose forefathers first embraced Mohammedanism form an aristocracy called "White Bones." All others are commoners and are known as "Black Bones." Intermarriage is forbidden between the two and, because of the prestige enjoyed by the former, its members are able to possess the greater part of the wealth.

The important unit in this society is the clan made up of a number of families tracing relationship in the male line. The clans own the pasture lands, give assistance to their members in time of need, and are responsible for their acts. They have distinctive crests which are placed on the dwellings and likewise serve as brands and property marks.

Within the clans are families, or kin groups, consisting of the father and his wives, his sons and their wives, unmarried daughters, and servants. The latter are usually descendants of slaves who are without property rights.

MONGOL TYPES
A great mixture of physical types
is evident, but the Mongoloid
strain is dominant.

CUSTODIAN OF THE LAW
IN MONGOLIA
This border official held up the
American Museum Expedition a
month.

All photos on this page courtesy
American Museum of Natural History,
New York

II—24

A kin group usually lives together during the winter, but in spring it spreads out over the land in smaller units. If feed allows, many tents may be pitched close together, but, if the season is bad, only three or four form a group. Since the father of the kin actually owns the greater part of the stock, he dictates their distribution.

Above the clan is a larger grouping known as the sök or phratry. This is made up of closely related clans which tend to live near one another if conditions permit. Formerly, it is said, they sometimes formed a unit in raiding parties or in defence of their lands.

An even more unstable unit is the tribe, made up of several phratries. Doubtless in days when warfare was more important the tribe had its functions, but now it is little more than a name.

The father or head of a kin group represents it in all matters of importance. One of these family heads who possesses wealth and prestige will be chosen to lead the clan and in earlier times he might have been made chief of the tribe.

KIRGHIZ AND HIS WIFE, WHO IS WEAVING

Courtesy American Museum of Natural History, New York

MONGOLS ERECTING A YURT

MOVING DAYS

Moving day comes frequently, but instead of looking for a new house the Kazak moves his dwelling. This is easily done, for his home is constructed with that in mind. Four or five sections of lattice work are set up to form the circular side walls. Above these is a dome-shaped frame with a circular opening at the top. All parts are tightly lashed together and then strips of felt are stretched tightly over the framework. Such a house is strong, cool, and weather proof, and it can be set up in a few moments.

Like the house, the furnishings must be of a kind easily moved. Beds are rolls of felt which, together with the pillows, are piled against the walls during the day. If the family is of great import-ance it may have a large couch covered with rugs and pillows in the place of honor at the back of the tent. Here the head of the family sleeps, and here he entertains his guests. Rugs of wool or felt also cover the floors of the more prosperous. Along the side walls are chests or leather bags filled with clothing or food. Cook-ing utensils surround the central fire and here, too, young animals are often cared for.

The largest of these structures may exceed twenty feet in diameter and be occupied by two or three families and their de-

Courtesy American Museum of Natural History, New York

A WAYSIDE MONGOL YURT WITH COVERING OF FELT

pendents. There is no privacy in such a home, but there is much companionship. Around the fires they sit to tell stories, to do string tricks, to play games, or just to gossip.

A visitor from a distance is gladly received, for he brings news of the outside world. While he is a guest he is under the protection of the family, but in former times it was quite proper to rob the visitor once he had left the shelter of the tents.

Suitable as these dwellings are for most of the year, they are not fitted to withstand the terrific blizzards of the winter. Late in the autumn, after the frosts have killed the flies and mosquitoes, the people go to the larger and more permanent camps along the streams, where they occupy rectangular earth lodges similar to those we saw in use among certain American Indian tribes. The floor is sunken and, around this, thick walls of sod are built up. Across the walls are timbers on which a sod roof is laid. A number of these huts constitute a settlement around which a high wall is built. Sheds erected against this wall afford protection for the flocks.

Practically all the wealth is in animals. Sheep are the most numerous, but horses and camels are more highly prized. On these animals they depend for food, clothing, shelter, and fuel. In a land without trees, animal dung is used as fuel for both cooking and warmth.

All the animals are eaten on occasion, but milk and milk products are the main foods. Most milk is made into butter and cheese, but mare's milk is reserved for special occasions. When placed in leather bags and allowed to sour, the result is kumiss, a highly prized and slightly intoxicating drink.

Animals are driven each day to the feeding grounds, but the young are kept tied near the camps so that the mothers will return frequently to feed them. The babies are allowed a little, then man takes the rest. Mares are often milked five or six times a day.

A KAZAK HORSEMAN

House work is simple, for only one dish is used at meal time. Fingers serve as knives and forks, and they can be licked off, so dishwashing is unnecessary. If a guest wishes to show his great appreciation of a meal he indulges in prolonged gulping and belching.

KICKING THE WOOL INTO FELT

Sheep are sheared in the autumn and the wool is packed into bales. When enough has been accumulated it is laid on hides where girls beat it with flat sticks; next it is pulled apart with the fingers, is thoroughly sprinkled with water, and made into a tight roll between two straw mats. Now comes the fun. Women and girls sit in two rows facing each other. At a signal all on one side push the roll away from them with their feet; as it reaches the other row they kick it back and so it rolls to and fro. After a time the mats are removed and the wool is beaten for hours by hand to make it more compact. The result is felt from which tent walls, rugs, and garments are made.

The Kazaks are not prepossessing at close quarters. They are short, heavily built, and on this frame they hang one or more long felt coats. Baggy trousers fit into high leather boots which are pointed at the toes. The dress of both sexes is much the same, but the men wear hats with upturned brims.

No matter how grotesque they may seem when on the ground, they make a fine appearance when on horseback. They seem to be a very part of the animal, so gracefully do they ride. Saddles and other horse-trappings often display a goodly share of the family wealth, yet wives of the well-to-do may wear elaborately decorated garments and considerable jewelry.

A question as to racial relationship is in place at this point, but the answer is not easy. Most of the people show distinct Mongoloid traits, yet many give evidence of intermixture with the Alpine peoples of western Asia and central Europe. Doubtless considerable intermixture has taken place in Asia, while marriage with captives, taken in the raids during the 12th and 13th centuries, may also account for the Caucasoid strain.

Marriage is always outside the clan and is arranged through purchase. Despite this, the groom is expected to "steal" his bride. When the time comes, she is clad in her best garments and has her trousseau ready, but she must be greatly surprised and put up a good fight. Payment is in animals, and the boy may not take the girl from her father's tent until all is settled. When the last animal is delivered, the couple goes to live with the groom's father.

Nominally the Kazaks are Mohammedans, and hence a man may have four wives if he can afford them. Women are quite independent; they never wear the veil, and they mingle freely with the men. As a matter of fact, the Mohammedan religion is only a very thin veneer below which old pagan practices and beliefs still flourish.

So it is in most affairs of life. This people once belonged to a great conquering horde; they were in touch with the highest cultures of the East and West. Yet today they live much as did their ancestors before Genghis Khan led them to the portals of Europe.

WE ARE ON OUR WAY.

WE. HAVE come to the end of our story.
The first beings we called man were quite different from modern men. Their crude stone tools gave little promise of development into the complicated machinery of the modern factory. Yet the advances of today rest on the achievements of yesterday, and they in turn on other yesterdays.

Human advance was at first slow and halting. The crude hand axe held sway for thousands of years before a primitive inventor added a handle. Many more generations came and went before the accomplishments of the cave man marked the greatest advance the world had seen. The pace quickened, and with the Neolithic Age a flood of new ideas spread over the world. On the foundations laid in the New Stone Age rests our own civilization. Likewise in America the high cultures of the south developed out of Stone Age beginnings.

With the coming of metals and of writing, civilization advanced rapidly in certain regions, but because of isolation and other reasons certain peoples were passed by. So today we have primitive tribesmen living under conditions not greatly different from those under which the ancestors of the civilized peoples must have developed. By studying them we have gained an insight into the nature of human society.

Of course no people of today is exactly the same as it was a hundred years ago, and no two have developed in exactly the same way.

Many people have contributed to the story of human development. Our studies have shown us that civilization is not the product of any one nation or race. Because of an earlier start, more favorable surroundings, or because of contacts, certain groups have forged ahead for a time. The backward people borrowed from the more advanced, and in time some of them became leaders. If in the future nations and peoples now lagging take the lead in civilization, history will be repeating itself.

We look over our world today with mixed feelings. Our industrial advances speak of great progress. Our inventions of the past fifty years exceed those of all prior history. We have practically annihilated time and space. Yet with all our advances we may be forging the materials for our own destruction.

Never in the world's history have so many men been withdrawn from productive enterprise to fill the ranks of the armies; never have such engines of warfare been devised. Suspicion between nations is intensified. Powerful states seize the lands of the weak, and hundreds of thousands of people are deprived of their homes and possessions on the false plea of racial purity. We appear to live in a world gone mad.

We have just read of a great conquering people who now must be ranked among the lowly. Tomorrow we shall read of other nations which sought to conquer the world. We shall read of oppression and cruelty, of intolerance and bigotry, and we shall read how those nations failed and others took the lead. Iroquois and Aztec, Inca and Kazak, Egypt and Babylon, each had its day of glory and sank into oblivion. The golden days of Greece and Rome were followed by the Dark Ages, but finally came the Renaissance.

Perhaps we have a warning and a promise. If we disregard the lessons of the past, we, too, may vanish from the scene, and others may take our place. But we have the background of their history and we may, if we will, profit by their struggles and avoid their mistakes. On the foundations of yesterday we may build our tomorrows.

Courtesy National Park Service, U. S. Department of the Interior

EL MORRO NATIONAL MONUMENT

THE MAYA MAIZE GOD
This deity is depicted as a youth, wearing
a corn head dress.

ACKNOWLEDGEMENT

In the preparation of this volume the authors have used considerable material drawn from their own field research, particularly in Malaysia and America. They have also drawn freely from the writings of many investigators, in the attempt to present a complete and authentic story of man's advance through the ages. To all of these they express sincere appreciation.

The value of such a study is greatly enhanced by good illustrations, and the authors and publishers are deeply indebted to our leading museums for the use of many photographs and the privilege of reproducing materials in their collections.

Among the institutions and organizations which were particularly helpful were:

> Field Museum of Natural History, Chicago
> American Museum of Natural History, New York
> Buffalo Museum of Science, Buffalo
> University Museum of the University of Pennsylvania
> Department of Anthropology of the University of Chicago
> Logan Museum of Beloit College
> Art Institute, Chicago
> Atchison, Topeka and Sante Fe Railway Company
> Illinois Central System
> Canadian National Railways

Among the individuals to whom special thanks is due for the use of original data, advice and encouragement in the preparation of this volume are: Dr. M. R. Harrington of the Southwest Museum, Los Angeles, Dr. Paul Martin of the Field Museum of Natural History, Dr. Henry Field of the Field Museum of Natural History, Dr. A. E. Jenks of the University of Minnesota.

DESIGNER'S NOTE

This volume was set in twelve point Linotype Garamond. The illustrations at the head of each chapter are typical of the subject matter treated in the respective chapter. Each drawing was made after original material collected by the authors.

The style of typography, the art work and illustrations received a treatment similar to that of volume one, in order to establish a certain consistency and uniformity of style throughout these volumes.

OTTO MAURICE FORKERT
Director of Design and Typography